THE RAZOR'S EDGE
SHARP THINKING IN WORLD HISTORY

Second Edition

Edited by
Glen C. Bowman, Jr.
Elizabeth City State University

KENDALL/HUNT PUBLISHING COMPANY
4050 Westmark Drive   Dubuque, Iowa 52002

On the cover: World image copyright © Photos.com; blade image copyright © PhotoDisc, Inc.

Copyright © 2005, 2007 by Kendall/Hunt Publishing Company

ISBN 978-0-7575-4362-3

All rights reserved. No part of this publication may be reproduced, stored in a retrieval system, or transmitted, in any form by any means, electronic, mechanical, photocopying, recording, or otherwise, without the prior written permission of the copyright owner.

Printed in the United States of America
10 9 8 7 6 5 4 3 2 1

CONTENTS

Preface to the Second Edition ... v

Chapter One: Evaluating Arguments: A Six-Step Guide ... 1

    Step One: Finding the Thesis ... 2
    Step Two: Determining Whether the Argument Cites Convincing Factual Evidence ... 9
    Step Three: Determining Whether the Argument Cites Convincing Statistics ... 9
    Step Four: Determining Whether the Argument Cites Convincing Opinions ... 11
    Step Five: Determining Whether the Argument Is Based on Acceptable Assumptions and Values ... 11
    Step Six: Looking for Logical Traps ... 22

Chapter Two: Timeless Questions Throughout World History: A Reader ... 35

    How Did the World Begin? ... 35
    What Is Criminal Justice? ... 40
    What Is Goodness? ... 44
    What Is Feminism? ... 50
    Who Gives Political Leaders Their Power? ... 54
    Does God Exist? ... 58
    Who Should Be Allowed to Vote? ... 62
    Should the Military Be Glorified? ... 66
    What Is Education? ... 70
    What Is Genocide? ... 76
    What Should Be the Relationship between Church and State? ... 80
    What Code Should the Military Follow? ... 84
    What Is Marriage? ... 88
    What Has Been the Impact of Disease in History? ... 92
    Is Violence Ever Justifiable to Enact Political Change? ... 98
    Who Should Set Prices? ... 102
    How Should Political Leaders Rule? ... 106
    What Is the Purpose of Government? ... 110
    What Are Civil Rights? ... 114
    What Is Society's Obligation to the Poor? ... 118
    How Should the Guilt or Innocence of the Accused Be Determined? ... 122
    How Will the World End? ... 126
    Is There an Afterlife? ... 130

Chapter Three: Time-Specific Questions Throughout World History: A Reader 135
   Why Did the Roman Empire Fall? 135
   What Was Africa Like Before 1500? 138
   Who "Discovered" America? 142
   Was Christopher Columbus a Hero? 148
   What Was Slavery Like? 152
   Was Martin Luther Right? 156
   Why Was the Transatlantic Slave Trade Abolished? 160
   What Were the Effects of Imperialism? 164
   What Were the Effects of the Industrial Revolution? 166
   What Is Nationalism? 170
   What Is Communism? 176
   What Does It Mean to Live under a Totalitarian Regime? 182
   Was It Right for the United States to Drop the Atomic Bomb on Japan during World War II? 186
   Should the United States Help End Communism in Vietnam? 190
   What Was Apartheid in South Africa? 196
   What Are the Causes of Africa's Problems? 200
   Why Did the Soviet Union Collapse? 204
   Who Should Control Palestine? 208
   What Is Fundementalism? 212

Bibliography 219
Endnotes 222

Preface to the Second Edition

When I wrote the preface for the first edition, I noted that one of my goals as a teacher and a writer was to help students develop the essential skills of critical thinking, reading, writing, and problem-solving. I also noted that *The Razor's Edge* was "a work in progress."

The second edition contains many changes, yet the objective remains the same. And, yes, this is still a work in progress.

I would have it no other way.

The [new] Razor's Edge is in many ways a more comprehensive world history reader. There are close to thirty documents that were not in the first edition. There is more from Africa's past. More Asian history, as well.

Nevertheless, much has remained the same. The focus is on primary documents, not on the individual interpretations of modern historians. The length of the documents is kept brief, often under five hundred words, so they are manageable for students who lack a detailed historical background.

The division between timeless debates through history and time-specific debates limited to a particular era has been maintained. Timeless questions expose students to comparative history, and to see just how certain questions are asked repeatedly. Sometimes instead of receiving answers, those who question discover that they only have more questions, as if life were some neverending Socratic dialogue. Time-specific questions cover the range from the decline of the Western Roman Empire, to Africa's ancient past, to the "discovery" of America, and to ongoing controversies, such as the rise of fundamentalism in Christianity and Islam. Although these are limited to a specific era in history, they are issues historians still regard as open to debate.

Most history readers in the marketplace are mere collections of excerpted documents. Although this is to be expected, it is easy to assume that students innately know how to bring their analytical tools to the task. *The Razor's Edge*—part reader, part guide to rhetoric—is different. The six-step process of understanding, comprehending, analyzing, and reacting to what one has read has been revised for this edition. Although many of these steps can be found in guides to university-level rhetoric, they are included here because I believe that the study of World History is a great medium for the teaching of critical thinking and critical writing across the curriculum.

Similar to the first edition, all authorial royalties will go to the Leonard Ballou Memorial Fund. Mr. Ballou had a special place in his heart for Elizabeth City State University and its students, and all of the proceeds in the fund go toward student research and travel.

My thanks to my colleagues in the Department of History and Political Science, particularly to those who teach World Civilizations. I also would like to thank my department chair, Dr. Flora Brown, and the Dean of Arts and Humanities, Dr. Jennifer Keane-Dawes, for their active support of this book and my other scholarly endeavors.

Thanks also belong to my students, past and present, whose attitudes and efforts make the work that went into this book all worth the while.

CHAPTER 1

EVALUATING ARGUMENTS: A SIX-STEP GUIDE

"If you cannot think for yourself, then someone else is going to do it for you."

Logicians would call this a conditional statement. I would also call it the truth.

But what does it mean to "think for yourself"? After all, no one wants to be accused of being led along like a puppy on a leash, but if you lack the ability to analyze arguments in order to determine if they are based on valid and sound premises, that is what you will be.

Wars are fought everyday, and not all of them are on the military battlefield. There is a war going on for your mind and money. People everywhere are trying to persuade you to believe something, buy something, or simply to do something. This is true whether you know it or not.

If you sit down in the morning to read the newspaper, you are going to have to go through a lot of advertisements in order to get to the news (in fact, if papers did not have ads, they would cost many times the typical 50 cents a paper). If you like music on the radio, get prepared to listen to car dealers barking out news about their upcoming sales and radio personalities telling you why their station is the "best" in the area. When you shop for groceries, you are being sold on certain grocery items the whole time you are in the store. Those "free samples" are effective marketing, as is that "free" coupon in Sunday's newspaper. Sometimes advertising is found in unusual places—the side of a city bus, the back of a church bulletin, even the restroom wall. Arguments are on billboards along highways, on the sides of city buses, and on T-shirts. Arguments are also all over any library in newspapers, magazines, and journals. They may even be on the side of that great cup of coffee from your favorite restaurant.

For those who want to escape arguments, staying at home will do no good, for they will find you there (probably uninvited) as well. If you like television, you better get used to the ads, unless you have HBO, and even then you have to deal with promotions for upcoming shows and new series. If you subscribe to magazines, or get junk mail, you will be exposed some more. If you own a telephone, get ready for the persistent telemarketer, who may be fortunate enough to sneak in two or more arguments before you hang up. Even if you choose to be placed on the "do-not-call" list, you will still have to deal with phone calls asking you to vote for a particular candidate, and give money to a local charity.

You can escape attempts to win your heart and your money only if you sit in an isolated room with a blanket over your head. But who wants to do that? Exactly!—that's why the ability to evaluate arguments critically and logically is crucial.

There are at least six steps in such an effort:

1. Finding the thesis, or main point or proposition.
2. Determining whether the argument cites convincing factual evidence.
3. Determining whether the argument cites convincing statistics.
4. Determining whether the argument cites convincing opinions.
5. Determining whether the argument is based on acceptable assumptions.
6. Looking for logical traps.

Let's consider each of these in turn.

STEP ONE: FINDING THE THESIS

The thesis is a fancy word for "main point" or "proposition." It is the foundation of any argument.

For example, when a historian writes a book analyzing the causes of the U.S. Civil War, he/she will certainly discuss what happened (battles, the actions of leading generals, the places where battles were fought). Although this information can be found in any number of books, this does not mean that all books are the same. Upon first glance, two books might seem to be reflections of each other: same length, same topic, maybe even similar covers.

Appearances can be deceiving. Each book is different, because each book reflects the assumptions, values, styles, and other qualities of the author. When historians write, they offer not just facts and figures, but interpretations. The main interpretation in a book, or an article, or an essay, is called the thesis.

This is not a principle limited only to historians or those interested in the past. It is a feature of daily life. For instance, an advertisement for suntan lotion might include the sun-tanned bodies of lean, muscular volleyball players, as well as images of some pristine beach in a tropical paradise. Yet these are not on television merely to entertain viewers. They are being used to sell a particular brand of suntan lotion. The sales pitch, in this way, can be seen as the thesis, or main point of the commercial. If viewers think "Nice commercial" yet do not buy the product being sold, the commercial will not be seen as a success.

A critical step in thinking for oneself is being able to pick up the message, the thesis. Before you can agree or disagree with it, one first needs to find it. How does one go about doing this?

In a book, the first place to look for it is in the first chapter and the last chapter, and sometimes it appears on the cover or dustjacket of the book. Often a writer will want the readers to know exactly what the thesis is right away and will therefore discuss the thesis in the very first chapter. At the very least, most authors will state what point they will attempt to prove in the book, as in "I am going to show in this book that the long-standing idea that slavery was the primary cause of the Civil War is still the best way to view the conflict." Almost always, an author will restate the thesis at the very end of the book. The middle chapters provide the evidence for the thesis.

Textbooks will not generally have a thesis. This does not mean that the interpretations of the author or authors will not be apparent. A historian who studies politics may write a textbook, for instance, that emphasizes government, political philosophy, or other parts of the political world.

Likewise, in a shorter essay of five hundred or so words (the average length of a newspaper or magazine editorial), one should consider the following steps:

1. Watch for the sales pitch. Expect that the author is going to try to persuade you to believe or do something. The author will include facts, but be aware that the author has a proposition, a thesis, that he or she is trying to prove.
2. Scan, focusing on the introduction and conclusion. The last sentence is often the most important.
3. Look for key words. Key words are sometimes used more than once. They are often the subjects of the sentences. Note the predicate verbs of these key words when they are the subjects of the sentences.
4. Understand the context in which these words are being used. For instance, the word "justice" has multiple meanings. Economic justice is different from criminal justice. What might be just to one person may be unjust to another.

Consider the following paragraph:

"The town council in Green Lane approved a resolution declaring God as the foundation of our national heritage. Government of all shapes and sizes can declare anything it wants, but it cannot change the facts. The reality, painful for many of the faithful, is that a good number of the founding fathers were not really Christians. Most believed in God but rejected the notion of a God who acts within creation, and considered the Incarnation and Resurrection impossible. Moreover, by taking up arms against England, they disregarded the New Testament prohibition against active political resistance. Jesus never advocated revolting against Rome. Neither did the apostle Paul, who in Romans 13 describes political leaders as God's chosen ministers who must be honored. He repudiated rebellion even against Nero, one of history's most vicious tyrants. If the founding fathers had viewed the Bible as their main source for political wisdom, they never would have revolted, and the United States might not have been established. Fortunately instead, they used their God-given abilities of reason, and determined that rebellion was the only way to secure their God-given rights. Unfortunately for us, our town council once again refuses to act like genuine leaders, choosing instead to make historical declarations instead of picking a mayor pro-tem. God help us."

Carefully reading the first sentences and the last sentences reveals the main point of the author: that the town council was wrong in approving a resolution stating that God is the foundation of our (apparently United States) national heritage. Note that "town council" appears both at the beginning and the end of the paragraph, and both times it is the subject of the sentence. According to these sentences, this council "approved a resolution," an act that according to the author shows that the council "refuses to act like genuine leaders" and chooses "to make historical declarations" instead of doing town business. In this case, the thesis is fairly easy to spot.

The author sets forth other arguments: that "a good number of the founding fathers were not really Christians"; that they "disregarded the New Testament prohibition against active political resistance" and therefore did not act as a Christian should; and that the founding fathers nevertheless "used their God-given abilities of reason, and determined that rebellion was the only way to secure their God-given rights." Although the author discusses the founding fathers frequently, the thesis is not about their actions. Rather, their actions instead show that they were not establishing a Christian nation, and that the town council, by passing this resolution, is neglecting history (or, rather, is going against the historical interpretation of the author. Clearly, their interpretation is different from that of the author).

Exercises for Finding the Thesis

Choose the best answer for the following questions. Explain the reasons you chose the answer you did, and why you did not choose the others. A few sentences per question should suffice.

"It's terrible that the poor man was shot to death yesterday by the Paris police who had reason to think he was a terrorist. But should we worry that the shoot-to-kill policy will result in more deaths? Really, it should be quite unlikely for the same sort of thing to happen again, just as it's very unlikely that anyone will ever again hijack an airplane with a small knife. That method of hijacking an airplane ended on the morning of September 11, 2001 . . ., Similarly, everyone—at least in Paris—now knows not to run from the police, especially not onto a train and while wearing bulky clothing. Is it not true that yesterday's sad mistake has already solved the problem it represents? In fact, a further good has been created: as ordinary persons change their behavior and drop the bulky clothing and unnecessary running, the real terrorists will stand out more. Indeed, if anyone ever behaves like John Menendez again, the presumption that he is a terrorist will be so overwhelmingly strong that the police really must kill him."

1. The main point of this argument is
   a) Menendez is (or was) a terrorist.
   b) no one will ever again use a small knife to hijack a plane.
   c) this tragic shooting might help to identify potential terrorists.
   d) no one wearing bulky clothing near a train should run from police.

"We have to figure out how to handle the immigration problem domestically. But we also must do something to get our neighbor to the south to clean up its act. The Pew Hispanic Center also released a new survey that included polling in Mexico as well as in the United States. When Mexican citizens were asked if they would move to the United States if they had the means and opportunity to do so, an incredible 46 percent of respondents said they would. Almost half of the Mexican population wants to leave! When asked if they would do it illegally, 21 percent of those polled responded affirmatively."

2. The thesis can be found in the _____ sentence.
   a) first   b) second   c) third   d) fourth

"A few months ago, at the urging of Gov. Jayson Johnson, the Legislature required that all new welfare applicants must spend four months in a full-time job search before formally entering the welfare system. Some say that this is cruel, but they're wrong. Work before welfare is only fair."

3. The main point is that
   a) Governor Johnson is an exceptional governor and potential president.
   b) welfare recipients are all lazy bums.
   c) Governor Johnson's welfare reforms are morally right because they're fair.
   d) Governor Johnson's welfare reforms have proven successful.

"The Justice Department must admit the truth already: law enforcement officers far too often engage in racial profiling. According to a study commissioned back in the 1990's by the N.A.A.C.P., people of color are much more likely than white drivers to be arrested following a traffic stop. The best way to stop future abuse is to have Congress hold a lengthy public hearing on the issue. Maybe that will shame the Justice Department to take racial profiling more seriously."

4. The main argument is that
   a) Congress has jurisdiction over the Justice Department.
   b) the NAACP conducted a study several years ago on racial profiling.
   c) racial profiling should be illegal only at the federal level.
   d) racial profiling is a major problem that must be addressed.

"Looting is often opportunistic. The apparent lapse in authority enables people to believe that they won't be discovered or charged. Looting also cascades through a group of people as one person believes that his contribution to the crime is lessened because someone else is looting, too. People may also believe that if the goods are not stolen, then they will simply be wasted, and see their act as a lesser of two evils. Finally, a looter may believe that if he doesn't steal the property, it will simply be stolen by someone else and he will gain nothing from his obedience. Looters are usually locals of the site of the disaster, and as such, may have lost a lot of their own property. This further encourages them to steal as it is reducing the negative impact of the disaster."

5. The main point is to
   a) attack looting as an immoral act.
   b) define looting.
   c) explain reasons for why people loot.
   d) inform law enforcement on ways to prevent looting.

"In the latest National Crime Victimization Survey, the Bureau of Justice Statistics reported that the U.S. murder rate for 2003 was about 5.6 per 100,000 persons, unchanged from 2001 and 2002. Executions during this time steadily increased. Former Attorney General Janet Reno noted that she had never seen any research that would prove that capital punishment is a deterrent. Indeed, back in the 1950's Thorsten Sellin applied his combination of qualitative and quantitative methods in an exhaustive study of capital punishment in American states. In addition, he used every scrap of data that was available, together with his knowledge of the history, economy, and social structure of each state, and went as far as comparing states to other states. He nevertheless concluded that executions have no discernable effect on homicide rates. It is therefore clear that _____ ."

6. The main point, which would fill in the blank at the end of the quote, is that
   a) Janet Reno was trained as a social scientist.
   b) capital punishment is always wrong.
   c) capital punishment seems to be an ineffective deterrent.
   d) life imprisonment is a better alternative to executions.

"Economic and social inequalities are only justified if they benefit all of society, especially its most disadvantaged members. Furthermore, all economically and socially privileged positions must be open to all people equally. For example, it is only justified that a doctor makes more money than a grocery clerk since if this were not the case, no one would study and train to be a doctor, and there would be no medical care. Therefore, the doctor's greater salary benefits not only him, but all of society, including the grocery clerk, since it permits the clerk to get medical care. This particular economic inequality benefits all of society, and leaves all its members better off."

7. The main point or thesis can be found in which sentence?
   a) first   b) second   c) third   d) fourth

8. The author supports the thesis primarily by
   a) citing statistics.   b) citing opinions from experts.   c) citing facts.   d) illustrating through an example.

"Strongly influenced by Platonism and neo-Platonism, Augustine was important to the 'baptism' of Greek thought and its entrance into the Christian, and was a key figure in the European intellectual tradition. Also important was his influential writings on the human will, a central topic in ethics, and one which became a focus for later philosophers such as Schopenhauer and Nietzsche. As William Henry, a biographer, noted, it is largely due to Augustine's arguments against the Pelagians, who did not believe in original sin, that Western Christianity has maintained the doctrine of original sin. Catholic theologians generally subscribe to Augustine's belief that God exists outside of time in the 'eternal present'; time existing only within the created universe."

9. The main point or thesis can be best paraphrased as:
   a) Augustine was not as significant as some scholars make him out to be.
   b) Augustine remains a central figure in Christianity and in the history of philosophy.
   c) Augustine was a Platonist and neo-Platonist.
   d) Augustine wrote about the human will.

"Egyptologists say that Cleopatra was descended from the Ptolemies, a Greek family, whose patriarch was once a general for Alexander the Great. They say the Ptolemies' family tree indicates that there was a great deal of interbreeding in the family, and that because Cleopatra was the first monarch to learn Egyptian, Cleopatra was white. Afrocentric historians, however, claim that ancient Egypt was a predominately black civilization and that most ancient Egyptians were black people. Even though they acknowledge Ptolemy was white, they believe there must have been sexual liaisons between the monarchs and the people of Egypt. Egyptologists say that belief in Cleopatra's being black is Afrocentric revisionism, designed to stir up pride amongst black youth. Afrocentric historians say the belief that Cleopatra was white is just another example of white people stealing black culture."

10. The main point or thesis can best be paraphrased as:
    a) Cleopatra was white.
    b) Cleopatra was black.
    c) Egyptologists and Afrocentric historians disagree about Cleopatra's skin color.
    d) The debate over Cleopatra is a part of the debate about race in America.

"Napoleon is credited with introducing the concept of the modern professional conscript army to Europe. In France, Napoleon is also seen as having preserved the French Revolution by creating and perpetuating its myth. Furthermore, the Napoleonic Wars also exported the Revolution to the rest of Europe, and it is believed that the movements of national unification and the rise of the nation state, notably in Italy and Germany, were rooted in and precipitated—if not caused—by the Napoleonic rule of those areas. In Great Britain, though, he is remembered as a tyrant.

"The Code Napoléon was adopted throughout much of Europe and remained after Napoleon's defeat. Professor Dieter Langewiesche of the University of Tübingen describes the code as a 'revolutionary project' which spurred the development of bourgeois society in Germany by expanding the right to own property and breaking the back of feudalism. Langewiesche also credits Napoleon with reorganizing what had been the Holy Roman Empire made up of more than 1,000 entities into a more streamlined network of 40 states providing the basis for the future unification of Germany under the Second Reich in 1871."

11. The main point or thesis in these two paragraphs would be best described as:
    a) Napoleon left a complicated and controversial legacy.
    b) Napoleon created the Code Napoleon.
    c) Napoleon is loved in France and hated in Great Britain.
    d) Napoleon was a founder of the modern country of Germany.

"Muslims believe that the Qur'an was revealed to the Prophet Muhammad by the Angel Gabriel on numerous occasions between the years 610 and Muhammad's death in 632. In addition to memorizing his revelations, his followers are said to have written them down on parchments, stones, and other media, so that the entire Qur'an was written down during the lifetime of Prophet Muhammad. Muhammad was illiterate, so someone else had to do the writing.

"Muslims believe that the Qur'an available today is the same as that revealed to Prophet Muhammad and by him to his followers, who memorized his words. Scholars accept that the version of the Qur'an used today was first compiled in writing by the third Caliph, Uthman ibn Affan, sometime between 650 and 656. He sent copies of his version to the various provinces of the new Muslim empire, and directed that all variant copies be destroyed. However, some skeptics doubt the recorded oral traditions (hadith) on which the account is based and will say only that the Qur'an must have been compiled before 750."

12. The main point or thesis in these paragraphs is best described as:
    a) The Qu'ran is the primary holy book of Muslims.
    b) The Qu'ran was written on parchment by Muhammad.
    c) The Qu'ran's history goes back to the early 600s.
    d) Muslims disagree about the authenticity of the Qu'ran.

"In at least two ways modern medicine has helped decrease the appeal of euthanasia. One is that many formerly devastating diseases can be cured, or at least managed. The other is that powerful painkilling drugs can eliminate much of the intense suffering of the sickly. The prospect of such suffering moved Mahatma Gandhi to consider the possibility of taking the life of his own child as the only means to end the anguish from incurable rabies." (based on *Death and Dying: Opposing Viewpoints* [St. Paul: Greenhaven, 1987], 142).

13. The main point or thesis appears in the ____ sentence.
    a) first   b) second   c) third   d) fourth

"Roger Braddock, curator at the British Museum, should allow the Krykos family to take back their ancient Greek artifacts. First, they are part of the cultural heritage of Greece, not Great Britain. Second, the only reason Braddock has them in the first place is that ninety years ago, thieves 'donated' the artifacts to the Museum. After all, if a kind father gave his child a car, but the car was actually stolen property, the child would still have to return the car, even if the father thought he was buying a legitimate automobile."

14. The main point or thesis appears in the ____ sentence.
    a) first   b) second   c) third   d) fourth

"Native American legends written before 1492 speak of contact with white men. The Vikings were able shipbuilders, and sailed across the Atlantic many times. A silver coin dating back to the mid-1000s was found in what is today Maine. Clearly the Vikings did make their way to North America in the 1000s. They, not Columbus, were the first Europeans in North America."

15. The main point or thesis can be found in the ____ sentences.
    a) first and second   b) second and third   c) third and fourth   d) fourth and fifth

Aristotle wrote, "Just as a murderer does not have the right to take a mother from her family, or a child from her parents, so the suicidal, even though he or she freely chooses to be his or her own victim, does not possess the right to therefore diminish the welfare of so many others."

16. Aristotle's main point or thesis can best be summarized as:
    a) Suicide is not a right.
    b) Murder is wrong.
    c) Those who commit suicide often murder other people first.
    d) The welfare of society is more important than the welfare of an individual.

"Attempts to curb what some define as price gouging are futile. Some might be uncomfortable that some gas stations have sold gasoline for substantially higher prices than they paid for it. However, these are the same sages who would think nothing of selling their own home for double the price they paid for it two years ago, even if they have not made a single improvement to that property."

17. The main point or thesis here is that
    a) it is wrong to sell a house for double the cost.
    b) it is wrong to sell gas at a price much higher than the cost.
    c) stopping price gouging is not worth the time.
    d) gas stations have sold gasoline at a price much higher than the cost.

"Serial killers Ted Bundy and David Berkowitz, 'Son of Sam,' grew up in broken homes. Clearly people brought up in that kind of environment have a hard time creating a sense of identity. A missing parent, therefore, can be a good predictor of a future life of crime, including murder."

18. The thesis statement can be found in the ____ sentence.
    a) first   b) second   c) third   d) fourth

STEP TWO: DETERMINING WHETHER THE ARGUMENT CITES CONVINCING FACTUAL EVIDENCE

1. Check to see if the evidence is current.

It is not surprising that people tend to accept newer evidence more readily than evidence which is a bit dated; there is often some kind of great interest in that which is supposedly "on the cutting edge". There seems to be some truth to this point. For one thing, the amount of data in the world keeps getting larger and larger, day by day. Science textbooks, for example, quickly become outdated as new research challenges, and often refutes, established points-of-view.

There are exceptions to this principle. Some older research may in fact be more accurate than new research; even though scientists of all stripes may have allegedly better research methods than their predecessors did, these innovations do not necessarily guarantee that current research is free from error. The odds are that a research report done two years ago contains more accurate information than one done, say, forty years ago. Still, it would be careless to assume that this is always true. The real test of an argument is in the evidence supporting it, not its age.

2. Check to see if there is enough evidence.

This principle is actually a "rule-of thumb", because it is hard to gauge what is enough (sufficient) evidence. It is usually sensible, however, to set high standards; demand several bits of evidence (some facts, some opinions, some statistics), not just one or two.

To be consistent with the "etiquette of argumentation," it is never appropriate to make up evidence so your audience accepts your argument. Certainly some people would not agree; to many of them, the ends may justify the means. They may try to win by any means necessary, and they may indeed win often. Still, it would appear that those who hide or make up evidence can get away with such practices only for so long.

3. Check to see if the evidence is relevant.

In other words, your evidence should pertain to your argument. This may seem fairly obvious, but many do not always follow it. It is true that some audiences may tend to react more to emotional evidence that is irrelevant to the argument than to relevant evidence. It is better not to depend on "reactions"; just because a piece of evidence might be persuasive to certain people does not mean that it should be used.

STEP THREE: DETERMINING WHETHER THE ARGUMENT CITES CONVINCING STATISTICS

1. Rely only on statistics with reliable sources.

Find the original source of the statistic. As statistics appear in other publications other than the source, statistics can be misquoted or even intentionally twisted. Hearsay or second-hand information should not be assumed to be reliable. To ensure accuracy, try to get as close as possible to the original source.

Be wary of statistics whose source is somehow involved with the subject of the statistics themselves. Observe this example:

"According to the Motor Drivers Association, 88% of surveyed owners would purchase this same car again."

The sample of those owners surveyed may be largely, and disproportionately, comprised of employees who work for the company that produces the automobiles. The directors of the "Motor Drivers Association" may also have a financial interest, and therefore a conflict of interest, in promoting the automobile. Such conflicts should be revealed, but unfortunately this does not always happen.

2. Make certain that the terms are defined clearly.

Terms such as "eighteen-year olds" and "women" are generally free from ambiguity. Other terms, however, may be open to interpretation. For examples, read the following statements:

"College students who work part-time jobs tend to earn grade-point averages 13% lower than those students not engaged in part-time employment."

This statistic may seem pretty straight forward, but is it? First, what does "part-time" precisely mean? To some, 30 hours a week is "full-time", whereas to others anything less than 40 hours is "part-time". In addition, some students may work 3 part-time jobs; the combined hours may be the equivalent of a full-time employee. Does the survey include these students?

"In a recent telephone survey, 71% of respondents expressed a great fear of crime."

There are at least three examples here of vaguely-defined terms, and many questions are not answered:

1. "telephone survey": Were the people contacted by telephone? How did the telemarketers get their names? Did the people whose opinions were sampled voluntarily call a certain number to complete a survey? Were they paid?
2. "great fear": How does one measure "great fear"? What is the difference between having a "fear" and having a "great fear"?
3. "crime": Does the survey intend to survey the responses just to violent crime, such as assault and murder, or does it also plan to consider less violent crimes such as credit card fraud?

3. Notice the SIZE of the sample.

If it is too small or too selective, the statistics might not accurately represent reality. Extremely small samples are often used in advertising:

> 55 percent of something could refer to a survey involving:
> 5 out of 9
> 11 out of 20
> 55 out of 100
> 5,500 out of 10,000

Excessively small samples may actually be evidence of a hasty generalization.

4. Check to see if any key information has been left out.

Failing to reveal some important details of a statistical survey may be as deceptive as providing some incorrect details.

"My employees are committed to helping the poor. 77% of my workers spend at least one day every two months in charity work. My company, clearly, is doing its job by willingly giving back to the community."

Helping those who are needy is certainly a decent thing to do, yet not all "charity" is alike. What if the employer who made that statement pays employees for their time? Does that coercion indicate that the company is "willingly giving back to the community"?

Other examples of failing to provide all essential information include elections by non-democratic governments. A victorious candidate may claim the support of 98% of voters, but if the candidate made certain that he or she was the only one on the ballot, is it fair to say that the person has the full support of the electorate?

5. Make certain it is clear what is being meant by "average".

"Average" has more than one meaning. It has three:

1. The MEAN is what usually comes to mind when one thinks of "average". The mean is computed by dividing the sum of the elements being measured by the number of the elements themselves.

"In the first five quizzes in geometry, my scores were 89, 75, 92, 84, and 80; and my average score is 84."

This average was tallied by adding the five scores together, the sum of which is 420 which, divided by five, is 84.

2. The MEDIAN is another "average". When several numbers are placed in the order from highest to lowest, or lowest to highest, the one in the middle is the median. Half of the rest of the numbers are above the median, and the other half are below it:

"There are three drycleaners in Madison County: one grosses $250,000 a year; another takes in $325,000 in the same span; and the final one, $150,000. The average (the median) drycleaner has a gross of $250,000."

Note that the median average is actually a bit higher than the mean average of around $241,300 (the sum of the three is $725,000 divided by three).

3. The MODE appears most frequently in a series:

"The weekly salaries for the 7 secretaries at the Healthy Life Insurance Company are as follows: $400, $300, $200, $350, $350, $225, and $275. The average secretary (the mode) makes $350 a week."

This total is more than the mean average of $300 (the sum of $2100 divided by 7). The median average is the same number, for 3 totals are less than $300 ($200, $225, $275) and three are more than $300 ($350, $350, and $400).

It is easy to use different interpretations of "average" in order to twist statistics to mean several things. When someone uses statistics that claim to represent a certain "average", find out which definition of "average" is being used.

STEP FOUR: DETERMINING WHETHER THE ARGUMENT CITES CONVINCING OPINIONS

1. Find out if the source is credible enough to give an opinion.

This advice is often neglected. It is easy to assume who appears authoritative may actually be a proper authority, but appearances can be deceiving. If you have any doubts, find out the qualifications of a source before citing it as a credible source.

If the credentials of the source are in your opinion respectable, then feel free to cite it as a source. Keep in mind that the audience may not be familiar with your quoted source. Point out the source's qualifications (education, experience, reputation, publications, positions, honors, etc.). Mentioning this information will not only make the reader more likely to listen to your argument, but may also make a good impression.

2. Consider whether the author of the opinion is one-sided for or against the interpretation.

It is easy, but also foolish, to assume that people will always try to be fair in presenting an argument and that they will seek to avoid twisting evidence to fit their predetermined conclusions. Even the best researchers will unintentionally contort the evidence to fit their own belief systems. Sometimes it is next to impossible—as people with feelings, personalities, and emotions—to be completely "objective" about anything.

Some arguments, though, take the element of bias and stretch it too far. How far is "too far"? It's hard to tell. Some who present arguments apparently do not try to find the most accurate and truthful position but instead aim to convince an audience by any means necessary. Advertisers are well-known for being biased toward a certain position. Some of them want you to buy a certain product, so they present only its good points. If another product is better, the advertiser will rarely admit that. Of course, most people expect this as part of a competitive marketplace in which the careful consumer prevails. No one expects Coca-Cola to be talking up Pepsi.

One must also be a shrewd consumer of ideas. Certainly there are some solid arguments that are presented by a biased messenger, but that does not mean that you have to reject them because they are "biased". You would have to wait a long, long time if you are that picky a customer. A more reasonable approach is to accept an argument because it provides convincing evidence, not because the messenger appears "unbiased".

STEP FIVE: DETERMINING WHETHER THE ARGUMENT IS BASED ON ACCEPTABLE ASSUMPTIONS AND VALUES

1. Identify the assumptions themselves

The ability to write and to identify a thesis statement is a key step, as is the understanding that one must support one's thesis with evidence. Yet this is not always enough to persuade the reader.

When writing about the past, historians, whether they know it or not, make several assumptions as they try to make the connection between their arguments and their supporting evidence.

- That the evidence cited, perhaps a person, is credible (credibility):

"According to Professor David Smith, Henry VIII was politically savvy."

This statement is persuasive only if one accepts that Professor Smith is a credible authority. If Smith has researched Henry VIII extensively and can cite evidence that further supports his conclusion, then one might surmise that Smith is reliable.

Consider this:

"According to Professor Smith, Henry VIII was politically savvy. Unfortunately, Smith himself was not too savvy, as he was recently reprimanded by the American Historical Association for plagiarism."

In this case, Smith's credibility has been challenged. One would certainly be less apt to listen to the professor if he was guilty of committing academic fraud.

- That a general statement, whether it be a thesis or a conclusion, can be drawn from specific examples (generalization):

"Contrary to some, not all professional athletes take steroids. Indeed, two teams in Major League Baseball had all of their players pass a drug test."

This statement is persuasive if one assumes that what is true of these two is also true for the rest of the teams. If one does not accept this assumption, one might instead believe this statement:

"Those two teams passed the drug test, but what about the other players on the other teams? Let's see their tests!"

- That certain observations indicate or signify a trend (sign):

"Terrorism has been around for centuries, if not millennia, but the news today is filled with reports of terrorists who hijack planes, bomb train stations, and plot to kill world leaders. Clearly, terrorism has become a much larger threat recently."

The writer of this assumes that the hijacking of planes, the bombing of train stations, and the plotting of assassinations signify a trend: terrorism as a threat is intensifying.

But what happens to the argument if the readers do **not** accept that these news events represent signs of change? Consider this example:

"Some commentators argue that terrorism is on the rise. They refer to hijackings, train bombings, murder plots and the like. Yet they forget that other news points to the opposite conclusion, that terrorism is a lesser threat. Estimates are that there are 56% fewer terrorists now than there were five years ago. Funding for terrorism has dried up due to embargos and political pressure. There was one hijacking last year: that of a 747 jumbo jet. Sure, 400 passengers were hijacked, but there was only one incident. There were five hijackings two years ago, all of smaller planes."

- That one condition causes another condition (cause and effect):

"Ironically, the economic reforms that East Germany launched to save the country from disaster actually hastened its decline."

This statement is based on the assumption that the reforms had damaging effects on the economy and therefore on East Germany. The problem is that the assumption of cause and effect is difficult, if not impossible, to prove. Two conditions might exist at the same time, but that does not mean that one causes the other. A skeptic to the above analysis of East German history might offer an alternative:

"Pollution severely damaged the East German economy to the point that even the most brilliant ideas for reform could not save the nation."

One can easily prove that the country suffered from pollution. But does it prove that it was responsible for the country's decline?

"Brezhnev and Chernenko were ineffective leaders who failed to inspire the country to reach its potential. Under them the Soviet Union was a mansion left to decay because of inattention. No reforms, even those of Gorbachev, could recoup decades of lost time."

Yet another "cause" is proposed: weak leadership.

- That what is true for this case is also true in another case because these two cases are similar (analogy):

"Recent elections in Spain show that on terrorism, Spanish voters are following the same policy of appeasement that Hitler took advantage of in 1938."

Among the many assumptions here are that Spain and Germany are similar in that they are both European countries. Since similar behavior brought disaster to Europe in 1938 it will bring disaster to Spain today, that the political background of 1938 is similar enough to that of the twenty-first century, and that Hitler's aggression is similar enough to modern terrorism.

But even things that have similarities **have** to have differences, unless the two are the exact same thing, which is impossible. Two cars of the same make, model, and year exhibit dissimilarities (although one might have to look closely). Even twins have differences between each other.

- That what is true for this case is also true in another case, even though these two cases seem dissimilar:

"The nuclear arms race was a waste of money, as both the U.S. and Soviet Union built enough weapons to kill each other off many times over. It was like a sword fight in which one combatant owns 478 swords, and the other, 523. One would think that ten swords would be enough, providing that the other nine fail!"

The assumption here is that even though the U.S. and U.S.S.R. never used swords in combat, or even really fought at all, that a sword fight was analogous to the Cold War.

- That the reader agrees with the underlying values:

"Statistics demonstrate that AIDS has spread widely in Africa since 1982. Boys and girls are dying. Africa is in crisis. The U.S. must therefore provide government funds to stop this tragedy."

The thesis—that the United States must fund the fight against AIDS in Africa—is persuasive only if the reader accepts the values assumed in the thesis: that stopping the spread of AIDS overseas is desirable, and that the U.S. has the moral obligation to alleviate world suffering.

Even if the author cites reams of statistics that prove that AIDS has spread, and the reader accepts the statistics as being accurate, that does not mean that the reader will necessarily agree with the thesis. Perhaps the reader believes that the United States is morally obligated to stay **out** of Africa, or that it should be individual Americans, and not the United States federal government, who should financially help out needy Africans.

Finding assumptions can be difficult. After all, they are not stated but implied; and we must therefore "read between the lines" to find them.

A helpful way to do this is to break down an argument into its component parts. If we find the conclusion (the main argument) and the premise (a statement from which the conclusion is drawn), then locating the assumption(s) can be easier.

Note the following examples:

Credibility:

1. "Tiger Woods, my favorite golfer, owns a Buick automobile and advertises for the brand. I had better buy a Buick too."

   Broken down, it looks something like this:

   Premise: Tiger Woods owns a Buick and advertises for the brand.
   Assumption (Unstated): Tiger Woods knows something about cars.
   Conclusion: I had better buy a Buick too.

   Does Tiger Woods know cars? That is difficult to say for sure. He certainly knows golf, but that does not make him a credible expert on other subjects.

2. "I talked to my barber while getting my hair cut, and he said that he expects Ohio State will be a #1 seed in the March Madness NCAA tournament. I think he's right—OSU will be a 1 seed."

   Premise: My barber thinks that Ohio State will be a #1 seed in the NCAAs.
   Assumption (Unstated): My barber is a credible authority on college basketball.
   Conclusion: Ohio State will probably be a #1 seed.

   The obvious question here is, how do you KNOW that the barber is an authority on basketball? Does he study the sport seriously? Is he simply a big talker who likes to keep his customers thinking that he knows something?

Generalization:

1. "I was a science major at Duke, and students talk all of the time about the Mathematics Department. Everyone I talk to said that MATH 200 is a hard course. MATH 250 is pretty hard too. You cannot say that I didn't warn you, but if you take math there, expect to have a tough course."

   Break this down into its component parts.

   Premise: At Duke University, MATH 200 is a hard course.
   Premise: MATH 250, also at Duke, is a really hard course.
   Assumption (Unstated): Two is enough of a number to know the difficulty of math courses at Duke.
   Conclusion: If you take a math course at Duke, it will be tough.

   If you do not accept the assumption that two is enough of a number to make an accurate generalization, you might not agree with the conclusion.

2. "During winter in 2004, it was warm. The same for 2005, and for 2006. I would venture to say that 2007 is going to be warm too."

   Premise: 2004 had a warm winter.
   Premise: 2005 had a warm winter.
   Premise: 2006 had a warm winter.
   Assumption (Unstated): Three consecutive seasons is enough to confirm a trend that will continue in the future.
   Conclusion: It is therefore probable that 2007 will have a warm winter.

   Some scientists might disagree with the assumption, arguing instead that winters in the past have little influence on winter weather in the future. Those who reject the assumption likely will not be persuaded.

Analogy:

1. "I read a news story that China executed three drug dealers. Maybe they ought to do that here."

   Premise: In China, drug dealers are put to death.
   Assumption (Unstated): China and the United States are similar countries.
   Conclusion: Therefore, the United States should put drug dealers to death as well.

   The question that needs to be asked—Is China that similar to the United States? If we can think of a lot of differences, then perhaps that assumption is not warranted.

2. "My grandparents live in Florida, and they don't have to file for state income tax. We should have that here in North Carolina, since I hate wasting my time filing."

   Premise: Florida has no income tax.
   Assumption (Unstated): Florida and North Carolina are similar states.
   Conclusion: Therefore, North Carolina should not require income tax either.

   How alike ARE the two states? Are there enough similarities to make the analogy stick?

Sign:

1. "My biology classroom was something like 80 degrees. Why don't they fix the air conditioner in there. We cannot study in that kind of environment."

   Premise: The classroom is hot.
   Assumption (Unstated): If the class is hot, the air conditioner is broken.
   Conclusion: Therefore, the air conditioner needs to be fixed.

   Perhaps it is a broken air conditioner, but there may be other reasons: an open window, an air conditioner that works but is not turned on, other possible sources of "hot air."

2. "My blood test revealed high blood sugar. I must have diabetes."

   Premise: My blood sugar is high.
   Assumption (Unstated): High blood sugar is a sign or symptom of diabetes.
   Conclusion: Therefore, I must have diabetes.

   High blood sugar can be a sign of diabetes, but some people with high blood sugar do not have diabetes. Therefore, a medical test would be necessary.

Cause and effect:

1. "Did you hear about Bob dying last Friday? He smoked like a chimney for thirty years, and then got cancer. That's what killed him."

   Premise: After smoking for thirty years, Bob died last week of cancer.
   Assumption (Unstated): It can be proven that smoking causes cancer and that cancer caused by smoking can kill.
   Conclusion: Therefore, smoking probably killed Bob.

2. "East Texas State University raised tuition big time. I can bet that some students will drop out to the point that their enrollment will be going down. They won't put up with that."

Premise: East Texas State University raised tuition.
Assumption (Unstated): Higher tuition can cause lower enrollment.
Conclusion: Therefore, East Texas State University will have fewer students.

Cause and effect is rarely this simple. Although there is proof that smoking causes deadly cancers, not everyone who dies from cancer smoked, or even was exposed to second-hand smoke. In addition, while it is true that students hate paying high tuition bills, students often transfer or leave universities for other reasons.

Values:

1. "Did you hear that a hurricane hit Mexico. Those poor people. The politicians in Washington, D.C. should do whatever possible to send them some aid."

Premise: A hurricane just hit Mexico.
Assumption (Unstated): If a neighboring country is suffering because of a hurricane, the federal government should care, and caring means sending aid.
Conclusion: Therefore, the federal government should send aid to Mexico.

If we do not accept the assumption, we cannot agree with the conclusion.

Some might feel badly about the people hurting in Mexico, but they might accept a different assumption: the government should not be involved in charity because that responsibility should be shouldered by individuals.

2. "Gary got caught drinking beer on his security guard job. They should fire him."

Premise: Gary drank on the job.
Assumption (Unstated): Employees who drink on the job should be fired.
Conclusion: Therefore, Gary should be fired.

Those who are more open about alcohol usage might not agree that a person should lose his or her job over one mistake. Perhaps to them getting suspended may be a better punishment. They may think that it is wrong to drink on the job, but they might not accept the assumption as stated above.

2. Understand that your reaction to an argument is usually consistent with your own value system.

Living in a diverse world means that most of us eventually encounter points-of-view that differ greatly from our own. It seems that most people can tolerate minor differences in opinion, but there are times when someone's opinion is so different from standard ones that it is easy to react very strongly against it. Why is this so?

A major reason for such a reaction may lie in competing value systems. We tend to accept an argument that is based on values similar to our own; if we can identify our own values, it is usually easier to understand our reactions to the arguments of others.

Values are concepts that are considered worthwhile. They are the foundations of our thoughts, our beliefs, and our actions.

Consider this small sample of values:

Honesty	Freedom of the press	Peace	Caution
Equality	Rationality	Security	Passion/emotions
Individualism	Order	Patriotism	Selflessness
Freedom of speech	Competition	Generosity	Selfishness/self-interest
Tradition	Individual responsibility	Safety	Obedience
Freedom of thought	Collective responsibility	Life	Creativity
Justice	Efficiency	Private property	
Piety	Privacy	Courage	

Just about everyone would agree with each of these values to a certain degree. What makes us all different is how each of us regards some values more highly than other values.

For instance, a person who believes that abortion should be legal, the so-called "pro-choice" position, might not necessarily like the fact that abortions take place. Often times, those who support abortion rights do so because they highly value the right of a woman to control her own body. They may also value highly the rights of the fetus that she carries, but in their judgment, the rights of the mother are more important.

On the contrary, a so-called "pro-life" position is based on the assumption that the rights of a fetus to life are more important than the rights of the mother to privacy. An advocate of this position generally would not support the right of a woman to terminate her pregnancy, and would support a government ban on abortions. Still, that does not mean that a "pro-life" position assumes that the government deserves total control over a person's physical body.

In addition, most teachers, without a doubt, believe that all students should value high academic achievement. At the same time, however, teachers also value academic honesty, and probably consider it higher up in the chain of values. A student who earns an "A+" but does it while cheating is not, in the eyes of the typical teacher, a good student (or a good person). Why not? Because honesty as a value, in their view, trumps academic achievement.

The best way to come to grips with our system of values is through self-discovery. When an issue arises, learn as much about it as possible, and then come to a preliminary conclusion. Seek other opinions and evaluate them; sometimes you will find something worth learning. In other words, determine why you accept a certain position. Trace the steps that lead to your conclusion.

Exercises for Assumptions

Choose the best answer for the following questions. Explain the reasons you chose the answer you did, and why you did not choose the others. A few sentences per question should suffice.

"A businessman offers baseball fans a free LA Dodgers ticket and bus ride in exchange for the bobblehead doll they receive at the gate. The fans attend the game, then willingly surrender their bobbleheads afterward. The Dodgers call this arrangement a scam. I call it good business."

1. Of the following four values, the writer of this statement especially believes in
    a) the right of government to regulate business.
    b) the right of baseball teams to give out free gifts to fans.
    c) the right of people to engage freely in a business transaction.
    d) the baseball team's right to control the behavior of fans.

"According to Sports Weekly Magazine, in the last month the starting catcher for the Oakland A's as well as TWO players from the Baltimore Orioles have tested positive for cocaine. Obviously, Major League Baseball needs to address the rising drug usage among its players."

2. What is being assumed here is that
    a) cocaine usage can lead to premature death.
    b) the cocaine busts of three players indicate a growing trend among ballplayers.
    c) the teams do not support drug testing, and that's why three tested positive.
    d) no other players in the league use cocaine.

"If David McCullough says that John Adams could be a bickering, not necessarily polite individual, then John Adams probably was sometimes a bickering, not necessarily polite individual."

3. This argument is based on the (unstated) assumption that
    a) David McCullough wrote a book on John Adams.
    b) David McCulough is a credible authority on John Adams.
    c) David McCullough is not a credible authority on John Adams.
    d) David McCullough teaches a course on American history.

"Sun Tzu said that a successful military campaign must move swiftly. No army can sustain a war for a protracted period of time. Adolf Hitler, by attacking Russia, ignored his wisdom. His decision committed him to a long and protracted war. It also committed him to failure."

4. This argument is based on the (unstated) assumption that
    a) Sun Tzu was a wise military strategist—or at least wrote wise strategy.
    b) Hitler attacked Russia.
    c) Adolf Hitler was involved in a long war, and, in the end, he lost this war.
    d) In a war with Russia, Adolf Hitler lost.

"Serial killers Ted Bundy and David Berkowitz, 'Son of Sam,' grew up in broken homes. Clearly people brought up in that kind of environment have a hard time creating a sense of identity. A missing parent, therefore, can be a good predictor of a future life of crime, including murder."

5. The assumption being made here is that
    a) what is true for Bundy and Berkowitz is generally true for other criminals.
    b) Ted Bundy was a serial killer.
    c) David Berkowitz is a serial killer.
    d) all serial killers grow up without both parents.

"Attempts to curb what some define as price gouging are futile. Some might be uncomfortable that some gas stations have sold gasoline for substantially higher prices than they paid for it. However, these are the same sages who would think nothing of selling their own home for double the price they paid for it two years ago, even if they have not made a single improvement to that property."

6. This argument is based on the (unstated) assumption that
    a) higher gas prices lead to higher real estate prices.
    b) higher gas prices lead to inflation.
    c) selling gas at a profit is similar to selling real estate at a profit.
    d) government has an obligation to stop unfair pricing of gas.

"Bismarck was a great political leader, since he mastered the fine art of diplomacy."

7. The (unstated) assumption here is that
    a) mastery of diplomacy is a sign of a great political leader.
    b) all political leaders have mastered the fine art of diplomacy.
    c) historians say that Bismarck was a great political leader.
    d) diplomacy is a fine art.

"Between 1405 and 1433, Ming emperors sent seven maritime expeditions probing down into the South Seas and across the Indian Ocean. The economic motive for these huge ventures may have been important, and many of the ships had large private cabins for merchants. But the chief aim was probably political, to enroll further states as tributaries and mark the reemergence of the Chinese Empire following nearly a century of barbarian rule."

8. This argument is based on the (unstated) assumption that
    a) the economic and political motivation of Ming emperors are known now.
    b) the Indian Ocean actually exists.
    c) some of the ships that were sent on the expeditions still exist.
    d) the Mings were in power between 1405 and 1433.

"Stealing is wrong. Because of this, taxation without representation is also wrong."

9. The (unstated) assumption here is that
    a) stealing is always wrong.
    b) taxation without representation is wrong.
    c) taxation without representation is a form of stealing.
    d) stealing is sometimes wrong—it depends what you steal.

"Indeed, Pittman accuses me of slander. My guess is that the guy has mental problems and probably has a non-sexual crush on Senator Jackson."

10. The (unstated) assumption here is that
    a) the author is an authority in determining whether someone has mental problems or not.
    b) slander is not a bad thing to be accused of doing.
    c) Pittman accuses the author of slander.
    d) Senator Jackson has mental problems too.

Exercises for Value Judgments

A Minneapolis, Minnesota official was the first in his family to earn a college degree, and he has come from a family of farmers to become a full-fledged "city slicker." He is on a committee looking to build a road into the suburbs. He has long believed that farmers have the right to use their land, because it is theirs, but in his quest to get a road built, he has run across a farmer who refuses to sell his land. As long as the farmer holds out, there will be no road to build. The city official believes that the new road will benefit all citizens, urban and rural, so he decides to strongarm the farmer and pressure him to sell.

1. Which of these statements best describes the value judgement made here?
   a) private property is the most important right of a citizen
   b) citizens do not have the right to private property
   c) the rights of many people take precedence over the rights of one person
   d) people in the city are smarter than those on a farm and therefore their needs must be met first

In Hungary, a child was near death from a rare, but curable, form of lymphoma. Gallen Biosciences, a pharmaceutical company, has just released an experimental drug that might save her life. There is one problem: a drug distributor in Hungary is charging $20,000 for a month's dosage, which is ten times the cost. The dying child's father worked three jobs, and went to everyone he knew to borrow the money, and tried every legal means, to raise the money, but could only raise $11,400, barely half the cost. He told the distributor that his child was dying and begged him to sell the drug to him for the $11,400 he had raised. The distributor flatly refused, citing the need and right to make a large profit.

2. The father believes in the Golden Rule. He also values the life of his child and believes that one must be honest, yet he would break the law rather than let his child die. What could he do while remaining true to his values?
   a) break into the warehouse and steal the drug
   b) hire someone else to steal the drug from the druggist
   c) find another supplier who might sell the drug at a lower price
   d) go to a new doctor, who will run a new series of tests on the child

Kenya Ray is an environmental compliance technician for a chemical producing plant. She knows that her company has produced pollution but within the legal limits. She believes, as a scientist, that the legal limits are not strict enough, that her company, even though it is following the law, is responsible for releasing significant amounts of dangerous pollutants. In her scientific research, she has come across a technique that will lower the level of pollutants her company produces, but will cost the company and its shareholders money. The company right now is barely profitable, and there are talks about imminent layoffs. Uncertain about what to do, she does nothing, keeping her mouth shut.

3. One possible reason Kenya remained quiet was because of an ethical conflict between
   a) losing her job and losing money in her company's falling stock
   b) protecting the environment and possibly losing her job
   c) remaining true to science and remaining faithful to her company
   d) obeying government regulations and obeying her conscience

A police officer in the Deep South is guarding a prisoner accused of kidnapping and then killing a ten-year old girl. A mob has formed outside, demanding that the police give them the prisoner so they can give him some "Southern justice." Although the officer feels that there is probably enough evidence against the accused murderer (why else would he be in jail in the first place), he refuses at first, arguing that every person deserves a fair trial. The mob gets increasingly angry. They even cut the phone lines. The officer knows that the mob is going to riot soon if they do not get what they want, and the officer knows that riots often kill many people. The officer panics and delivers the prisoner to the mob.

4. His actions reflect that he does not highly value
   a) the lives of others
   b) the right of every citizen to a fair trial
   c) people living in the Deep South
   d) the right to life of a convicted murderer

Two teenagers live in poverty in a town that has a few wealthy citizens, one of whom is a former corporate executive who was convicted of fraud by his own company. One of the teenagers confesses to the other that he sneaked into the man's house and stole some jewelry worth less than $1000. The other teenager knows that this amount is like pocket change to the wealthy former executive, but nevertheless decides to turn his friend in to the authorities.

5. The teenager who turned his friend in to the police MOST LIKELY believes
   a) it is OK to steal some objects, but not jewelry, from the wealthy
   b) it is wrong to steal, even from the rich
   c) friendship is more important than obeying the law
   d) getting a reward from a rich person is more important than friendship

In *Crime and Punishment* the main character, a young man, murders a frail, elderly woman who happens to be wealthy, and then steals her money. He justifies the theft by noting that she was a miserable, miserly hag anyway, and that he will do more good with her money than she would have. He is going to school with the money, whereas all she would have done was hoard it for a brief time until her death.

6. This character has violated all of the following EXCEPT
   a) the old woman's right to life
   b) the old woman's right to private property
   c) the old woman's religious freedom
   d) society's prohibition against the strong harming the weak

During the final days of World War I, a German officer surrendered to an American officer. The German handed his gun and binoculars to the American and raised his hands. Without a doubt, he was unarmed. The American said "thank you" and, seemingly in a daze and without the slightest bit of anger, shot the German through the head. A soldier who witnessed the incident asked a friend for advice on what to do. "Should I turn him in?" the witness asked. His friend admitted that shooting the unarmed man was probably a bad thing to do, but he saw someone else do the same thing the day before. Besides, the American officer was a good man who was probably not quite right in the head—this is war, after all, and none of us are completely sane. Turning the officer in would not bring the dead man back anyway, so just forget about it. To the witness, this outlook made a lot of sense, so he decided to keep quiet. When he wrote about the incident years later, he did not identify the name of the American officer.

7. The witness would likely agree with all of the following EXCEPT
   a) "killing is wrong, even during war"
   b) "a person is not responsible for a crime if he is mentally ill"
   c) "killing is wrong, except in self defense"
   d) "no use crying over spilled milk"

A fundamentalist Christian high school sincerely aims to prepare their students to be educated, and effective, Christian citizens. To fulfill the school's mission, the school's administrators place some anti-pornographic software on all campus computers. The software is so restrictive that students cannot study the writings of famous historian Peter Gay, the world's foremost expert on the eighteenth century. This is in addition to a long-standing rule banning all books containing sexual content or profanity, even if they are literary classics, from the library.

8. According to their actions, the administrators strongly believe that
   a) it is more important to be educated than to be moral
   b) it is more important to obey the Bible than to be educated
   c) it is acceptable to censor material that might threaten young minds
   d) students need to study all of history, even the more disturbing parts

A homeowner is a pacifist who eats meat on occasion but strongly believes that animals should be treated humanely. His house has become the home to a family of mice, who eat his food, chew up his floorboards, and leave a musky odor wherever they go. He decides that he needs to remove the intruders but does not want to kill them, so instead of buying a typical mouse trap, he purchases a more expensive, but more humane, trap that allows the user to release the rodent outside, preferably in some vacant field far from his house.

9. The homeowner apparently accepts that
    a) animals deserve more rights than humans
    b) animals have the same rights as humans
    c) animals have fewer rights than humans but have rights nonetheless
    d) animals have no rights whatsoever

A shy woman has long believed that far too many people sue, and usually for frivolous reasons. However, while recently shopping for groceries, she slipped and broke her leg in two places when she unknowingly walked into a puddle of salad oil. She has missed work for two weeks and is not being paid, because she never signed up for disability insurance. She feels that the store was negligent for not cleaning up its messes and has decided to hire a lawyer, yet is still uncertain whether she will sue.

10. She would likely agree with all of the following statements EXCEPT
    a) "the grocery store is responsible for the safety of its customers"
    b) "a broken leg is a significant injury"
    c) "the grocery store owners have property rights and can therefore do what they want on their property"
    d) "the grocery store violated her right to work"

A student is running late for class and risks missing an examination. There seem to be no police officers around, so he drives 60 in a 50 MPH zone.

11. The actions of the student most closely parallel a
    a) police officer who sells drugs to earn extra money
    b) a tax cheat who thinks the IRS won't audit her return and who cheats because she needs the money for birthday presents
    c) a prostitute who sells her body to earn money for drugs
    d) a student who cheats on an examination

STEP SIX: LOOKING FOR LOGICAL TRAPS

Hall of Fame pitcher Phil Niekro retired many years ago, yet even casual baseball fans remember that he was a master at manipulating a baseball. Sometimes he obeyed the rules of the game; sometimes he took liberty with them. He would use sandpaper, vaseline, and other banned substances—anything—to gain an advantage over a batter. He was such a talented pitcher that he did not have to do that. He knew better, but did it anyway.

Propagandists, and other artists of persuasion, likewise tend to be highly intelligent and well-educated. As Niekro manipulated the baseball, so they are experts at manipulating words and language. They know all about logic and reason, and perhaps more importantly, know that most other people do not. They take advantage of this lack of knowledge by bending the rules of fair debate in order to deceive others. Sometimes it is because they know that their evidence is weak, that they are going to have to find other ways to win people over to their side. The tricks they employ are like the foreign objects in Niekro's pocket—if something works, then it is worth trying. Propagandists tend to use the same tricks again and again. Here are the most common ones.

1. Begging the Question:

This common fallacy involves assuming something that needs to be proven (in other words, mistaking an assumption for a claim).

"Professor Adams is too demanding; no one in her class received a final grade higher than a 'B+'."

This argument assumes that someone in the class actually deserved a higher grade. Perhaps that is true, but such a statement requires evidence.

A cruder version of this fallacy is circular reasoning. Note this example:

"The minimum drinking age should not be reduced from 21 to 18 because eighteen-year olds are too young to drink."

That 18 is "too young" has not been established but rather just assumed.

The way to challenge an argument guilty of question-begging is to point out the skipped step and to demand that the argument go back to it.

2. Appeal to Tradition

In this fallacy, it is assumed that because something worked or appeared to be true in the past, it has to work or be true today. Arguments falling into this logical trap usually assume that the past and present are really not very different. For if something worked in the past, it must also work at the present time. Note this example:

"The military draft instilled a sense of pride in recruits. Ever since it was abolished, the quality of the armed forces has suffered. To save the military, it is important to go back to what once worked: Restore the draft."

Appealing to tradition, as this example illustrates, often assumes the existence of some glorious "Golden Age" from the past whose presence cannot be easily verified (what may be "glorious" to some may not have been so to others). The problem with this fallacy is that most things in life eventually change. The reasons that made a certain policy effective in the past may no longer be present.

When faced with an argument that in some way appeals to a past tradition, ask yourself: Are the pieces that made this argument true in the past still in place, or has the world changed so much that this past idea may no longer be applicable?

3. Appeal to Precedent

This fallacy is very similar to "Appeal to Tradition". The difference is that in appealing to tradition, one is usually referring to some vague ideal or way of life in the past. When one appeals to precedent, one is calling upon an actual event to show that a current event is similar to a past one. In other words, the approach to the past event should be applied to the present one. As an illustration, observe this example:

"As the school principal, I do not tolerate academic dishonesty. The last time I had to deal with a suspected student, he was given an "F" for the class and was suspended for three days. That is the same punishment I am giving to you."

Past students who were accused of cheating served as the precedent in this example; their punishment will also be the same for the student to whom the principal was speaking.

"Appeal to precedent" is commonly used in judicial matters. For example, higher courts, when faced with resolving an issue, look to past decisions on the same (or at least very similar) issue. If both the past and present manifestations of the issue are similar enough, court members may decide that the present manifestation should be resolved in a manner like the past one.

When an argument appeals to precedent, it is important to determine whether there are good reasons to do so.

4. Appeal to Authority

This fallacy appeals to the authority of a certain person who may be unqualified to give an expert opinion. Another way to appeal to authority is to assume that just because someone with authority has made a claim, the soundness of the claim does not have to be verified.

This fallacy has many disguises, some of which are very obvious. For example, when you were a child, it is likely that at one time your parents, or other adults, told you to do something. If you questioned their command and dared to ask them why, you might have heard a version of "Because I told you so." As adults, we may laugh at that now, yet it is no laughing matter to trust someone who may appear to be credible but may not be.

Some advertisers promote their products by citing the opinion of someone called "Doctor." Often this person is wearing a white lab coat, probably to give more credibility as a person of science.

But what kind of "doctor" is this person? A person with a Ph.D., for example, may be able to give opinions within a particular field; a leading biologist, however, may not be qualified to offer a credible opinion on geology. Should a person with a Ph.D. in herbal science be giving opinions on the radio about politics? It is an impressive accomplishment to earn a doctorate in anatomy, but does that mean that the good doctor should be regarded as a respected authority on human behavior (as in her knowledge of the muscles in the thigh somehow give her the authority to treat psychological disorders)?

A famous movie star or athlete, even a popular one, may not be a proper authority to consult when buying consumer products. Tiger Woods signed a $60 million contract with Nike to sell golf footwear, and NASCAR would not be the same without the ubiquitous ads on the driver's jacket and on the car. That's all nice, but does that make Nike golf spikes better than those put out by Adidas? Just because Jeff Gordon is sponsored by Hardees, does that mean that you yourself should buy a hamburger and fries from that fast-food chain?

The issue at stake is not whether a celebrity or authoritative person believes something, but whether a certain claim has sufficient evidence backing it up. But people are not generally critical thinkers. That is why companies hire spokespeople.

5. Appeal to Pity

This fallacy involves appealing to ideals of compassion rather than respecting evidence. When appealing to pity, excuses often take the place of convincing argumentation:

"I know I haven't completed my term paper, but I really think that I should be excused. This has been a difficult quarter for me: I've been sick, and my car broke down. Please grant me an extension."

The problem with this argument is that even though the reasons to support the premise may be true, they are not necessarily relevant to the conclusion.

Often times an elderly person who kills one's spouse for health reasons is given a much lighter sentence than a young person who commits the same crime. Sometimes this is done out of an appeal to pity: "Look at the poor, pathetic old man. He shouldn't go to prison. He's harmless." This statement is one with which his murdered wife might not concur.

6. Appeal to Fear

Those guilty of this fallacy try to persuade by intimidation and scare tactics (fear of some kind of loss, including that of money, job, or possessions). Arguments guilty of this fallacy, in other words, try to scare you into agreement.

"If you vote for him, he will raise your taxes, mark my word. Vote for me instead."

There are two problems here. First, one cannot know for certain if the first candidate will raise taxes unless he is first elected. Second, a vote against one person begs the question as to why you should elect a certain other candidate. If not A, then B, works only if there is no C or D.

Sometimes businesses employ this when they issue coupons that expire on a certain date, or especially when they pressure a consumer to buy an item on sale NOW, because "supplies are limited" (for that matter, so is the oxygen in the atmosphere!) and "the sale can end at any time" (as can the world!). The fear that is being capitalized on is fear of loss. They want you to rush to the store to buy the item out of fear that if you do not do it now, you will lose the chance to get a bargain.

7. Appeal to Ignorance

In this fallacy, either a conclusion is alleged to be true because it cannot be proven false, or a conclusion is alleged to be false because it cannot be proven true. Here is an example of the first version:

"You say God doesn't exist, but can you prove that? If you can't, you then must accept that God does in fact exist."

This argument is not sound; simply because an opponent cannot disprove the conclusion does not prove that it is right. "Negative proof" is not really proof at all.

"If you cannot prove that God exists, then God does not exist."

This argument is unsound as well. Simply because an opponent cannot prove the conclusion does not necessarily mean that the conclusion CANNOT be proven, either now or in the future.

"There is no extraterrestrial life. If there were, we would have found it already."

People say this, sometimes.

"Polio is incurable."

People USED to say this. They do not say this anymore.

8. Appeal to Force

This fallacy involves using force or the threat of force to convince someone to take a certain position.

"Hand over your money, or I will slice you open."

The main point here is simple: someone may have the power or strength to force you to accept a conclusion, but force alone does not make it sound. Still, to be safe, it may be better to avoid arguing and just hand over the money.

Consider a more subtle (but not THAT much more subtle) example:

"If you do not tell me all you know about Peter's cheating on the mid-term, then I will do everything I can to expel you from this university."

Or, this paraphrase from many a crime drama:

"If you do not testify against your brother, then I will simply arrest you and charge you with being an accomplice to murder."

9. Attack on the Person

Those committing this fallacy do not attack the argument but rather the person advocating it. A common example of this fallacy (Latin name *ad hominem*) is name-calling: ridiculing a person on the basis of weight, intelligence, hair length or color, political orientation, salary, place of origin, level of education, occupation, ethnic or religious background, age, or other characteristics is to reveal ignorance of proper argumentation. Worthwhile debate involves claims and evidence, not personal attacks.

"The senator from Tennessee knows nothing about crime; he's just a hick. Just look at his hair."

"I don't want that kid working for me. Look how he refuses to pull up his pants all the way."

The home of the Tennessee legislator may have little to do with his knowledge of crime. Likewise, the teenager might be a good worker, even if his rear is hanging out of his pants.

"Your opinion does not matter. You're a fundamentalist flake."

"You are motivated only by your politically-correct ideology. Your arguments should not be taken seriously."

This is not only ad-hominem (the labels "politically correct" and "ideology"), but also begging the question. How does the person know anything about the other person's motivations?

10. False Cause

(Latin name *post hoc ergo propter hoc*) This fallacy involves an assumption: event "A" caused event "B" because event "B" happened after event "A". Note the following humorous example:

"It always rains after I wash my car; therefore, washing the car caused the rain."

This example is probably mere coincidence mixed with a bit of Murphy's Law, which itself is based on a *post hoc* argument.

False cause is a very common argument that is often hard to avoid because it is very difficult—if not impossible—to demonstrate cause-and-effect convincingly. The major problem with trying to determine causes and effects is that there are almost always many more than two elements (one "cause" and one "effect") involved. There are usually many causes and many effects.

"President Clinton's policies were most responsible for the prosperity of the 1990's."

"The G.W. Bush tax cuts made the recession of 2001 less painful than it would have been."

"President Johnson's policies lowered poverty rates."

All of these sound good, and many people believe them, but causation is much more complex than this. There may well be some truth in each of these statements. They are nevertheless difficult to prove with any degree of certainty.

11. Appeal to People (Jumping on the Bandwagon)

This fallacy substitutes popular appeal for evidence. It assumes that a conclusion is sound because a great number of people already accept it. There are clear problems with such a line of thinking; even if a high number of credible authorities advocate a certain position, it may still have problems.

"Sign up for this credit card. Over 3.4 million people already use it."

The issue at stake here is not the number of users of the card, but rather its interest rate, credit limit, and annual fee, among other things.

"Most people in this county are Democrats. You should register as a Democrat too."

The way to overcome this fallacy is, first, to point out that people often are wrong, and then to judge the argument by its evidence. Just because "Everyone's doing it" does not mean it is the right thing to do. "Join in the revolution" only when there is enough good evidence to justify doing so.

12. False Analogy

This fallacy involves making a comparison between two similar cases and arguing that what is true in one of them must necessarily be true in the other (in other words, because two things are similar on some levels, they are therefore comparable).

It is important to point out that not all analogies are fallacies. Analogies can be useful, in fact, but only when they compare two things having many significant (in other words, more than just one or two minor) points of similarity. The significant points must be central points, and the differences must be minor. One who decides to argue through analogy must be ready to defend the comparison. Analogies are used often in argumentation; notice the following example, which also appeals to tradition:

"We must not stop until our goal has been reached. We must persevere. Our battle is just like that of the abolitionists in the 1800's; their movement started as a small group of concerned individuals, but it continued until the slaves were free. We are going to follow in the abolitionists' footsteps, and we won't stop until we succeed."

The nineteenth century is in the distant past, and many things have changed since then. It is probably not fair to compare anything today with something from that time. The analogy is weak.

Having the government authorize an evacuation in order to escape a hurricane is very much unlike having the government forcibly round up thousands of Japanese and intern them as was done in 1942 during World War II. This might sound obvious, but someone actually employed this analogy in print to defend Japanese internment.

"If we follow the policy of appeasement in Iraq, then we'll fall into the same trap that snared Neville Chamberlain in 1938, when he felt he could "appease" Hitler. If we do not crush Saddam now, we'll be on the road to World War III."

This is yet another analogy that has some similarities yet many more differences. Hitler and Saddam Hussein were similar in some regards while very, very different in others. The question as to whether there were "enough" similarities is open to debate.

13. Slippery Slope

This fallacy assumes that one undesirable action will lead to a worse action, which will lead to an even worse one, and so on. "Slippery slope" is a mixture of "false cause" and "appeal to fear" and is often a powerful fallacy. It is often used in claims of policy; many involve morality or government programs.

"Don't take that first drink, or else you will start drinking every weekend, and then you will be getting drunk every weekend. Before you know it, you will be a full-fledged alcoholic."

"Don't start funding that new government program, or then we have to support that other program. Soon we're going to be giving money away to everyone, and we'll end up just like France and the other Socialists."

Examples like these may often work, but they are still based on sloppy thinking. The truth is that it is hard enough to try to demonstrate how something causes something else, but to attempt to do this in a long chain is next to impossible. A person may take one drink and never take another drink. The person may indeed one day become an alcoholic, but it is impossible to predict that fate after the person takes one drink.

There is no evidence either that the funding of certain programs has to lead to the funding of everything.

14. Hasty Generalization

It is impossible to avoid using generalizations. What makes a hasty generalization a fallacy is that it is based on a very small sample. The larger the sample, the more reliable the generalization will tend to be.

"My ex-boyfriend is a creep; therefore, it's obvious. All men are creeps. So don't even think about asking me out."

The ex-boyfriend is just one person; there are billions of men in the world. One possible example cannot support such a broad claim.

"Government is corrupt. Congressman Jacobson was accused of taking a bribe, and Senator Lightfoot was expelled for the same offense. You can't trust politicians."

Once again, two possible examples are probably not sufficient evidence. How do these two elected officials compare with the rest of "government"?

"The former convict, who was recently released on parole, ended up killing someone. All criminals should serve all of their time."

This one incident, while it should be considered, needs to be seen in the context of all parolees.

15. False Dilemma

This fallacy, also known as the "either/or" or "black and white" fallacy, or "bifurcation," implies that there are only two (often extreme) alternatives and no other ones.

"You're either a liberal or a conservative. Which is it?"

"You can go to college, or you have to work on the farm."

"If you don't vote for him, then you must be for the murderers."

Members of other parties—Libertarian, Communist, Independent, or whatever—would disagree with that first point. Also, one does not necessarily have to work as a farmer if one decides not to attend college. There are other jobs. The third example is a particularly egregious one, but it has been said.

16. Non Sequitur

This fallacy, an extreme kind of false generalization, involves taking otherwise sound premises to form an invalid conclusion (one that does not follow from the premises).

"Dysfunctional families are common tragedies, and the ones who endure the most suffering are the children. The government should break up such families to save young people from repeating their parents' example."

There are several problems with this argument, and one is that government intervention is not discussed until the end. The argument, moreover, does not demonstrate that government is obligated to intervene in the family unit.

"North Korea is on the rise, and it needs to be stopped. The United Nations has failed and therefore needs to be abolished."

Although facts exist that North Korea has increased in power in recent years, and although few would argue with the claim that it needs to be stopped, there is no evidence presented here that this is a result of the United Nations. Additional evidence would be required to support the abolition of the U.N.

17. Loaded Language

This fallacy involves using emotionally-charged language, instead of solid evidence, to demonstrate a position. "Loaded language", a subtler form of *ad hominem*, overstates the negative or positive qualities of a person or policy and is often used in propaganda.

"It is unfair at this time to offer a tax cut. If anything, the working people should have their taxes cut. The rich leeches have already sucked enough money."

It is one thing, for example, to say that someone is wealthy; it is another to call that person a "leech," or for that matter, a "rich dirt-bag", "robber baron", or a "money-grubber." Likewise, it is not always fair to call a person receiving government assistance a "welfare-queen" or a "parasite", or an elected official who wants to limit government assistance a "Scrooge" or someone who wants to "take food out of the mouths of starving children."

Fair debate involves accurate descriptions, not emotional distortions based on a bit of truth. Using loaded language is a way to overstate an argument and is a poor substitute for reasoned dialogue.

18. Straw Man

This fallacy has two forms. First, it can occur when a person claims to be addressing a contrary opinion but instead distorts it. The person first claims to provide "evidence" which disproves the distortion and then contends that the contrary opinion has been successfully refuted.

"She argues that the United States should provide, for all citizens, national health care. What she is really advocating, though, is socialism, a failed philosophy of government."

It may not be fair to equate "national health coverage" with "socialism". They may have similar elements but may not necessarily be the same thing. This fallacy also may be guilty of ambiguous definition; it would be sensible to define "socialism" precisely.

Sometimes a qualifying word such as "apparently" or a phrase such as "I suppose he is saying . . ." or "I guess what he means . . ." is used.

"He voted against the senator. Apparently he hates America."

This argument takes a fact (a vote) and links it with an opinion, so it appears that the opinion is actually factual. In this case, the opinion that a voter "hates America" is not supported merely by a voter exercising his rights at the ballot box.

19. Two Wrongs Make a Right

This fallacy is another example of denying a valid conclusion. It involves pointing out an opponent's possible weaknesses in a case when these weaknesses are irrelevant. Instead of providing evidence to overcome an objection, a person may try to change the topic and try to place the burden of proof back on the challenger.

"Two wrongs make a right" is often committed in issues of morality or character:

"I know the project was late, and I am sorry for the inconvenience. Still, last year I asked you for a project, and you were two weeks late."

What happened last year is irrelevant to the present question: Was the current project on time?

"The Republicans smeared President Clinton, so it is perfectly OK for Bush to get the same."

"Evening the score," this is called. Some would also call it "two wrongs make a right."

20. Red Herring

This fallacy is also known as "changing the subject". It is committed when a person is unable to present a convincing argument on a certain topic. Instead of trying to stick to the topic, the person will introduce a new subject—one that might have some emotional appeal with the audience.

The fallacy of "red herring" is often committed in debate. Let's suppose Mike is debating Barbara, but she is out of evidence and in trouble. Out of desperation for the win, she might try to change the subject of the debate to a topic that may not be entirely relevant to the debate. Barbara has thrown Mike a "red herring". If he is wise, he won't jump for the bait and will instead point out that Barbara has changed the topic. He should then declare that since she has brought up an irrelevant issue, the original topic has been resolved, and that he has won.

21. Repeated Assertion

This fallacy involves continually repeating an argument without providing evidence, and then saying that the argument is therefore true (in other words, substituting repetition for evidence).

Propagandists are often guilty of committing this fallacy, even though repeating something again and again does not make it so. A factual wrong statement is wrong the first time, the second time, the fiftieth time, and even the one-millionth time it is told. Then again, too many people forget this, and this is why propagandists are still in business.

22. Card Stacking (Selective Omission)

This fallacy uses evidence selectively. What happens usually is that a person will emphasize only the evidence that supports the claim and will ignore that which might damage it.

Consider this technique, the rhetorical equivalent of a bodybuilder who wears a muscle shirt to show off his biceps yet wears long pants because he does not want everyone to see his untrained legs. Card stacking involves cherry picking only the facts that help your case while ignoring those uncomfortable facts that weaken it. There might be more facts that contradict rather than support the argument, yet one would not know this if there is card stacking going on. Anyone can find a few facts that support just about any argument, but a well-established argument should address—and attempt to refute—contrary facts.

When it comes to selling oneself, card stacking is fairly innocuous. For instance, a candidate running for office is naturally going to emphasize her strengths, not her weaknesses. For that matter, a person going out with someone for the first time is probably going to be on his best behavior and will keep his bad habits, annoying behavior, and gross body functions to himself. There is nothing wrong with that, to a certain extent. Attacking one's opponent in an election is a given, and is to be expected.

The critical listener should remember he is getting only one side. No person is either one thing or the other; people have good sides, and they have bad sides. Just because one side is not being presented does not mean that it does not exist.

23. Anecdotal Evidence

One of the simplest fallacies is to rely on anecdotal evidence. For example,

"This cow pancreas extract definitely works in helping arthritis. I took it for two weeks, and I feel better."

The placebo effect and the ability of the mind to control the body are both well documented. The Food and Drug Administration, fortunately, has much more stringent standards of proof.

"Prayer must work. I prayed that the Phillies would win the 1980 World Series, and they finally did (but they won only once)."

I say this only because it was true (at least I thought so at the time). I did pray—hard!—and the Phillies did win the 1980 World Series, but this does not mean that they won because of my prayers. Certainly there were twelve-year old boys in Kansas City who were praying for the Royals to win. Their prayers were not answered.

"Tupac is alive. I saw him at Wal-Mart."

Well, you might think you saw the dead rapper, but more evidence would be necessary in order to prove that he is alive. The same goes with "Elvis is alive!" and other "urban legends."

Exercises for Fallacies

Choose the best answer for the following questions. Explain the reasons you chose the answer you did, and why you did not choose the others. A few sentences per question should suffice.

There are two groups of people in the business world: the "winners" and the "losers".

1. This statement is logically misleading because
   a) it employs the either or fallacy
   b) it is an attack on the person
   c) it is a sweeping generalization

The United Nations acted appropriately in arguing for African independence. Obviously, every nation who voted for the measure is reasonable.

2. The problem with this statement, at least in a logical sense, is that
   a) it is a hasty generalization, since nations voting for the measure might act unreasonably in other ways
   b) it is an appeal to authority, the authority of the United Nations
   c) it is a sweeping generalization, because the UN might be wrong
   d) it is a straw man, the UN being the straw man

"During the 1990s, 40 million children were injected with thimerosal-based vaccines, receiving unprecedented levels of mercury during a period critical for brain development. As the number of vaccines increased, the rate of autism among children exploded."

3. This argument possibly contains the fallacy
   a) attack on the person   b) false cause   c) hasty generalization   d) false analogy

Physicians are all alike. This is the fourth time I have heard this month about some doctor committing insurance fraud by ripping off Medicare.

4. All of these are possible problems with this EXCEPT
   a) unless proven, hearsay is insufficient evidence
   b) four is a small number; perhaps many more physicians are honest
   c) one month is too short a period to make such a rash conclusion
   d) it is an example of an either/or fallacy

Since tax revenues have come up short, we have two choices: cut some services drastically while keeping some services fully funded, or cut all services moderately.

5. A good counter to this argument would be to point out that
   a) taxes were cut by an irresponsible Congress
   b) the people voted for the tax cut
   c) there is a third option: raise taxes
   d) there is only one option: trim down services

"Thirty million Americans cannot be wrong. Join your local Southern Baptist church."

6. This argument is relying on the fallacy
   a) appeal to fear   b) appeal to force   c) jumping on the bandwagon   d) false cause

Bob said, "On my radio program I attacked illegal immigrants, using a so-called slur, and now the liberals are calling me a racist. This is anti-Christian prejudice, plain and simple. I am not surprised that they are criticizing me, since Christians are discriminated against everywhere."

7. The last two sentences are examples of
    a) an appeal to pity, since Bob is claiming that he is being persecuted for his faith
    b) an appeal to force, since Christians are persecuted by force
    c) a hasty generalization, since not all immigrants are illegal
    d) a hasty generalization, since Christians are not persecuted everywhere

I don't like to hear that I as president cannot both solve domestic problems and fight a war overseas at the same time. I have two daughters, and I took care of both of them. I never said that I had to choose between caring for one or for the other.

8. This is a false analogy because
    a) presidents cannot do two things equally well
    b) solving problems as president is not the same as caring for children
    c) the president did not provide adequately for his own daughters
    d) a war at home (domestic) is not the same as a war overseas

Civil disobedience must be stopped, because it leads to riots, and riots lead to revolution.

9. Logically, this is weak because it employs the fallacy
    a) false analogy
    b) slippery slope
    c) hasty generalization
    d) appeal to ignorance

Democracy is a poor way to elect a leader. Too many voters are like children who think they know what's best for them. The reality is, they don't.

10. This argument contains an analogy that is probably false because
    a) children are too young to vote
    b) voters are not always this self-confident
    c) in many ways voters are not at all similar to the young
    d) democracy is not at all like monarchy

Some people believe that we must adopt a national energy policy of conservation. They are wrong to think that conservation will create a utopia in which there are no problems, because there can never be a utopia.

11. The red herring here is
    a) the claim that critics are necessarily seeking a utopia
    b) the impossibility of ever having a utopia
    c) the impossibility of ever having a national energy policy
    d) the claim that a national policy is impractical

"Biotech companies time and time again come up with drugs that are supposed to cure disease, but what happens is that the FDA takes the drugs off the market because they are discovered to be killers. These poisoners should be heavily fined to the point of bankruptcy. This is the only way to stop this abuse of the public."

12. The writer concludes that heavy financial penalties represent the "the only way to stop this abuse of the public." Why is this argument weak?
    a) there might be other ways to stop abuse, not just one
    b) the public might be too stupid to protect itself
    c) the only way to solve anything is to have stronger government regulation
    d) natural cures are the only way to go

Hall-of-Fame batter Wade Boggs had a routine that he believed was essential for his success. He headed to the ballpark at the same time before every game, ate chicken and cheesecake before the first pitch, and after the game had two hot dogs, a bag of barbecue potato chips and an iced tea.

13. This superstition, like all superstitions, are examples of the fallacy
    a) slippery slope
    b) false cause
    c) appeal to ignorance
    d) loaded language

North Carolina should legalize casino gambling. Look what it did to Nevada and New Jersey.

14. This argument would be most weakened if it could be proven that
    a) North Carolina has already allowed gambling
    b) Nevada and New Jersey are very different from North Carolina
    c) Nevada and New Jersey are much like North Carolina
    d) Nevada was the first state to legalize casino gambling

"The first president, George Washington, started serving in 1789. He died soon after leaving office. Every United States president elected in twenty-year intervals beginning with 1840 (starting with William Henry Harrison) died in office: Harrison 1840, Lincoln 1860, Garfield 1880, McKinley 1900, Harding 1920, Roosevelt 1940, JFK, 1960. President Bush, elected in 2000, might well be careful, as he might die in office as well."

15. The fallacy here is that of
    a) false analogy   b) false cause   c) begging the question   d) appeal to fear

"Please allow me to enlighten those who are so shocked at the Vatican's policy banning priests from marrying. The debate over clerical marriage was settled a long time ago. For centuries the Roman Catholic Church has banned priests from marrying. The church, therefore, should continue to do the same. If it ain't broke, don't fix it."

16. This argument is possibly an example of an appeal to
    a) tradition   b) pity   c) force   d) ignorance

"St. Thomas Aquinas wrote this paragraph on just war, and since Aquinas was one of the greatest thinkers in Christian history, he probably was right."

17. This statement might well be an example of
    a) appeal to authority
    b) appeal to pity
    c) false cause
    d) jumping on the bandwagon

18. An example of "two wrongs make a right" would be
    a) There is no way that Copernicus can be right that the sun is the center of the solar system, because Aristotle rejected that idea.
    b) You tell me that smoking is bad for my health, but yet you smoke! It cannot be true.
    c) Torture is justifiable. Peoples have used it since the dawn of time. If it didn't work, wouldn't we all know it by now?
    d) Reverend Smith obviously does not care about Catholics, since she is a Protestant minister.

19. An example of an appeal to precedent would be
    a) The United States needs to remain in the United Nations because it has been a member since it was founded after World War II
    b) Why worry about failing schools when it is the war on terrorism that we should be more concerned about?
    c) We should cut welfare because too many single mothers are getting benefits already.
    d) Both presidential candidates went to Yale, so either of them would make a great president.

Universal health care will lead to socialized medicine and ultimately to socialism.

20. This statement is an example of the fallacy
    a) slippery slope
    b) either/or
    c) repeating an assertion
    d) insinuation through rumor

Michael Foley attacked me in his autobiography, so it is time, now that I am writing the story of my life, to return the favor.

21. Someone who believed this would also accept that
    a) saying something more than once makes it more valid
    b) one should use force or threats of force to persuade
    c) two wrongs make a right
    d) it is proper to use loaded language

Michael said, "Ecological wackos have burned thousands of SUVs."
David said, "Prove it."
Michael said, "65 SUVs were spraypainted in Santa Cruz, California, and 40 more were vandalized in Alabama."

22. An example of ad hominem, attacking the person, appears above:
    a) "SUVS"
    b) "Ecological wackos"
    c) "spraypainted"
    d) "thousands of SUVS"

"Many of history's most brilliant scientists and mathematicians had a keen interest in music, including Sir Isaac Newton and Albert Einstein. Those with children should consider having them take music lessons, so they can too become scientific and mathematical geniuses."

23. It can be said that this argument relies on false cause, because
    a) some athletes like music too, so that contradicts the argument
    b) it is easy to forget that Albert Einstein also liked politics
    c) mathematics and music require similar mental abilities
    d) liking music does not necessarily make one a genius

24. It can also be said that this argument makes a hasty generalization, because
    a) many other mathematicians and scientists are great musicians also
    b) R Kelly is a musician, but he hates both math and science
    c) two examples of genius are not enough; more are needed
    d) Einstein was not a brilliant mathematician, but rather a brilliant physicist

Although no one likes to use torture on another human being, in the war of terrorism, it will sometimes have to be done. You have to make choices. Which is worse: terrorists in pain or terrorists who gain?

25. The biggest problem with the logical reasoning here is that
    a) rarely are there ever just two alternatives
    b) torture is a form of appeal to force
    c) both alternatives are undesirable
    d) some people are disturbed enough that they like torturing others

CHAPTER 2

TIMELESS QUESTIONS THROUGHOUT WORLD HISTORY: A READER

HOW DID THE WORLD BEGIN?

The Hebrews: Genesis 1-2[1]

This creation account is from the Old Testament of the Bible and is a part of the Judeo-Christian tradition. It has been alleged that Moses wrote this sometime around the thirteenth century BCE.

In the beginning God created the heaven and the earth. And the earth was without form, and void; and darkness was upon the face of the deep. And the Spirit of God moved upon the face of the waters. And God said, Let there be light: and there was light. And God saw the light, that it was good: and God divided the light from the darkness. And God called the light Day, and the darkness he called Night. And the evening and the morning were the first day.

And God said, Let there be a firmament in the midst of the waters, and let it divide the waters from the waters. And God made the firmament, and divided the waters which were under the firmament from the waters which were above the firmament: and it was so. And God called the firmament Heaven. And the evening and the morning were the second day.

And God said, Let the waters under the heaven be gathered together unto one place, and let the dry land appear: and it was so. And God called the dry land Earth; and the gathering together of the waters called he Seas: and God saw that it was good. And God said, Let the earth bring forth grass, the herb yielding seed, and the fruit tree yielding fruit after his kind, whose seed is in itself, upon the earth: and it was so. And the earth brought forth grass, and herb yielding seed after his kind, and the tree yielding fruit, whose seed was in itself, after his kind: and God saw that it was good. And the evening and the morning were the third day.

And God said, Let there be lights in the firmament of the heaven to divide the day from the night; and let them be for signs, and for seasons, and for days, and years: And let them be for lights in the firmament of the heaven to give light upon the earth: and it was so. And God made two great lights; the greater light to rule the day, and the lesser light to rule the night: he made the stars also. And God set them in the firmament of the heaven to give light upon the earth, and to rule over the day and over the night, and to divide the light from the darkness: and God saw that it was good. And the evening and the morning were the fourth day.

And God said, Let the waters bring forth abundantly the moving creature that hath life, and fowl that may fly above the earth in the open firmament of heaven. And God created great whales, and every living creature that moveth, which the waters brought forth abundantly, after their kind, and every winged fowl after his kind: and God saw that it was good. And God blessed them, saying, Be fruitful, and multiply, and fill the waters in the seas, and let fowl multiply in the earth. And the evening and the morning were the fifth day.

And God said, Let the earth bring forth the living creature after his kind, cattle, and creeping thing, and beast of the earth after his kind: and it was so. And God made the beast of the earth after his kind, and cattle after their kind, and every thing that creepeth upon the earth after his kind: and God saw that it was good. And God said, Let us make man in our image, after our likeness: and let them have dominion over the fish of the sea, and over the fowl of the air, and over the cattle, and over all the earth, and over every creeping thing that creepeth upon the earth. So God created man in his own image, in the image of God created he him; male and female created he them. And God blessed them, and God said unto them, Be fruitful, and multiply, and replenish the earth, and subdue it: and have dominion over the fish of the sea, and over the fowl of the air, and over every living thing that moveth upon the earth. And God said, Behold, I have given you every herb bearing seed, which is upon the face of all the earth, and every tree, in the which is the fruit of a tree yielding seed; to you it shall be for meat. And to every beast of the earth, and to every fowl of the air, and to every thing that creepeth upon the earth, wherein there is life, I have given every green herb for meat: and it was so. And God saw every thing that he had made, and, behold, it was very good. And the evening and the morning were the sixth day.

Thus the heavens and the earth were finished, and all the host of them. And on the seventh day God ended his work which he had made; and he rested on the seventh day from all his work which he had made. And God blessed the seventh day, and sanctified it: because that in it he had rested from all his work which God created and made.

These are the generations of the heavens and of the earth when they were created, in the day that the LORD God made the earth and the heavens, And every plant of the field before it was in the earth, and every herb of the field before it grew: for the LORD God had not caused it to rain upon the earth, and there was not a man to till the ground. But there went up a mist from the earth, and watered the whole face of the ground. And the LORD God formed man of the dust of the ground, and breathed into his nostrils the breath of life; and man became a living soul.

And the LORD God planted a garden eastward in Eden; and there he put the man whom he had formed. And out of the ground made the LORD God to grow every tree that is pleasant to the sight, and good for food; the tree of life also in the midst of the garden, and the tree of knowledge of good and evil. And a river went out of Eden to water the garden; and from thence it was parted, and became into four heads . . .

And the LORD God took the man, and put him into the garden of Eden to dress it and to keep it. And the LORD God commanded the man, saying, Of every tree of the garden thou mayest freely eat: But of the tree of the knowledge of good and evil, thou shalt not eat of it: for in the day that thou eatest thereof thou shalt surely die.

And the LORD God said, It is not good that the man should be alone; I will make him an help meet for him. And out of the ground the LORD God formed every beast of the field, and every fowl of the air; and brought them unto Adam to see what he would call them: and whatsoever Adam called every living creature, that was the name thereof. And Adam gave names to all cattle, and to the fowl of the air, and to every beast of the field; but for Adam there was not found an help meet for him. And the LORD God caused a deep sleep to fall upon Adam, and he slept: and he took one of his ribs, and closed up the flesh instead thereof; And the rib, which the LORD God had taken from man, made he a woman, and brought her unto the man. And Adam said, This is now bone of my bones, and flesh of my flesh: she shall be called Woman, because she was taken out of Man. Therefore shall a man leave his father and his mother, and shall cleave unto his wife: and they shall be one flesh. And they were both naked, the man and his wife, and were not ashamed.

Japanese: Nihongi[2]

Completed in 720 CE, Nihongi is the second oldest surviving source on Japanese mythology and history.

Of old, Heaven and Earth were not yet separated, and the In and Yo not yet divided. They formed a chaotic mass like an egg which was of obscurely defined limits and contained germs.

The purer and clearer part was thinly drawn out, and formed Heaven, while the heavier and grosser element settled down and became Earth . . .

Thereafter Divine Beings were produced between them.

Hence, it is said that when the world began to be created, the soil of which lands were composed floated about in a manner which might be compared to the floating of a fish sporting on the surface of the water. At this time a certain thing was produced between Heaven and Earth. It was in form like a reed-shoot. Now this became transformed into a God, and was called Kuni-toko-tachi-no-Mikoto . . .

Being formed by the mutual action of Heavenly and Earthly principles, they were made male and female. From Kuni-no-toko-tachi-no-Mikoto to Izanagi-no-Mikoto and Izanami-no-Mikoto are called the seven generations of the age of the Gods.

Izanagi-no-Mikoto and Izanami-no-Mikoto stood on the floating bridge of Heaven, and held counsel together, saying, "Is there not a country beneath?" Thereupon they thrust down the jewel-spear of Heaven and groping about therewith found the Ocean. The brine which dripped from the point of the spear coagulated and became an island. The two Deities thereupon descended and dwelt in this island. Accordingly they wished to become husband and wife together, and to produce countries. Hereupon the male and female first became united as husband and wife. Now when the time of birth arrived [they gave birth to one island after another in all eight islands which were known as Oho-ya-shima country] . . .

They next produced the sea, then the rivers, and then the mountains. Then produced Ku-ku-no-chi, the ancestor of the trees, and next the ancestor of herbs, Kaya-no-hime . . .

They then together produced the Sun-Goddess . . . The resplendent luster of this child shone throughout . . .

They next produced the Moon God. His radiance was next to that of the Sun in splendor. This God was to be the consort of the Sun-Goddess, and to share in her government. They therefore sent him also to Heaven [with the Sun-Goddess].

Their next child was Sosano-wo-no-Mikoto. This God had a fierce temper and was given to cruel acts. Moreover he made a practice of continually weeping and wailing. So he brought many of the people of the land to an untimely end. Again he caused the green mountains to become withered. Therefore the two Gods, his parents, addressed him, saying "Thou art exceedingly wicked, and it is not meet that thou shouldst reign over the world. Certainly thou must depart far away to the Nether-Land." So they at length expelled him.

Upon this Sosa-no-wo-no-Mikoto made petition, saying, "I will not obey thy instructions and proceed to the Nether-Land. Therefore I wish for a short time to go to the Plain of High Heaven and meet with my elder sister, after which I will go away for ever." Permission was granted him, and he therefore ascended to Heaven . . .

Now at first when Sosa-no-wo-no-Mikoto went up to Heaven, by reason of the fierceness of his divine nature there was a commotion in the sea and the hills and mountains groaned aloud. [The Sun Goddess], knowing the violence and wickedness of this Deity, was startled and changed countenance, when she heard the manner of his coming. She said [to herself], "Is my younger brother coming with good intentions? I think it must be his purpose to rob me of my kingdom . . .

After this Sosa-no-wo-no Mikoto's behavior was exceedingly rude. In what way? The [Sun Goddess] had made august rice fields of Heavenly narrow rice fields and Heavenly long rice fields. The Sosa-no-wo-no Mikoto, when the seed was sewn in the spring, broke down the divisions between the plots of rice, and in autumn let loose the Heavenly piebald colts, and made them lie down in the midst of the rice fields. Again, when he saw that the [Sun Goddess] was about to celebrate the feast of first fruits, he secretly voided excrement in the New Place.

Moreover, when he saw that the [Sun Goddess] was in her sacred weaving hall, engaged in weaving the garments of the Gods, he flayed the piebald colt of Heaven, and breaking a hole in the roof-tiles of the hall, flung it in. Then the [Sun Goddess] startled with alarm, and wounded herself with the shuttle. Indignant at this, she straightway entered the Rock-cave of Heaven, and having fastened the Rock-door, dwelt there in seclusion. Therefore, constant darkness prevailed on all sides, and the alteration of night and day was unknown.

Questions for Contemplation and Discussion

1. What is one similarity that you see between the Hebrew creation account and the Japanese creation account?

   Both Man + Women were involved in the creation of the Heavens + Earth in religions.

2. What is one significant difference between the two accounts?

   God had make the earth within a week.
   Within Japanese - tree branch of families members to assemble the world.

3. Some have criticized these accounts because they are scientifically impossible. The Genesis account, some say, contains a scientific error, for how could God create the sun a day after creating grass, because grass needs sunlight to exist through the scientific process called photosynthesis? Would you agree that neither the Hebrew or Japanese account is to be taken literally as scientific fact? Explain.

   In most cases, no it cannot be taken scientifically because science They cannot be proven scientifically. Somewhat myths as looked as — must believe

4. What do these accounts tell us about the divinity or divinities? Are the creators discussed in these passages a force for good? Are they supportive of humanity? Explain.

   The only evil in Hebrew's perspective was detected through the deception of the fruit from the tree.

5. What do these documents say about good and evil? Explain.

   Disobedience = evil
   good = divinity
   simple unity

WHAT IS CRIMINAL JUSTICE?

Code of Hammurabi[3]

Hammurabi (c. 1792–1750 BCE) was king in ancient Babylon in Mesopotamia, an area that is in modern Iraq. The entire code consisted of 282 clauses, but only those pertaining to murder are reprinted below.

- If a man, in a case (pending judgment), bear false (threatening) witness, or do not establish the testimony that he has given, if that case be a case involving life, that man shall be put to death.
- If any one steal the property of a god (temple) or palace, that man shall be put to death, and he who receives from his hand the stolen (property) shall also be put to death.
- If a man purchase silver or gold, a male or female slave, ox, sheep, or ass, or anything else from a man's son, or from a man's servant without witnesses or contracts, or if he receive the same in trust, he shall be put to death as a thief.
- If any one steal ox or sheep, ass or pig, or goat, if it be from a god (temple) or a palace, he shall restore thirtyfold; if it be from a freed man he shall render tenfold; if the thief has nothing with which to pay he shall be put to death.
- If any one steal a man's son, who is a minor, he shall be put to death.
- If a man harbor in his house a male or female slave who has fled from the palace or from a freeman, and do not bring him (the slave) forth at the call of the commandant, the owner of that house shall be put to death.
- If a man make a breach [break a hole] in a house, they shall put him to death in front of that breach and they shall thrust him therein.
- If a man is committing a robbery and be captured, that man shall be put to death.
- If a priestess . . . open a wineshop or enter a wineshop for a drink, they shall burn that woman.
- If a man force the (betrothed) wife of another who has not known a male and is living in her father's house, and he lie in her bosom and they take him, that man shall be put to death and that woman shall go free.
- If a man lie in the bosom of his mother after (the death of) his father, they shall burn both of them.
- If a son strike his father, they shall cut off his fingers.
- If a man strike a man's daughter and bring about a miscarriage, he shall pay ten shekels of silver for her miscarriage.
- If that woman die, they shall put his daughter to death.
- If, through a stroke [being hit], he bring about a miscarriage to the daughter of a freeman, he shall pay five shekels of silver
- If that woman die, he shall pay one-half mina of silver.
- If he strike the female slave of a man and bring about a miscarriage, he shall pay two shekels of silver.
- If that female slave die, he shall pay one-third mina of silver.
- If a physician operate on a man for a severe wound . . . and cause the man's death; or open an abscess (in the eye) of a man . . . and destroy the man's eye, they shall cut off his fingers.
- If a physician operate on a slave of a freeman for a severe wound . . . and cause his death, he shall restore a slave of equal value.
- If a builder build a house for a man, and do not make its construction firm, and the house which he has built collapse and cause the death of the owner of the house, that builder shall be put to death.
- If he cause the death of a son of the owner of the house, they shall put to death a son of that builder.
- If it cause the death of a slave of the owner of the house, he shall give to the owner of the house a slave of equal value.

The Yuan Code[4]

During the Yuan Dynasty (1271–1368), China was ruled by the Mongols. The dynasty was established by Kublai Khan, grandson of the great Genghis Khan.

- A person who kills another person is punishable by death. The family of the victim is entitled to receive from the family of the killer fifty taels of silver for funeral expenses. The amount could be reduced if the family of the killer is too poor, but under no circumstances should it be less than ten taels of silver in paper currency. If a general clemency is declared before the death sentence is carried out, the payment to the injured family will be doubled.

Source: Reprinted with the permission of Scribner, an imprint of Simon & Schuster Adult Publishing Group, from *The Civilization of China: From the Formative Period to the Coming of the West* by Dun J. Li. Copyright © 1975 by Dun J. Li. All rights reserved.

- A person who, after having killed another person, chooses to commit suicide but fails in his attempt is punishable by death nonetheless.
- A person who kills another person is eligible for clemency if he has accumulated good deeds after the killing, provided that the killing is accidental rather than intentional.
- In a physical fight between two persons, the person who has no intention to kill at the beginning but acquires such intention during the process of fighting is regarded as having harbored the intention to kill, if the physical fight ends with the death of the other person.
- If a man kills a prostitute who has refused to elope with him, the man will be regarded as guilty as if he had killed a person other than a prostitute.
- A person who beats to death the person who has killed his father is regarded as guiltless. The family of the person who has killed his father is responsible for the payment of fifty taels of silver for his father's funeral expenses.
- If a Mongol, in a physical fight or in a state of drunkenness, kills a Chinese, the Mongol will be punished by exile to an expeditionary army, in addition to the payment of funeral expenses for the dead person.
- If a man beats to death another man who has been flirting with his wife, he will receive a punishment one degree lower than the death sentence. He will be responsible for the dead man's funeral expenses.
- If a person beats to death a notorious outlaw who would have been sentenced to death if captured by governmental authorities, he is guiltless. He is not responsible for the dead man's funeral expenses.
- If a father, with valid reason, beats a son or daughter of his and accidentally causes his or her death, the father is guiltless.
- A man or woman who mistreats his or her daughter-in-law and causes her death will be punished by 107 blows, despite the fact that the woman, before her death, has not been a good daughter-in-law.
- A man who kills his wife for flimsy reasons will be punished by death.
- If a man beats his wife and subsequently causes her death for her arrogant attitude toward his parents, the man will be punished by 77 blows.
- If a man beats to death his slave who has verbally and physically abused him, the man is guiltless.
- If a person kills his or her slave who has been faultless, he or she will be punished by 87 blows. If he or she is in a state of drunkenness when the killing takes place, the punishment will be reduced by one degree [i.e., 77 blows].
- If a person in a state of insanity beats another person who subsequently dies as a result of injury, the person is guiltless. He is responsible, however, for the dead person's funeral expenses.
- If a physician, because of his insufficient knowledge, kills a patient with his needle or medicine, the physician will be punished by 107 blows. He shall pay for the dead person's funeral expenses.

Questions for Contemplation and Discussion

1. What do these documents tell us about how the Mongols and the ancient Babylonians defined "murder"? Explain.

2. What do these documents tell us about gender and social standing? In other words, do some laws reflect differing punishment for different social classes of individuals? Was a man's death regarded as different from that of a woman? Explain.

3. Is it ever right to have different standards of justice for people of different social standing or wealth? Why? Why not?

4. Were these law codes just? Explain.

5. Should society today adopt these law codes? Why? Why not?

6. Were these laws, in your opinion, overly harsh? Explain.

7. What role did the rights to private property (home, land, slaves) have in Hammurabi's code? Explain.

WHAT IS GOODNESS?

Confucius Analects[5]

Until 1949, when China became communist, Confucius, or Master Kung (551-479 BCE) was the country's most important moral and political philosopher. The *Analects* are a compilation of his sayings.

V. 1. The Master said, "Riches and honours are what men desire. If it cannot be obtained in the proper way, they should not be held. Poverty and meanness are what men dislike. If it cannot be obtained in the proper way, they should not be avoided.

XVII. The Master said, "Man is born for uprightness. If a man lose his uprightness, and yet live, his escape *from death* is the effect of mere good fortune."

XVIII. The Master said, "They who know *the truth* are not equal to those who love it, and they who love it are not equal to those who find delight in it."

VIII. The Master said, "I do not open up the truth to one who is not eager *to get knowledge*, nor help out anyone who is not anxious to explain himself. When I have presented one corner of a subject to anyone, and he cannot from it learn the other three, I do not repeat my lesson."

XXXV. The Master said, "Extravagance leads to insubordination, and parsimony to meanness. It is better to be mean than to be insubordinate."

XXXIV. The Master said, "The superior man is satisfied and composed; the mean is always full of distress."

II. 1. The Master said, "Respectfulness without the rules of propriety, becomes laborious bustle; carefulness, without the rules of propriety, becomes timidity; boldness, without the rules of propriety, becomes insubordination; straightforwardness, without the rules of propriety, becomes rudeness.

2. "When those who are in the high stations perform well all their duties to their relations, the people are aroused to virtue. When old ministers and friends are not neglected by them, the people are preserved from meanness."

I. 1. Yen Yuen asked about perfect virtue. The Master said, "To subdue one's self and return to propriety, is a perfect virtue. If a man can for one day subdue himself and return to propriety, all under heaven will ascribe perfect virtue to him. Is the practice of perfect virtue from a man himself, or is it from others?"

II. Chung-kung asked about perfect virtue. The Master said, "*It is*, when you go abroad, *to behave to every one* as if you were receiving a great guest; to employ the people as if you were assisting at a great sacrifice; not to do to others as you would not wish done to yourself; to have no murmuring against you in the country, and none in the family." Chung-kung said, "Though I am deficient in intelligence and vigour, I will make it my business to practice this lesson."

2. The Master said, "The man of perfect virtue is cautious and slow in his speech."

XIV. Tsze-chang asked about government. The Master said, "*The art of governing* is to keep *its affair* before the mind without weariness, and to practice them with undeviating consistency."

XV. The Master said, "By extensively studying all learning, and keeping himself under the restraint of the rules of propriety, *one* may thus likewise not err from what is right."

XVI. The Master said, "The superior man *seeks* to perfect the admirable qualities of men, and does not *seek* to perfect their bad qualities. The mean man does the opposite of this."

XVII. Ke K'ang asked Confucius about government. Confucius replied, "To govern means to rectify. If you lead on *the people* with correctness, who will dare not to be correct?"

XXII. Fan Ch'e asked about benevolence. The Master said, "It is to love *all men*." He asked about knowledge. The Master said, "It is to know *all men*."

XI. The Master said, "If good men were to govern a country in *succession* for a hundred years, they would be able to transform the violently bad, and dispense with capital punishments. True indeed is this saying!"

XII. The Master said, "If a truly royal ruler were to arise, it would *still* require a generation, and then virtue would prevail."

XIII. The Master said, "If a minister make his own conduct correct, what difficulty will he have in assisting in government? If he cannot rectify himself, what has he to do with rectifying others?"

Source: From *Library of Original Sources* by Oliver Thatcher, Ed.

I. Heen asked what might be considered shameful. The Master said, "When good government prevails in a State, *to be thinking only of his* salary; and, when bad government prevails, *to be thinking in the same way, only of his* salary;—this is shameful."

VII. Confucius said, "There are three things which the superior man guards against. In youth, when the physical powers are not yet settled, he guards against lust. When he is strong, and the physical powers are full of vigour, he guards against quarrelsomeness. When he is old, and the animal powers are decayed, he guards against covetousness."

Aristotle, Nichomachaean Ethics[6]

Aristotle (c. 384–322 BCE) lived in Athens, Greece. He is regarded as one of the greatest thinkers in human history. A student of Plato, Aristotle wrote on politics, science, logic, and many other subjects.

Every art and every kind of inquiry, and likewise every act and purpose, seems to aim at some good: and so it has been well said that the good is that at which everything aims . . .

Let us again return to the good we are seeking, and ask what it can be. It seems different in different actions and arts; it is different in medicine, in strategy, and in the other arts likewise. What then is the good of each? Surely that for whose sake everything else is done. In medicine this is health, in strategy victory, in architecture a house, in any other sphere something else, and in every action and pursuit the end; for it is for the sake of this that all men do whatever else they do. Therefore, if there is an end for all that we do, this will be the good achievable by action, and if there are more than one, these will be the goods achievable by action.

So the argument has by a different course reached the same point; but we must try to state this even more clearly. Since there are evidently more than one end, and we choose some of these for the sake of something else, clearly not all ends are final ends; but the chief good is evidently something final. Therefore, if there is only one final end, this will be what we are seeking, and if there are more than one, the most final of these will be what we are seeking. Now we call that which is in itself worthy of pursuit more final than that which is worthy of pursuit for the sake of something else, and that which is never desirable for the sake of something else more final than the things that are desirable both in themselves and for the sake of that other thing, and therefore we call final without qualification that which is always desirable in itself and never for the sake of something else.

Now such a thing happiness, above all else, is held to be; for this we choose always for self and never for the sake of something else, but honour, pleasure, reason, and every virtue we choose indeed for themselves (for if nothing resulted from them we should still choose each of them), but we choose them also for the sake of happiness, judging that by means of them we shall be happy. Happiness, on the other hand, no one chooses for the sake of these, nor, in general, for anything other than itself . . .

Happiness, then, is something final and self-sufficient, and is the end of action.

Presumably, however, to say that happiness is the chief good seems a platitude, and a clearer account of what it is still desired. This might perhaps be given, if we could first ascertain the function of man. For just as for a flute-player, a sculptor, or an artist, and, in general, for all things that have a function or activity, the good and the "well" is thought to reside in the function, so would it seem to be for man, if he has a function. Have the carpenter, then, and the tanner certain functions or activities, and has man none? Is he born without a function? Or as eye, hand, foot, and in general each of the parts evidently has a function, may one lay it down that man similarly has a function apart from all these? What then can this be? Life seems to be common even to plants, but we are seeking what is peculiar to man. Let us exclude, therefore, the life of nutrition and growth. Next there would be a life of perception, but it also seems to be common even to the horse, the ox, and every animal. There remains, then, an active life of the element that has a rational principle; of this, one part has such a principle in the sense of being obedient to one, the other in the sense of possessing one and exercising thought. And, as "life of the rational element" also has two meanings, we must state that life in the sense of activity is what we mean; for this seems to be the more proper sense of the term . . .

We state the function of man to be a certain kind of life, and this to be an activity or actions of the soul implying a rational principle, and the function of a good man to be the good and noble performance of these, and if any action is well performed when it is performed in accordance with the appropriate excellence: if this is the case, human good turns out to be activity of soul in accordance with virtue, and if there are more than one virtue, in accordance with the best and most complete.

Source: Aristotle, translated by F. H. Peters.

But we must add "in a complete life." For one swallow does not make a summer, nor does one day; and so too one day, or a short time, does not make a man blessed and happy . . .

The question we have now discussed confirms our definition. For no function of man has so much permanence as virtuous activities (these are thought to be more durable even than knowledge of the sciences), and of these themselves the most valuable are more durable because those who are happy spend their life most readily and most continuously in these; for this seems to be the reason why we do not forget them. The attribute in question, then, will belong to the happy man, and he will be happy throughout his life; for always, or by preference to everything else, he will be engaged in virtuous action and contemplation, and he will bear the chances of life most nobly and altogether decorously, if he is 'truly good . . .

Now many events happen by chance, and events differing in importance; small pieces of good fortune or of its opposite clearly do not weigh down the scales of life one way or the other, but a multitude of great events if they turn out well will make life happier (for not only are they themselves such as to add beauty to life, but the way a man deals with them may be noble and good), while if they turn out ill they crush and maim happiness; for they both bring pain with them and hinder many activities. Yet even in these nobility shines through, when a man bears with resignation many great misfortunes, not through insensibility to pain but through nobility and greatness of soul.

If activities are, as we said, what gives life its character, no happy man can become miserable; for he will never do the acts that are hateful and mean. For the man who is truly good and wise, we think, bears all the chances life becomingly and always makes the best of circumstances, as a good general makes the best military use of the army at his command and a good shoemaker makes the best shoes out of the hides that are given him; and so with all other craftsmen. And if this is the case, the happy man can never become miserable . . .

Nor, again, is he many-coloured and changeable; for neither will he be moved from his happy state easily or by any ordinary misadventures, but only by many great ones, nor, if he has had many great misadventures, will he recover his happiness in a short time, but if at all, only in a long and complete one in which he has attained many splendid successes.

When then should we not say that he is happy who is active in accordance with complete virtue and is sufficiently equipped with external goods, not for some chance period but throughout a complete life? Or must we add 'and who is destined to live thus and die as befits his life'? Certainly the future is obscure to us, while happiness, we claim, is an end and something in every way final. If so, we shall call happy those among living men in whom these conditions are, and are to be, fulfilled—but happy men. So much for these questions.

Jesus, from The Sermon on the Mount, Matthew 5–7 [7]

To many, the Sermon represents the core values of the Christian faith. Jesus (c. 5 BCE-28 CE) gave this near the start of his public ministry in Jerusalem.

Blessed are the poor in spirit,
For theirs is the kingdom of heaven.
Blessed are those who mourn,
For they shall be comforted.
Blessed are the meek,
For they shall inherit the earth.
Blessed are those who hunger and thirst for righteousness,
For they shall be filled.
Blessed are the merciful,
For they shall obtain mercy.
Blessed are the pure in heart,
For they shall see God.
Blessed are the peacemakers,
For they shall be called sons of God.
Blessed are those who are persecuted for righteousness' sake,
For theirs is the kingdom of heaven . . .

You have heard that it was said to those of old, "You shall not murder, and whoever murders will be in danger of the judgment." But I say to you that whoever is angry with his brother without a cause shall be in danger of the judgment. And whoever says to his brother, "Raca!" shall be in danger of the council. But whoever says, "You fool!" shall be in danger of hell fire. Therefore if you bring your gift to the altar, and there remember that your brother has something against you, leave your gift there before the altar, and go your way. First be reconciled to your brother, and then come and offer your gift. Agree with your adversary quickly, while you are on the way with him, lest your adversary deliver you to the judge, the judge hand you over to the officer, and you be thrown into prison. Assuredly, I say to you, you will by no means get out of there till you have paid the last penny.

You have heard that it was said to those of old, "You shall not commit adultery." But I say to you that whoever looks at a woman to lust for her has already committed adultery with her in his heart. If your right eye causes you to sin, pluck it out and cast it from you; for it is more profitable for you that one of your members perish, than for your whole body to be cast into hell. And if your right hand causes you to sin, cut it off and cast it from you; for it is more profitable for you that one of your members perish, than for your whole body to be cast into hell.

Furthermore it has been said, "Whoever divorces his wife, let him give her a certificate of divorce." But I say to you that whoever divorces his wife for any reason except sexual immorality causes her to commit adultery; and whoever marries a woman who is divorced commits adultery.

Again you have heard that it was said to those of old, "You shall not swear falsely, but shall perform your oaths to the Lord." But I say to you, do not swear at all: neither by heaven, for it is God's throne; nor by the earth, for it is His footstool; nor by Jerusalem, for it is the city of the great King. Nor shall you swear by your head, because you cannot make one hair white or black. But let your "Yes" be "Yes," and your "No," "No." For whatever is more than these is from the evil one.

You have heard that it was said, "An eye for an eye and a tooth for a tooth." But I tell you not to resist an evil person. But whoever slaps you on your right cheek, turn the other to him also. If anyone wants to sue you and take away your tunic, let him have your cloak also. And whoever compels you to go one mile, go with him two. Give to him who asks you, and from him who wants to borrow from you do not turn away.

You have heard that it was said, "You shall love your neighbor and hate your enemy." But I say to you, love your enemies, bless those who curse you, do good to those who hate you, and pray for those who spitefully use you and persecute you, that you may be sons of your Father in heaven; for He makes His sun rise on the evil and on the good, and sends rain on the just and on the unjust. For if you love those who love you, what reward have you? Do not even the tax collectors do the same? And if you greet your brethren only, what do you do more than others? Do not even the tax collectors do so? Therefore you shall be perfect, just as your Father in heaven is perfect.

Take heed that you do not do your charitable deeds before men, to be seen by them. Otherwise you have no reward from your Father in heaven. Therefore, when you do a charitable deed, do not sound a trumpet before you as the hypocrites do in the synagogues and in the streets, that they may have glory from men. Assuredly, I say to you, they have their reward. But when you do a charitable deed, do not let your left hand know what your right hand is doing, that your charitable deed may be in secret; and your Father who sees in secret will Himself reward you openly . . .

For if you forgive men their trespasses, your heavenly Father will also forgive you. But if you do not forgive men their trespasses, neither will your Father forgive your trespasses . . .

Do not lay up for yourselves treasures on earth, where moth and rust destroy and where thieves break in and steal; but lay up for yourselves treasures in heaven, where neither moth nor rust destroys and where thieves do not break in and steal. For where your treasure is, there your heart will be also.

Judge not, that you be not judged. For with what judgment you judge, you will be judged; and with the measure you use, it will be measured back to you. And why do you look at the speck in your brother's eye, but do not consider the plank in your own eye? Or how can you say to your brother, "Let me remove the speck from your eye"; and look, a plank is in your own eye? Hypocrite! First remove the plank from your own eye, and then you will see clearly to remove the speck from your brother's eye.

Do not give what is holy to the dogs; nor cast your pearls before swine, lest they trample them under their feet, and turn and tear you in pieces . . .

And so it was, when Jesus had ended these sayings, that the people were astonished at His teaching, for He taught them as one having authority, and not as the scribes.

Questions for Contemplation and Discussion

1. Which values does Confucius, "The Master," hold in high esteem? Explain by referring to specific statements in the reading.

2. To Confucius, what qualities does a good person possess? Explain.

3. Which statement of Confucius was your favorite? Why?

4. To Aristotle, how does a person become a good person? What is the relationship between acting good and becoming good?

5. Which is better: to think about what is right, or to live according to what is right? Explain.

6. What is the thesis, or main point, of Jesus in Matthew 5-7?

7. Which values does Jesus promote?

8. What does Jesus mean when he says "love your enemies"? Refer to other parts of the Sermon on the Mount as you explain your answer.

WHAT IS FEMINISM?

Malleus Maleficarum[8]

Malleus Maleficarum, "The Hammer of Witches," was published for the first time in 1486. It was used for centuries as a handbook on how to identify, prosecute, and eliminate "witches". Both men and women were accused of the practice, and many thousands were executed because of this book.

Others again have propounded other reasons why there are more superstitious women found than men. And the first is, that they are more credulous; and since the chief aim of the devil is to corrupt faith, therefore he rather attacks them. See *Ecclesiasticus* xix: He that is quick to believe is light-minded, and shall be diminished.

The second reason is, that women are naturally more impressionable, and more ready to receive the influence of a disembodied spirit; and that when they use this quality well they are very good, but when they use it ill they are very evil.

The third reason is that they have slippery tongues, and are unable to conceal from their fellow-women those things which by evil arts they know; and, since they are weak, they find an easy and secret manner of vindicating themselves by witchcraft. See *Ecclesiasticus* as quoted above: I had rather dwell with a lion and a dragon than to keep house with a wicked woman. All wickedness is but little to the wickedness of a woman. And to this may be added that, as they are very impressionable, they act accordingly.

There are also others who bring forward yet other reasons, of which preachers should be very careful how they make use. For it is true that in the Old Testament the Scriptures have much that is evil to say about women, and this because of the first temptress, Eve, and her imitators; yet afterwards in the New Testament we find a change of name, as from Eva to Ave (as S. Jerome says), and the whole sin of Eve taken away by the benediction of Mary. Therefore preachers should always say as much praise of them as possible.

But because in these times this perfidy is more often found in women than in men, as we learn by actual experience, if anyone is curious as to the reason, we may add to what has already been said the following: that since they are feebler both in mind and body, it is not surprising that they should come more under the spell of witchcraft.

For as regards intellect, or the understanding of spiritual things, they seem to be of a different nature from men; a fact which is vouched for by the logic of the authorities, backed by various examples from the Scriptures. Terence* says: Women are intellectually like children. And Lactantius (Institutiones, III): No woman understood philosophy except Temeste.[†] And *Proverbs* xi, as it were describing a woman, says: As a jewel of gold in a swine's snout, so is a fair woman which is without discretion.

But the natural reason is that she is more carnal than a man, as is clear from her many carnal abominations. And it should be noted that there was a defect in the formation of the first woman, since she was formed from a bent rib, that is, a rib of the breast, which is bent as it were in a contrary direction to a man. And since through this defect she is an imperfect animal, she always deceives. For Cato says: When a woman weeps she weaves snares. And again: When a woman weeps, she labours to deceive a man. And this is shown by Samson's wife, who coaxed him to tell her the riddle he had propounded to the Philistines, and told them the answer, and so deceived him. And it is clear in the case of the first woman that she had little faith; for when the serpent asked why they did not eat of every tree in Paradise, she answered: Of every tree, etc.—lest perchance we die. Thereby she showed that she doubted, and had little faith in the word of God. And all this is indicated by the etymology of the word; for *Femina* comes from *Fe* and *Minus*, since she is ever weaker to hold and preserve the faith. And this as regards faith is of her very nature; although both by grace and nature faith never failed in the Blessed Virgin, even at the time of Christ's Passion, when it failed in all men.

Therefore a wicked woman is by her nature quicker to waver in her faith, and consequently quicker to abjure the faith, which is the root of witchcraft.

And as to her other mental quality, that is, her natural will; when she hates someone whom she formerly loved, then she seethes with anger and impatience in her whole soul, just as the tides of the sea are always heaving and boiling. Many authorities allude to this cause. *Ecclesiasticus* xxv: There is no wrath above the wrath of a woman. And Seneca (*Tragedies*, VIII): No might of the flames or of the swollen winds, no deadly weapon, is so much to be feared as the lust and hatred of a woman who has been divorced from the marriage bed.*

This is shown too in the woman who falsely accused Joseph, and caused him to be imprisoned because he would not consent to the crime of adultery with her (*Genesis* xxx). And truly the most powerful cause which contributes to the increase of witches is the woeful rivalry between married folk and unmarried women and men. This is so even among holy women, so

---

Source: Malleus Maleficarum, translated by Rev. Montague Summers.

what must it be among the others? For you see in *Genesis* xxi. how impatient and envious Sarah was of Hagar when she conceived: how jealous Rachel was of Leah because she had no children (*Genesis* xxx): and Hannah, who was barren, of the fruitful Peninnah (I. *Kings* i): and how Miriam (*Numbers* xii) murmured and spoke ill of Moses, and was therefore stricken with leprosy: and how Martha was jealous of Mary Magdalen, because she was busy and Mary was sitting down (*S. Luke* x). To this point is *Ecclesiasticus* xxxvii: Neither consult with a woman touching her of whom she is jealous. Meaning that it is useless to consult with her, since there is always jealousy, that is, envy, in a wicked woman. And if women behave thus to each other, how much more will they do so to men.

A Vindication of the Rights of Woman[9]

Mary Wollstonecraft (1759–1797) is seen as one of the modern founders of the feminist movement. Her daughter, Mary Wollstonecraft Shelley, was herself a famous writer, penning *Frankenstein*.

In the present state of society, it appears necessary to go back to first principles in search of the most simple truths, and to dispute with some prevailing prejudice every inch of ground. To clear my way, I must be allowed to ask some plain questions, and the answers will probably appear as unequivocal as the axioms on which reasoning is built; though, when entangled with various motives of action, they are formally contradicted, either by the words or conduct of men.

In what does man's pre-eminence over the brute creation consist? The answer is as clear as that a half is less than the whole; in Reason.

What acquirement exalts one being above another? Virtue; we spontaneously reply.

For what purpose were the passions implanted? That man by struggling with them might attain a degree of knowledge denied to the brutes: whispers Experience.

Consequently the perfection of our nature and capability of happiness, must be estimated by the degree of reason, virtue, and knowledge, that distinguish the individual, and direct the laws which bind society: and that from the exercise of reason, knowledge and virtue naturally flow, is equally undeniable, if mankind be viewed collectively.

The rights and duties of man thus simplified, it seems almost impertinent to attempt to illustrate truths that appear so incontrovertible: yet such deeply rooted prejudices have clouded reason, and such spurious qualities have assumed the name of virtues, that it is necessary to pursue the course of reason as it has been perplexed and involved in error, by various adventitious circumstances, comparing the simple axiom with casual deviations.

Men, in general, seem to employ their reason to justify prejudices, which they have imbibed, they cannot trace how, rather than to root them out. The mind must be strong that resolutely forms its own principles; for a kind of intellectual cowardice prevails which makes many men shrink from the task, or only do it by halves. Yet the imperfect conclusions thus drawn, are frequently very plausible, because they are built on partial experience, on just, though narrow, views . . .

Questions for Contemplation and Discussion

1. What is the thesis, or main point, of the chapter from the *Malleus Maleficarum*? What do the authors use as evidence to support their thesis? What kinds of evidence do the authors **not** use?

2. Would a person who agreed with the ideas in *Malleus Maleficarum* support education for women? Would one who agreed with the ideas be more likely to feel threatened and intimidated by an educated woman? Explain.

3. Why do you think Mary Wollstonecraft wrote *Vindication*?

4. Wollstonecraft wrote that "Men, in general, seem to employ their reason to justify prejudices." What do you think she meant by that? What is your reaction to that statement? Do you agree with her? If so, why? If not, why not?

WHO GIVES POLITICAL LEADERS THEIR POWER?

James I[10]

James I of England was also king of Scotland, where he was James VI. He was the first monarch of the Stuart dynasty, which took control of the English throne in 1603. James wrote political philosophy and on occasion gave speeches defending his power. This is from a speech he gave to Parliament in 1609.

The state of monarchy is the supremest thing upon earth; for kings are not only God's lieutenants upon earth, and sit upon God's throne, but even by God himself they are called gods. There be three principal similitudes that illustrate the state of monarchy: one taken out of the word of God; and the two other out of the grounds of policy and philosophy. In the Scriptures kings are called gods, and so their power after a certain relation compared to the divine power. Kings are also compared to fathers of families; for a king is truly *parens patriae*, the politic father of his people. And lastly, kings are compared to the head of this microcosm of the body of man.

Kings are justly called gods, for that they exercise a manner or resemblance of divine power upon earth; for if you will consider the attributes to God, you shall see how they agree in the person of a king. God hath power to create or destroy, make or unmake at his pleasure, to give life or send death, to judge all and to be judged nor accountable to none, to raise low things and to make high things low at his pleasure, and to God are both soul and body due. And the like power have kings: they make and unmake their subjects, they have power of raising and casting down, of life and of death, judges over all their subjects and in all causes and yet accountable to none but God only. They have power to exalt low things and abase high things, and make of their subjects, like men at the chess,—a pawn to take a bishop or a knight,—and to cry up or down any of their subjects, as they do their money. And to the king is due both the affection of the soul and the service of the body of his subjects . . .

I would wish you to be careful to avoid three things in the matter of grievances:

First, that you do not meddle with the main points of government; that is my craft: *tractent fabrilia fabri,*—to meddle with that were to lessen me. I am now an old king; for six and thirty years have I governed in Scotland personally, and now have I accomplished my apprenticeship of seven years here; and seven years is a great time for a king's experience in government; therefore there should not be too many Phormios to teach Hannibal: I must not be taught my office.

Secondly, I would not have you meddle with such ancient rights of mine as I have received from my predecessors, possessing them, *more majorum*; such things I would be sorry should be accounted for grievances. All novelties are dangerous as well in a politic as in a natural body, and therefore I would be loath to be quarreled in my ancient rights and possessions; for that were to judge me unworthy of that which my predecessors had and left me.

And, lastly, I pray you beware to exhibit for grievance anything that is established by settled law, and whereunto (as you have already had a proof) you know I will never give a plausible answer; for it is an undutiful part in subjects to press their king, wherein they know beforehand he will refuse them.[1]

John Locke, Two Treatises on Government[11]

John Locke (1632–1704) is regarded as one of the great political philosophers in early modern England. He also wrote a treatise on epistemology, the study of how people obtain knowledge. His political thinking shaped the minds of Thomas Jefferson and other Founding Fathers.

Man being born, as has been proved, with a title to perfect freedom, and an uncontrouled enjoyment of all the rights and privileges of the law of nature, equally with any other man, or number of men in the world, hath by nature a power, not only to preserve his property, that is, his life, liberty and estate, against the injuries and attempts of other men; but to judge of, and punish the breaches of that law in others, as he is persuaded the offence deserves, even with death itself, in crimes where the heinousness of the fact, in his opinion, requires it. But because no political society can be, nor subsist, without having in itself the power to preserve the property, and in order thereunto, punish the offences of all those of that society; there, and there only is political society, where every one of the members hath quitted this natural power, resigned it up into the hands of the community in all cases that exclude him not from appealing for protection to the law established by it . . .

Those who are united into one body, and have a common established law and judicature to appeal to, with authority to decide controversies between them, and punish offenders, are in civil society one with another: but those who have no such

---

Source: James Harvey Robinson, Ed.
Source: John Locke, edited by Henry Morley.

common appeal, I mean on earth, are still in the state of nature, each being, where there is no other, judge for himself, and executioner; which is, as I have before shewed it, the perfect state of nature . . .

Hence it is evident, that absolute monarchy, which by some men is counted the only government in the world, is indeed inconsistent with civil society, and so can be no form of civil-government at all: for the end of civil society, being to avoid, and remedy those inconveniencies of the state of nature, which necessarily follow from every man's being judge in his own case, by setting up a known authority, to which every one of that society may appeal upon any injury received, or controversy that may arise, and which every one of society ought to obey; where-ever any persons are, who have not such an authority to appeal to, for the decision of any difference between them, there those persons are still in the state of nature; and so is every absolute prince, in respect of those who are under his dominion . . .

For he being supposed to have all, both legislative and executive power in himself alone, there is no judge to be found, no appeal lies open to any one, who may fairly, and indifferently, and with authority decide, and from whose decision relief and redress may be expected of any injury or inconveniency, that may be suffered from the prince, or by his order: so that such a man, however intitled, Czar, or Grand Seignior, or how you please, is as much in the state of nature, with all under his dominion, as he is with the rest of mankind: for where-ever any two men are, who have no standing rule, and common judge to appeal to on earth, for the determination of controversies of right betwixt them, there they are still in the state of nature, and under all the inconveniencies of it, with only this woful difference to the subject, or rather slave of an absolute prince: that whereas, in the ordinary state of nature, he has a liberty to judge of his right, and according to the best of his power, to maintain it; now, whenever his property is invaded by the will and order of his monarch, he has not only no appeal, as those in society ought to have, but as if he were degraded from the common state of rational creatures, is denied a liberty to judge of, or to defend his right; and so is exposed to all the misery and inconveniencies, that a man can fear from one, who being in the unrestrained state of nature, is yet corrupted with flattery, and armed with power.

To take away all such mutual grievances, injuries and wrongs, i.e. such as attend men in the state of nature, there was no way but only by growing into composition and agreement amongst themselves, by ordaining some kind of government public, and by yielding themselves subject thereunto, that unto whom they granted authority to rule and govern, by them the peace, tranquillity and happy estate of the rest might be procured. Men always knew that where force and injury was offered, they might be defenders of themselves; they knew that however men may seek their own commodity, yet if this were done with injury unto others, it was not to be suffered, but by all men, and all good means to be withstood.

Finally, they knew that no man might in reason take upon him to determine his own right, and according to his own determination proceed in maintenance thereof, in as much as every man is towards himself, and them whom he greatly affects, partial; and therefore that strifes and troubles would be endless, except they gave their common consent, all to be ordered by some, whom they should agree upon, without which consent there would be no reason that one man should take upon him to be lord or judge over another . . .

Questions for Contemplation and Discussion

1. What does James I mean when he said "kings are justly called gods, for they exercise a manner or resemblance of divine power on earth"? Explain.

2. What are some possible problems that can result when a leader says that God has given him or her the power to rule?

3. Would John Locke agree with James I, or not? Explain.

4. Locke also said, in a part of the *Two Treatises* not reprinted here, that a leader can be removed from power if that leader violates the people's rights to life, liberty, and property. Would you agree with this approach to government? Explain.

5. Is it essential that government leaders protect the private property of its citizens? Why? Why not?

DOES GOD EXIST?

Thomas Aquinas[12]

Aquinas (1225–1274) was one of the leading thinkers of the Roman Catholic Church. Following a precedent set by Muslim thinkers, he sought to apply Aristotle's principles of logic to make church doctrine more intellectually rigorous. This comes from his Summa Theologica, his "summary" of church doctrine.

I answer that it can be proved in five ways that God exists. The first and plainest is the method that proceeds from the point of view of motion. It is certain and in accord with experience, that things on earth undergo change. Now everything that is moved is moved by something; nothing, indeed, is changed, except it is changed to something which it is in potentiality. Moreover, anything moves in accordance with something actually existing; change itself, is nothing else than to bring forth something from potentiality into actuality. Now nothing can be brought from potentiality to actual existence except through something actually existing: thus heat in action, as fire, makes fire-wood, which is hot in potentiality, to be hot actually, and through this process, changes itself. The same thing cannot at the same time be actually and potentially the same thing, but only in regard to different things. What is actually hot cannot be at the same time potentially hot, but it is possible for it at the same time to be potentially cold. It is impossible, then, that anything should be both mover and the thing moved, in regard to the same thing and in the same way, or that it should move itself. Everything, therefore, is moved by something else. If, then, that by which it is moved, is also moved, this must be moved by something still different, and this, again, by something else. But this process cannot go on to infinity because there would not be any first mover, nor, because of this fact, anything else in motion, as the succeeding things would not move except because of what is moved by the first mover, just as a stick is not moved except through what is moved from the hand. Therefore it is necessary to go back to some first mover, which is itself moved by nothing, and this all men know as God.

The second proof is from the nature of the efficient cause. We find in our experience that there is a chain of causes: nor is it found possible for anything to be the efficient cause of itself, since it would have to exist before itself, which is impossible. Nor in the case of efficient causes can the chain go back indefinitely, because in all chains of efficient causes, the first is the cause of the middle, and these of the last, whether they be one or many. If the cause is removed, the effect is removed. Hence if there is not a first cause, there will not be a last, nor a middle. But if the chain were to go back infinitely, there would be no first cause, and thus no ultimate effect, nor middle causes, which is admittedly false. Hence we must presuppose some first efficient cause, which all call God.

The third proof is taken from the natures of the merely possible and necessary. We find that certain things either may or may not exist, since they are found to come into being and be destroyed, and in consequence potentially, either existent or nonexistent. But it is impossible for all things that are of this character to exist eternally, because what *may* not exist, at length *will* not. If, then, all things were merely possible (mere accidents), eventually nothing among things would exist. If this is true, even now there would be nothing, because what does not exist, does not take its beginning except through something that does exist. If then nothing existed, it would be impossible for anything to begin, and there would now be nothing existing, which is admittedly false. Hence not all things are mere accidents, but there must be one necessarily existing being. Now every necessary thing either has a cause of its necessary existence, or has not. In the case of necessary things that have a cause for their necessary existence, the chain of causes cannot go back infinitely, just as not in the case of efficient causes, as proved. Hence there must be presupposed something necessarily existing through its own nature, not having a cause elsewhere but being itself the cause of the necessary existence of other things,—which all call God.

The fourth proof arises from the degrees that are found in things. For there is found a greater and a less degree of goodness, truth, nobility, and the like. But more or less are terms spoken of various things as they approach in diverse ways toward something that is the greatest, just as in the case of hotter (more hot) which approaches nearer the greatest heat. There exists therefore something that is the truest, and best, and most noble, and in consequence, the greatest being. For what are the greatest truths are the greatest beings, as is said in the Metaphysics Bk. II. 2. What moreover is the greatest in its way, in another way is the cause of all things of its own kind (or genus) ; thus fire, which is the greatest heat, is the cause of all heat, as is said in the same book (cf. Plato and Aristotle). Therefore there exists something that is the cause of the existence of all things and of the goodness and of every perfection whatsoever—and this we call God.

The fifth proof arises from the ordering of things for we see that some things which lack reason such as natural bodies are operated in accordance with a plan. It appears from this that they are operated always or the more frequently in this same way

---

Source: Excerpts from *"Summa Theologica"* by Thomas Aquinas. Oliver Thatcher, Ed.

the closer they follow what is the Highest; whence it is clear that they do not arrive at the result by chance but because of a purpose. The things, moreover, that do not have intelligence do not tend toward a result unless directed by some one knowing and intelligent; just as an arrow is sent by an archer. Therefore there is something intelligent by which all natural things are arranged in accordance with a plan,—and this we call God.

In response to the first objection, then, I reply what Augustine says; that since God is entirely good, He would permit evil to exist in His works only if He were so good and omnipotent that He might bring forth good even from the evil. It therefore pertains to the infinite goodness of God that he permits evil to exist and from this brings forth good.

My reply to the second objection is that since nature is ordered in accordance with some defined purpose by the direction of some superior agent, those things that spring from nature must be dependent upon God, just as upon a first cause. Likewise what springs from a proposition must be traceable to some higher cause which is not the human reason or will, because this is changeable and defective and everything changeable and liable to non-existence is dependent upon some unchangeable first principle that is necessarily self-existent as has been shown.

David Hume, An Enquiry Concerning Human Understanding[13]

Hume (1711–1776) was a Scottish philosopher regarded as one of the leading figures in the Enlightenment.

When anyone tells me, that he saw a dead man restored to life, I immediately consider with myself, whether it be more probable, that this person should either deceive or be deceived, or that the fact, which he relates, should really have happened. I weigh the one miracle against the other; and according to the superiority, which I discover, I pronounce my decision . . .

The many instances of forged miracles, and prophecies, and supernatural events, which, in all ages, have either been detected by contrary evidence, or which detect themselves by their absurdity, prove sufficiently the strong propensity of mankind to the extraordinary and the marvellous, and ought reasonably to beget a suspicion against all relations of this kind . . .

You find certain phenomena in nature. You seek a cause or author. You imagine that you have found him. You afterwards become so enamoured of this offspring of your brain, that you imagine it impossible, but he must produce something greater and more perfect than the present scene of things, which is so full of ill and disorder. You forget, that this superlative intelligence and benevolence are entirely imaginary, or, at least, without any foundation in reason; and that you have no ground to ascribe to him any qualities, but what you see he has actually exerted and displayed in his productions . . .

I deny a providence, you say, and supreme governor of the world, who guides the course of events, and punishes the vicious with infamy and disappointment, and rewards the virtuous with honour and success, in all their undertakings. But surely, I deny not the course itself of events, which lies open to every one's inquiry and examination. I acknowledge, that, in the present order of things, virtue is attended with more peace of mind than vice, and meets with a more favourable reception from the world. I am sensible, that, according to the past experience of mankind, friendship is the chief joy of human life, and moderation the only source of tranquillity and happiness. I never balance between the virtuous and the vicious course of life; but am sensible, that, to a well-disposed mind, every advantage is on the side of the former.

And what can you say more, allowing all your suppositions and reasonings? You tell me, indeed, that this disposition of things proceeds from intelligence and design. But whatever it proceeds from, the disposition itself, on which depends our happiness or misery, and consequently our conduct and deportment in life is still the same. It is still open for me, as well as you, to regulate my behaviour, by my experience of past events. And if you affirm, that, while a divine providence is allowed, and a supreme distributive justice in the universe, I ought to expect some more particular reward of the good, and punishment of the bad, beyond the ordinary course of events; I here find the same fallacy, which I have before endeavoured to detect. You persist in imagining, that, if we grant that divine existence, for which you so earnestly contend, you may safely infer consequences from it, and add something to the experienced order of nature, by arguing from the attributes which you ascribe to your gods. You seem not to remember, that all your reasonings on this subject can only be drawn from effects to causes; and that every argument, deducted from causes to effects, must of necessity be a gross sophism; since it is impossible for you to know anything of the cause, but what you have antecedently, not inferred, but discovered to the full, in the effect . . .

While we argue from the course of nature, and infer a particular intelligent cause, which first bestowed, and still preserves order in the universe, we embrace a principle, which is both uncertain and useless. It is uncertain; because the subject lies entirely beyond the reach of human experience. It is useless; because our knowledge of this cause being derived entirely from the course of nature, we can never, according to the rules of just reasoning, return back from the cause with any new inference, or making additions to the common and experienced course of nature, establish any new principles of conduct and behaviour . . .

Source: David Hume.

The Deity is known to us only by his productions, and is a single being in the universe, not comprehended under any species or genus, from whose experienced attributes or qualities, we can, by analogy, infer any attribute or quality in him. As the universe shews wisdom and goodness, we infer wisdom and goodness. As it shews a particular degree of these perfections, we infer a particular degree of them, precisely adapted to the effect which we examine. But farther attributes or farther degrees of the same attributes, we can never be authorised to infer or suppose, by any rules of just reasoning.

Now, without some such licence of supposition, it is impossible for us to argue from the cause, or infer any alteration in the effect, beyond what has immediately fallen under our observation. Greater good produced by this Being must still prove a greater degree of goodness: a more impartial distribution of rewards and punishments must proceed from a greater regard to justice and equity. Every supposed addition to the works of nature makes an addition to the attributes of the Author of nature; and consequently, being entirely unsupported by any reason or argument, can never be admitted but as mere conjecture and hypothesis . . .

The great source of our mistake in this subject, and of the unbounded licence of conjecture, which we indulge, is, that we tacitly consider ourselves, as in the place of the Supreme Being, and conclude, that he will, on every occasion, observe the same conduct, which we ourselves, in his situation, would have embraced as reasonable and eligible. But, besides that the ordinary course of nature may convince us, that almost everything is regulated by principles and maxims very different from ours; besides this, I say, it must evidently appear contrary to all rules of analogy to reason, from the intentions and projects of men, to those of a Being so different, and so much superior . . .

Questions for Contemplation and Discussion

1. Aquinas argues that there is an "efficient cause." What does Hume say about causation?

2. Which of Aquinas's proofs did you find most persuasive?

3. Which of Aquinas's proofs did you find least persuasive?

4. What does Hume say about the possibility of miracles? Does his interpretation make sense? Do you believe in miracles: Why? Why not?

5. Some would say that both Aquinas and Hume are wrong to look for proof of God's existence in nature, because it is impossible to prove beyond a shadow of a doubt that God exists. God's existence, rather, is a matter of faith and is outside the realm of human understanding and reason. How would you respond to that interpretation? Explain.

WHO SHOULD BE ALLOWED TO VOTE?

Robert Lowe[14]

Robert Lowe (1811–1892) was a leading member of Parliament (MP) in Great Britain. He was known mostly for his opposition to expanding the electorate.

If the working classes, in addition to being a majority in the boroughs, get a redistribution of the seats in their favor, it will follow that their influence will be enormously increased. They will then urge the House of Commons to pass another Franchise Bill, and another Redistribution Bill to follow it. Not satisfied with these, yet another Franchise Bill and another redistribution of seats will perhaps follow. No one can tell where it will stop, and it will not be likely to stop until we get equal electoral districts and a qualification so low that it will keep out nobody. There is another matter with which my honorable friend has not dealt. I mean the point of combination among the working classes. To many persons there appears great danger that the machinery which at present exists for strikes and trade unions may be used for political purposes.

I come now to the question of the representatives of the working classes. It is an old observation that every democracy is in some respect similar to a despotism. As courtiers and flatterers are worse than despots themselves, so those who flatter and fawn upon the people are generally very inferior to the people, the objects of their flattery and adulation. We see in America, where the people have undisputed power, that they do not send honest, hard-working men to represent them in Congress, but traffickers in office, bankrupts, men who have lost their character and been driven from every respectable way of life, and who take up politics as a last resource.

In the colonies they have got democratic assemblies. And what is the result? Why, responsible government becomes a curse, instead of a blessing. In Australia there is no greater evil to the stability of society, to industry, to property, and to the well-being of the country, than the constant change which is taking place in the government, and the uncertainty that it creates and the pitting of rival factions against each other . . .

Now, Sir, democracy has yet another tendency, which it is worth while to study at the present moment. It is singularly prone to the concentration of power. Under it individual men are small and the government is great. That must be the character of a government which represents the majority, and which absolutely tramples down and equalizes everything except itself. And democracy has another strong peculiarity. It looks with the utmost hostility on all institutions not of immediate popular origin, which intervene between the people and the sovereign power which the people have set up.

The Declaration of Sentiments[15]

This document was the product of the 1848 Seneca Fall Convention, New York. Among those signing this were Elizabeth Cady Stanton and Lucretia Mott.

When, in the course of human events, it becomes necessary for one portion of the family of man to assume among the people of the earth a position different from that which they have hitherto occupied, but one to which the laws of nature and of nature's God entitle them, a decent respect to the opinions of mankind requires that they should declare the causes that impel them to such a course.

We hold these truths to be self-evident: that all men and women are created equal; that they are endowed by their Creator with certain inalienable rights; that among these are life, liberty, and the pursuit of happiness; that to secure these rights governments are instituted, deriving their just powers from the consent of the governed. Whenever any form of government becomes destructive of these ends, it is the right of those who suffer from it to refuse allegiance to it, and to insist upon the institution of a new government, laying its foundation on such principles, and organizing its powers in such form, as to them shall seem most likely to effect their safety and happiness. Prudence, indeed, will dictate that governments long established should not be changed for light and transient causes; and accordingly all experience hath shown that mankind are more disposed to suffer while evils are sufferable, than to right themselves by abolishing the forms to which they are accustomed.

But when a long train of abuses and usurpations, pursuing invariably the same object, evinces a design to reduce them under absolute despotism, it is their duty to throw off such government, and to provide new guards for their future security. Such has been the patient sufferance of the women under this government, and such is now the necessity which constrains them to demand the equal station to which they are entitled. The history of mankind is a history of repeated injuries and usurpations

---

Source: Speech by Robert Lowe. James Harvey Robinson and Charles Beard, Eds.
Source: "Declaration of Sentiments" from the 1848 Seneca Fall Convention. Elizabeth Cady Stanton, S.B. Anthony & M. J. Gage, Eds.

on the part of man toward woman, having in direct object the establishment of an absolute tyranny over her. To prove this, let facts be submitted to a candid world.

He has never permitted her to exercise her inalienable right to the elective franchise.

He has compelled her to submit to laws, in the formation of which she had no voice.

He has withheld from her rights which are given to the most ignorant and degraded men—both natives and foreigners.

Having deprived her of this first right of a citizen, the elective franchise, thereby leaving her without representation in the halls of legislation, he has oppressed her on all sides.

He has made her, if married, in the eye of the law, civilly dead. He has taken from her all right in property, even to the wages she earns.

He has made her, morally, an irresponsible being, as she can commit many crimes with impunity, provided they be done in the presence of her husband.

In the covenant of marriage, she is compelled to promise obedience to her husband, he becoming, to all intents and purposes, her master—the law giving him power to deprive her of her liberty, and to administer chastisement.

He has so framed the laws of divorce, as to what shall be the proper causes, and in case of separation, to whom the guardianship of the children shall be given, as to be wholly regardless of the happiness of women—the law, in all cases, going upon a false supposition of the supremacy of man, and giving all power into his hands.

After depriving her of all rights as a married woman, if single, and the owner of property, he has taxed her to support a government which recognizes her only when her property can be made profitable to it.

He has monopolized nearly all the profitable employments, and from those she is permitted to follow, she receives but a scanty remuneration. He closes against her all the avenues to wealth and distinction which he considers most honorable to himself. As a teacher of theology, medicine, or law, she is not known.

He has denied her the facilities for obtaining a thorough education, all colleges being closed against her.

He allows her in Church, as well as State, but a subordinate position, claiming Apostolic authority for her exclusion from the ministry, and, with some exceptions, from any public participation in the affairs of the Church.

He has created a false public sentiment by giving to the world a different code of morals for men and women, by which moral delinquencies which exclude women from society, are not only tolerated, but deemed of little account in man.

He has usurped the prerogative of Jehovah himself, claiming it as his right to assign for her a sphere of action, when that belongs to her conscience and to her God.

He has endeavored, in every way that he could, to destroy her confidence in her own powers, to lessen her self-respect and to make her willing to lead a dependent and abject life.

Now, in view of this entire disfranchisement of one-half the people of this country, their social and religious degradation—in view of the unjust laws above mentioned, and because women do feel themselves aggrieved, oppressed, and fraudulently deprived of their most sacred rights, we insist that they have immediate admission to all the rights and privileges which belong to them as citizens of the United States.

In entering upon the great work before us, we anticipate no small amount of misconception, misrepresentation, and ridicule; but we shall use every instrumentality within our power to effect our object. We shall employ agents, circulate tracts, petition the State and National legislatures, and endeavor to enlist the pulpit and the press in our behalf. We hope this Convention will be followed by a series of Conventions embracing every part of the country.

Questions for Contemplation and Discussion

Good ex.
Country like the U.S.

1. What is Lowe's thesis, or main point?

   The main point that Lowe's — is that the vote should be decided on democracy. It should be respectfully decided among the people.

2. Do you agree with his view of democracy and of working people? Explain.

   Yes I agree, everyone is equal and has the right to vote for the leader of their country. Working people also to know whom their dictator will be.

3. The *Declaration of Sentiments* was purposely written to look like the *Declaration of Independence*. Both begin with "When, in the course of human events," and include "We hold these truths to be self-evident." Why do you think the authors of the *Declaration of Sentiments* did this? Explain.

   The Dec. of Sentiments was made in contrast of the Dec. of Ind. It is more so spiritual belief than a political belief. Depends on Men or head of Household.

4. What does the *Declaration of Sentiments* say about the status of women, how it is and how it should be? Explain.

   Despite the fact it being a document made in the U.S. it says that the men have the full rights not the women. Says Men should have tyranny over women.

5. Do you agree with the values and assumptions in the *Declaration of Sentiments*?

   Personally I do not agree with the values and assumptions made by Dec. of Sent. Women have all rights to do so and vote.

6. Some have criticized democracy because it is based on the principle that the majority is always right, yet the truth is that sometimes the majority is wrong. What is your reaction to that criticism?

   Majority can be right - depending on the type of situation that arouses. Majority is not always right.

   In smaller situations - for ex. Saving animals the majority can be wrong

   Voting - ~~Presid~~ George Bush (2x)

SHOULD THE MILITARY BE GLORIFIED?

Du Fu, "Song of the War Chariot"[16]

Du Fu (712–770) has been called the greatest Chinese poet. He lived during the Tang Dynasty, one of the more tumultuous periods in China's history.

> The war-chariots rattle,
> The war-horses whinny.
> Each man of you has a bow and a quiver at his belt.
> Father, mother, son, wife, stare at you going,
> Till dust shall have buried the bridge beyond Changan [an ancient Chinese city].
> They run with you, crying, they tug at your sleeves,
> And the sound of their sorrow goes up to the clouds;
> And every time a bystander asks you a question,
> You can only say to him that you have to go . . .
>
> We remember others at fifteen sent north to guard the river
> And at forty sent west to cultivate the campfarms.
> The mayor wound their turbans for them when they started out.
> With their turbaned hair white now, they are still at the border,
> At the border where the blood of men spills like the sea—
> And still the heart of Emperor Wu is beating for war . . .
>
> Do you know that, east of China's mountains, in two hundred districts
> And in thousands of villages, nothing grows but weeds,
> And though strong women have bent to the ploughing,
> East and west the furrows all are broken down? . . .
>
> Men of China are able to face the stiffest battle,
> But their officers drive them like chickens and dogs.
> Whatever is asked of them,
> Dare they complain?
> For example, this winter
> Held west of the gate,
> Challenged for taxes,
> How could they pay? . . .
>
> We have learned that to have a son is bad luck-
> It is very much better to have a daughter
> Who can marry and live in the house of a neighbour,
> While under the sod we bury our boys . . .
>
> Go to the Blue Sea, look along the shore
> At all the old white bones forsaken—
> New ghosts are wailing there now with the old,
> Loudest in the dark sky of a stormy day.

Source: "Song of the War Chariot" by Du Fu from *An Introduction to Chinese Literature*, edited by Wu-Chi Liu. Copyright © 1966. Reprinted by permission of Indiana University Press.

Count Helmuth Von Moltke, "Letter to Professor Bluntschli"[17]

Von Moltke (1800-1891) possessed one of the great military minds of modern European history. He was one of the architects of Prussia's army. Prussia no longer exists as an independent nation, but it makes up the foundation of modern Germany.

Professor Bluntschli had sent a manual that was produced by an organization called the Institute of International Law to Count Moltke, and expressed the hope, in a letter dated November 19, 1880, that it would meet with his approval. Count Moltke replied as follows:

My dear Professor:

You have been good enough to send me the manual published by the Institute of International Law, and you ask for my approval. In the first place, I fully recognize your humane endeavors to lessen the sufferings which war brings in its train.

Eternal peace, however, is a dream, and not even a beautiful dream, for war is part of God's scheme of the world. In war the noblest virtues of man develop courage and renunciation, the sense of duty and abnegation, and all at the risk of his life. Without war the world would be swallowed up in the morass of materialism.

With the principle stated in the preface, that the gradual advance of civilization should be reflected in the conduct of war, I fully agree; but I go further, and believe that civilization alone, and no codified laws of warfare, can have the desired result.

Every law necessitates an authority to watch over it and to direct its execution, but there is no power which can enforce obedience to international agreements. Which third state will take up arms because one—or both—of two powers at war with each other have broken the loi de la guerre? [law of war] The human judge is lacking. In these matters we can hope for success only from the religious and moral education of the individuals, and the honor and sense of right of the leaders, who make their own laws and act according to them, at least to the extent to which the abnormal conditions of war permit it.

Nobody, I think, can deny that the general softening of men's manners has been followed by a more humane way of waging war.

Compare, if you will, the coarseness of the Thirty Years' War with the battles of recent dates.

The introduction in our generation of universal service in the army has marked a long step in the direction of the desired aim, for it has brought also the educated classes into the army. Some rough and violent elements have survived, it is true, but the army no longer consists of them exclusively.

The governments, moreover, have two means at hand to prevent the worst excesses. A strong discipline, practiced and perfected in times of peace, and a commissariat equipped to provide for the troops in the field.

Without careful provision, discipline itself can be only moderately well enforced. The soldier who suffers pain and hunger, fatigue and danger, cannot take merely en proportion avec les ressources du pays, [resources of countries] but he must take whatever he needs. You must not ask of him superhuman things.

The greatest blessing in war is its speedy termination, and to this end all means must be permitted which are not downright criminal. I cannot at all give my approval to the Déclaration de St. Petersbourg, [St. Petersburg Declaration] that "the weakening of the hostile army" is the only justifiable procedure in war. On the contrary, all resources of the hostile government must be attacked—its finances, railways, provisions, and even its prestige.

The last war against France was waged in this way, and yet with greater moderation than any earlier war. The campaign was decided after two months; and fierceness became characteristic of the fighting only when a revolutionary government continued the war through four more months, to the detriment of the country.

I am glad to acknowledge that your manual, with its clear and short sentences, does greater justice than former attempts to what is needed in war. But even the acceptance of your regulations by the governments would not ensure their observance. It has long been a universally accepted rule of warfare that no messenger of peace should be shot at. But in the last campaign we frequently saw this done.

No paragraph learned by heart will convince the soldier that the unorganized natives who spontaneously (that is, of their own free will) take up arms and threaten his life every moment of the day and night should be recognized as lawful opponents . . .

In war, where everything must be treated individually, only those regulations will work well which are primarily addressed to the leaders. This includes everything that your manual has to say concerning the wounded and the sick, the physicians and their medicines. The general recognition of these principles, and also of those which have to do with the prisoners of war, would mark a notable step in advance and bring us nearer the end which the Institute of International Law is pursuing with such admirable perseverance.

Very respectfully,

COUNT MOLTKE.

Questions for Contemplation and Discussion

1. What does Du Fu say about war? Is his view a positive view, or more a negative one?

2. Does Du Fu's description of war ring true to you? Is he being fair?

3. In his letter to the professor, Von Moltke says "Eternal peace, however, is a dream, and not even a beautiful dream, for war is part of God's scheme of the world." What is your reaction to that statement?

4. In Von Moltke's view, why can war be a good thing?

5. Would you agree with him that there is a need for some rules/guidelines regarding war? If so, what are some that warring nations should agree to follow?

6. "War is justifiable only if it is in self-defense." Do you agree with this statement? Cite reasoning and evidence in support of your position.

WHAT IS EDUCATION?

Confucius, Analects: On Learning[18]

This work became one of the required readings for the Chinese civil service exams, which were taken from the early fourteenth century to 1905.

BOOK I

A saying of the Scholar Yu:

"It is rarely the case that those who act the part of true men in regard to their duty to parents and elder brothers are at the same time willing to turn currishly upon their superiors: it has never yet been the case that such as desire not to commit that offence have been men willing to promote anarchy or disorder.

"Men of superior mind busy themselves first in getting at the root of things; and when they have succeeded in this the right course is open to them. Well, are not filial piety [the respect of children for parents and ancestors] and friendly subordination among brothers a root of that right feeling which is owing generally from man to man?"

The Master observed, "Rarely do we meet with the right feeling due from one man to another where there is fine speech and studied mien."

The Scholar Tsang [a Chinese Buddhist scholar from the 600's B.C.E] once said of himself: "On three points I examine myself daily . . . whether, in looking after other people's interests, I have not been acting whole-heartedly; whether, in my intercourse with friends, I have not been true; and whether, after teaching, I have not myself been practicing what I have taught."

The Master once observed that to rule well one of the larger States meant strict attention to its affairs and conscientiousness on the part of the ruler; careful husbanding of its resources, with at the same time a tender care for the interests of all classes; and the employing of the masses in the public service at suitable seasons.

"Let young people," said he, "show filial piety at home, respectfulness towards their elders when away from home; let them be circumspect, be truthful; their love going out freely towards all, cultivating good-will to men. And if, in such a walk, there be time or energy left for other things, let them employ it in the acquisition of literary or artistic accomplishments."

Sayings of the Master:—

"Give prominent place to loyalty and sincerity."

"Have no associates in study who are not advanced somewhat like yourself."

"When you have erred, be not afraid to correct yourself."

A saying of the Scholar Tsang:—

"The virtue of the people is renewed and enriched when attention is seen to be paid to the departed, and the remembrance of distant ancestors kept and cherished."

Tsz-kung [Chinese for Confucius; Confucius is a Latin name for Tsz-Kung] answered, "Our Master is a man of pleasant manners, and of probity, courteous, moderate, and unassuming: it is by his being such that he arrives at the facts. Is not his way of arriving at things different from that of others?"

A saying of the Master:—

"The man of greater mind who, when he is eating, craves not to eat to the full; who has a home, but craves not for comforts in it; who is active and earnest in his work and careful in his words; who makes towards men of high principle, and so maintains his own rectitude—that man may be styled a devoted student."

Tsz-kung asked, "What say you, sir, of the poor who do not cringe and fawn; and what of the rich who are without pride and haughtiness?" "They are passable," the Master replied; "yet they are scarcely in the same category as the poor who are happy, and the rich who love propriety."

"It does not greatly concern me," said the Master, "that men do not know me; my great concern is, my not knowing them."

Letters from Medieval Universities[19]

Letters from or to Students at the University of Paris

(1) A CERTAIN D. WRITES TO A CERTAIN PRIOR CONCERNING HIS STUDIES AT THE UNIVERSITY OF PARIS. (1109–1112.)

I am now in Paris in the School of Master William of Champeaux, the greatest of all the men of his time whom I have known, in every branch of learning. When we hear his voice we think that no man, but, as it were, an angel from heaven, is speaking; for the melody of his words and the profundity of his ideas transcends, as it were, human limitations. . . .

Here, my revered friend, I am training my youth that I may not utterly succumb to those vices which, unless conquered, are wont, as a rule, to overturn this period of life. Here I am doing my best to illumine by doctrine and study my untaught mind, emancipated from the shades of ignorance and the sin of the first man, so far as God, from whom alone comes every blessing of wisdom, shall himself deign to permit. Because the blessing of wisdom, when sought and acquired with pure interest, is rightly believed and considered by all men of discernment as the surmnuni bonum [the highest good]. For, as the Apostle [Paul] says: Knowledge without charity puffeth up but, with charity edifieth: for it uproots vices and grafts in virtues; it instructs itself in its duty to itself, its neighbor, and its Creator; finally, by its presence, it fortifies and defends the mind, over which it presides in person, against all the ills of this life that come to it from without.

(2) PHILIP OF HARVENGT TO HERGALD, A STUDENT AT PARIS (DATE BETWEEN 1154 AND 1181)

Know that I have both read carefully and when read, accepted gratefully the letters which your affection, with memorable feeling, led you to send to me . . . because in them I thought I saw evidence of your progress in learning. . . . Just as the Queen of Sheba is said to have come with a large retinue, that by the sight of her own eyes she might have surer knowledge of those things whose fame she had eagerly absorbed from afar, so you too, drawn by love of knowledge, came to Paris and found a much desired model of Jerusalem, sought for by many. For here David strikes his harp of ten chords, here with mystic touch he composes the psalms. Here Isaiah is read and in the reading his prophecies are revealed; here the rest of the prophets present their diverse strains of harmonious melody. Here the wisdom of Solomon is open for the instruction of those who have gathered from all parts of the world; here his treasure house is thrown open to eager students. Here to stimulate so great a concourse of students there is so great a throng of clerks that it vies with the numerous multitude of the laity. Happy city! in which the Sacred Codes are pored over with so much zeal and their involved mysteries are solved by the gift of the outpoured Spirit, in which there is so much diligence on the part of the readers, and, in short, so much knowledge of Scriptures that it truly deserves to be called Cariath Sepher, that is The City of Letters. Therein would I have you instructed like Gothoniel, not so much in letters as in the spirit, and so to grasp the Scriptures that you may take delight in searching out their inner sweetness. . . . Farewell.

(3) DESCRIPTION OF PARIS ABOUT 1175 BY GUY DE BASOCHES

To a youth who is noble and so like himself as to be a second self, Guy de Basoches [seeks] to match his nobility of birth by high-bred manners. . . .

My situation then is this: I am indeed in Paris, happy because of soundness of both mind and body, happier were you enjoying it too, and happiest had it but been my lot to have you with me. I am indeed in Paris, in that City of Kings, which not only holds, by the sweet delight of her natural dowry, those who are with her, but also alluringly invites those who are far away. For as the moon by the majesty of its more brilliant mirror overwhelms the rays of the stars, not otherwise does said city raise its imperial head with its diadem of royal dignity above the rest of the cities. It is situated in the lap of a delightful valley, surrounded by a coronet of mountains which Ceres and Bacchus adorn with fervent zeal. The Seine [major river in France], no humble stream amid the army of rivers, superb in its channel, throwing its two arms about the head, the heart, the very marrow of the city, forms an island. Two suburbs reach out to right and left, the less excellent, even, of which begets envy in envious cities. From the two suburbs two stone bridges stretch over to the island and one of them which has been named for its size, for it is Great, faces the north and the English Sea, while the opposite one, which opens towards the Loire, they call the Little Bridge. . . .

On this island Philosophy, of old, placed a royal throne for herself, Philosophy, who, despised in her solitude, with a sole attendant, Study, now possesses an enduring citadel of light and immortality, and under her victorious feet tramples the withered flowers of a world already in its dotage.

On this island, the seven sisters, to wit, the Liberal Arts, have secured an eternal abiding place for themselves, and, with the ringing clarion of their nobler eloquence, decrees and laws are proclaimed.

Here the healing fount of learning gushes forth, and as it were evoking from itself three most limpid streams, it makes a threefold division of the knowledge of the sacred page into History, Allegory and Morals.

(4) JOHANN VON JENZENSTEIN TO MASTER BENESCH OF HORSCHOWITZ, CONCERNING PARIS. (1375.)

Master Bennessius, dearest comrade and friend. If recent doings at Paris are unknown to you, if the fecundity of pleasures, the abundance of all things edible, the manners of the men, the bountiful supply of all the sciences, even the clever teaching in very many material crafts,—if you could but see the mere shadow of all these, surely, overpowered by their arguments, you would throw off your sluggishness and generously enter into the aforesaid enjoyments; and your eyes, grown old in old sights would renew their youth in these new sights. . . .

For here (says the writer sarcastically) are distinguished doctors of many faculties, some of whom by their crazy ways of thinking, and still others by crazy ways of acting, others, indeed, by inflicting wounds, and still others by abusive words, furnish enjoyment that is exceeding pleasing; and (he adds more seriously) there are other Masters subtly trained in the seven liberal Arts, by whose example and teaching the entire earth, like the heavens, is adorned with stars; and some of these masters are illuminated by the three trivials [grammar, logic, and rhetoric] and some by the four quadrivials [arithmetic, geometry, astronomy, and music] and some by both the trivials and the quadrivials.

Now the three trivials are grammar, which teaches clearly the agreement of speech; and starting from that, the youth who holds on to his first teaching makes a beginning whereby he may obtain a deeper taste of the profundities of other knowledge also; the second is rhetoric, which by the charm of its colors adorns as with pearls the subject matter, and ennobles grammar, and instills acceptably into the ears of men that which is heard; the third is logic by means of which the method of skilful deductive reasoning is assigned to the individual sciences, without which the powers of all the sciences are quiescent, and by whose addition all the sciences are regularly organized. (The letter ends with a similar description of the quadrivials.)

TWO UNIVERSITY OF OXFORD LETTERS OF THE FIFTEENTH CENTURY

(1) OXFORD UNIVERSITY [the oldest university in England and in the English-speaking world] TO THE DUKE OF GLOUCESTER, ACKNOWLEDGING A GIFT OF BOOKS. (1439.)

Most illustrious, most cultured and magnificent Prince, the enduring value of the benefits you have conferred on the English nation, and the meritorious deeds of your most powerful Highness in its behalf can never die, but, with distinguished fame destined to endure, will flourish with ever-renewed praise and happy remembrance. How delightful it certainly is for us to reflect upon these again and again! Among the rest, however, that deed itself redounds to the splendor of your most mighty Highness, namely, that after having brought about the repression of heretic plotting against the church of God, you have chosen to reinvigorate the vineyard of the Lord, your hand-maid, the University of Oxford, with books on all the sciences and virtues, out of which the abundant wine of knowledge and truth may be squeezed by the press of study. For this reason we set forth in this humble letter our thanks, our praise, and our prayers, but we cannot express ourselves adequately.

Which of the Universities has found a Prince so munificent, so illustrious, so magnificent?—whose service in the field has ever been successful, whose mind is most liberal, and who displays charity to all, justice to each, and harm to none. What respecter of the wise was ever so pious, what supporter of them so efficient, what patron of the sciences, of virtues, and of books so generous? And by these not only are the hearts of the living enlightened to the glory of God and the advance of virtue, but even more in coming ages will posterity be illumined. Can the happy memory of deeds so great pass away? Nay, but it will be a benediction forever.

A statute has been made in the words of your supplicant, and is to be forever in force, which will never fail in prayers in your behalf but will serve as an enduring memorial. Wherefore, although the fame of others may ebb with the flow of time or perish through being overshadowed by the rising of greater men, yet your fame cannot perish under the cloud of oblivion nor can it, of a truth, be obscured by the shadow of greater benefactions.

If the great conquests of Alexander [Alexander the Great, leader of Macedonia and conqueror of the Greeks from the 300's B.C.E.] come to our ears, renewed day by day through the devices of the wise Greeks who committed such deeds to writing, how much more will this University, your devoted supplicant, bear witness to your magnificent deeds to the end of time, not only by her prayers but also in her writings? Nay, were the tongues of all to be silent the fact itself would bear witness more than speech, the fact, to wit, that one hundred and thirty-nine most precious volumes of theology, medicine, and the seven liberal sciences have been deposited in our library from your own collection, as an eternal witness to your surpassing virtues and munificence.

We pray therefore that you may be willing to look upon this University as your vineyard and your handmaid and perpetual supplicant. And may the Lord Himself most glorious, who chose your serenity for the bestowing of such benefactions, grant to you the fruits of the spirit and guide you to the University of the saints. Written at Oxford in our congregation in the twenty-fifth day of the month of January.

TESTIMONIAL LETTER FOR MR. JOHN KING OF OXFORD

To all the children of Holy Church, our Mother, to whom this letter may come, the Chancellor of the University of Oxford and the whole assembly of masters ruling in the same send greeting in the arms of our Saviour. We believe that we present an offering in the sight of the highest truth, as often as we furnish a testimony of high praise to one excellent in virtue and in knowledge. Therefore we,—wishing all whom it may concern to know of the commendable life and the fragrance of honest conversation of our beloved brother, Master John King, M.A. [holder of the degree of Master of Arts] and student in Sacred Theology, a prudent Procurator of our University who has filled his office most efficiently; we therefore, as we have said, wishing all to know, as we are bound to do,—and to prevent so bright a light from being hid beneath the bushel of silence,—do bear witness by this letter that, through the commendable merits of our aforesaid brother and his study, he has attained such proficiency that the fragrant fame of his name—which the praise of his excellent action has exalted to the pinnacle of glory with us—could not be concealed: but from the height of its exalted pedestal it has furnished a living example to all scholars for emulation, and a great light to all people for profitable instruction. And so, while adorning our University with his presence and outshining all in the maturity and dignity of his character, he won the love of all by his spotless name. We commend him therefore to your worshipful reverences, earnestly praying that you will show yourselves favorable and kind to him, both out of regard for our University and for his deserts. In witness of which, and that all may know more fully about his laudable character, we have caused this letter to be sealed for said Master John with the seal of our University.

Given at Oxford in the Congregation-house, February 9th, 1434.

John Dewey, Democracy and Education[20]

John Dewey (1859–1952) was an American philosopher who wrote on education, philosophy, and psychology. His influence on American higher education was significant, for he emphasized the teaching of skills and the development of the person as a responsible civic individual over the rote teaching of knowledge.

From "Education as Training of Faculties"

There is no such thing as an ability to see or hear or remember in general; there is only the ability to see or hear or remember something. To talk about training a power, mental or physical, in general, apart from the subject matter involved in its exercise, is nonsense. Exercise may react upon circulation, breathing, and nutrition so as to develop vigor or strength, but this reservoir is available for specific ends only by use in connection with the material means which accomplish them. Vigor will enable a man to play tennis or golf or to sail a boat better than he would if he were weak.

But only by employing ball and racket, ball and club, sail and tiller, in definite ways does he become expert in any one of them; and expertness in one secures expertness in another only so far as it is either a sign of aptitude for fine muscular coordinations or as the same kind of coordination is involved in all of them. Moreover, the difference between the training of ability to spell which comes from taking visual forms in a narrow context and one which takes them in connection with the activities required to grasp meaning, such as context, affiliations of descent, etc., may be compared to the difference between exercises in the gymnasium with pulley weights to "develop" certain muscles, and a game or sport. The former is uniform and mechanical; it is rigidly specialized. The latter is varied from moment to moment; no two acts are quite alike; novel emergencies have to be met; the coordinations forming have to be kept flexible and elastic. Consequently, the training is much more "general"; that is to say, it covers a wider territory and includes more factors. Exactly the same thing holds of special and general education of the mind.

A monotonously uniform exercise may by practice give great skill in one special act; but the skill is limited to that act, be it bookkeeping or calculations in logarithms or experiments in hydrocarbons. One may be an authority in a particular field and yet of more than usually poor judgment in matters not closely allied, unless the training in the special field has been of a kind to ramify into the subject matter of the other fields.

Consequently, such powers as observation, recollection, judgment, esthetic taste, represent organized results of the occupation of native active tendencies with certain subject matters. A man does not observe closely and fully by pressing a button for the observing faculty to get to work (in other words by "willing" to observe); but if he has something to do which can be accomplished successfully only through intensive and extensive use of eye and hand, he naturally observes. Observation is an outcome, a consequence, of the interaction of sense organ and subject matter. It will vary, accordingly, with the subject matter employed.

It is consequently futile to set up even the ulterior development of faculties of observation, memory, etc., unless we have first determined what sort of subject matter we wish the pupil to become expert in observing and recalling and for what purpose. And it is only repeating in another form what has already been said, to declare that the criterion here must be social.

We want the person to note and recall and judge those things which make him an effective competent member of the group in which he is associated with others. Otherwise we might as well set the pupil to observing carefully cracks on the wall and set him to memorizing meaningless lists of words in an unknown tongue—which is about what we do in fact when we give way to the doctrine of formal discipline. If the observing habits of a botanist or chemist or engineer are better habits than those which are thus formed, it is because they deal with subject matter which is more significant in life.

In concluding this portion of the discussion, we note that the distinction between special and general education has nothing to do with the transferability of function or power. In the literal sense, any transfer is miraculous and impossible. But some activities are broad; they involve a coordination of many factors. Their development demands continuous alternation and readjustment. As conditions change, certain factors are subordinated, and others which had been of minor importance come to the front. There is constant redistribution of the focus of the action, as is seen in the illustration of a game as over against pulling a fixed weight by a series of uniform motions.

Thus there is practice in prompt making of new combinations with the focus of activity shifted to meet change in subject matter. Wherever an activity is broad in scope (that is, involves the coordinating of a large variety of sub-activities), and is constantly and unexpectedly obliged to change direction in its progressive development, general education is bound to result. For this is what "general" means; broad and flexible. In practice, education meets these conditions, and hence is general, in the degree in which it takes account of social relationships. A person may become expert in technical philosophy, or philology, or mathematics or engineering or financiering, and be inept and ill-advised in his action and judgment outside of his specialty.

If however his concern with these technical subject matters has been connected with human activities having social breadth, the range of active responses called into play and flexibly integrated is much wider. Isolation of subject matter from a social context is the chief obstruction in current practice to securing a general training of mind. Literature, art, religion, when thus dissociated [broken apart from each other], are just as narrowing as the technical things which the professional upholders of general education strenuously oppose.

Summary. The conception that the result of the educative process is capacity for further education stands in contrast with some other ideas which have profoundly influenced practice. The first contrasting conception considered is that of preparing or getting ready for some future duty or privilege. Specific evil effects were pointed out which result from the fact that this aim diverts attention of both teacher and taught from the only point to which it may be fruitfully directed—namely, taking advantage of the needs and possibilities of the immediate present.

Consequently it defeats its own professed purpose. The notion that education is an unfolding from within appears to have more likeness to the conception of growth which has been set forth . . .

Another influential but defective theory is that which conceives that mind has, at birth, certain mental faculties or powers, such as perceiving, remembering, willing, judging, generalizing, attending, etc., and that education is the training of these faculties through repeated exercise. This theory treats subject matter as comparatively external and indifferent, its value residing simply in the fact that it may occasion exercise of the general powers. Criticism was directed upon this separation of the alleged powers from one another and from the material upon which they act. The outcome of the theory in practice was shown to be an undue emphasis upon the training of narrow specialized modes of skill at the expense of initiative, inventiveness, and re-adaptability—qualities which depend upon the broad and consecutive interaction of specific activities with one another . . .

Questions for Contemplation and Discussion

1. What are the values expressed in the *Analects*?

2. Do the *Analects* focus more on book knowledge, or on attitude? Explain.

3. According to the *Analects*, "When you have erred, be not afraid to correct yourself." Do you agree with this philosophy? Support your answer with evidence and reasoning.

4. What do the letters tell us about medieval universities?

5. In particular, how were medieval universities different from universities today?

6. According to Dewey, what is education?

7. What role should education (secondary education, a university education) play in American democracy?

8. If you were a teacher in your major (if you don't have a major, pretend it is history), how do you think John Dewey would teach your subject?

9. Why should taxpayers help pay for your education? In your answer, refer to John Dewey's theories (you may agree or disagree with them).

WHAT IS GENOCIDE?

Iris Chang, The Rape of Nanking[21]

Iris Chang (1968–2004) was a journalist and historian who wrote the first detailed account of the Japanese massacre of the Chinese city of Nanking.

On December 13, 1937, thirty Japanese soldiers came to the Chinese home at 5 Hsing Lu Kao in the southeastern part of Nanking. They killed the landlord when he opened the door, and then Mr. Hsia, a tenant who had fallen to his knees to beg them not to kill anyone else. When the landlord's wife asked why they murdered her husband, they shot her dead. The Japanese then dragged Mrs. Hsia from under a table in the guest hall where she had tried to hide with her one-year-old baby. They stripped her, raped her, then bayoneted her in the chest when they were finished. The soldiers thrust a perfume bottle in her vagina and also killed the baby by bayonet. Then they went into the next room, where they found Mrs. Hsia's parents and two teenage daughters. The grandmother, who tried to protect the girls from rape, was shot by revolver; the grandfather clasped the body of his wife and was killed immediately.

The soldiers then stripped the girls and took turns raping them: the sixteen-year-old by two or three men, the fourteen-year-old by three. The Japanese not only stabbed the older girl to death after raping her but rammed a bamboo cane into her vagina. The younger one was simply bayoneted and "spared the horrible treatment meted out to her sister and mother," a foreigner later wrote of the scene. The soldiers also bayoneted another sister, aged eight, when she hid with her four-year-old sister under the blankets of a bed. The four-year-old remained under the blankets so long she nearly suffocated. She was to endure brain damage for the rest of her life from the lack of oxygen.

Before leaving, the soldiers murdered the landlord's two children, aged four and two; they bayoneted the older child and split the head of the younger one with a sword. When it was safe to emerge, the eight-year-old survivor, who had been hiding under the blankets, crawled to the next room where she lay beside the body of her mother. Together with her four-year-old sister, they lived for fourteen days on rice crusts that their mother had prepared before the siege. When a member of the International Committee arrived at the house weeks after the slaughter, he saw that one young girl had been raped on the table. "While I was there," he testified later, "the blood on the table [was] not all dry yet."

The Pit"[22]

This is a first hand account of the Nazi persecution and murder of Jews. This is from 1942.

Execution of the Jews at Dubno, October 5, 1942*

On October 5, 1942, when I visited the building office at Dubno, my foreman told me that in the vicinity of the site, Jews from Dubno had been shot in three large pits, each about 30 metres long and 3 metres deep. About 1,500 persons had been killed daily. All the 5,000 Jews who had still been living in Dubno before the pogrom were to be liquidated. As the shooting had taken place in his presence, he was still much upset.

Thereupon, I drove to the site accompanied by my foreman and saw near it great mounds of earth, about 30 metres long and 2 metres high. Several trucks stood in front of the mounds. Armed Ukrainian militia drove the people off the trucks under the supervision of an S.S. man. The militiamen acted as guards on the trucks and drove them to and from the pit. All these people had the regulation yellow patches on the front and back of their clothes, and thus could be recognized as Jews.

My foreman and I went directly to the pits. Nobody bothered us. Now I heard rifle shots in quick succession from behind one of the earth mounds. The people who had got off the trucks—men, women and children of all ages—had to undress upon the orders of an S.S. man, who carried a riding or dog whip. They had to put down their clothes in fixed places, sorted according to shoes, top clothing and underclothing. I saw a heap of shoes of about 800 to 1,000 pairs, great piles of underlinen and clothing.

Without screaming or weeping, these people undressed, stood around in family groups, kissed each other, said farewells, and waited for a sign from another S.S. man, who stood near the pit, also with a whip in his hand. During the fifteen minutes that I stood near I heard no complaint or plea for mercy. I watched a family of about eight persons, a man and a woman both about fifty with their children of about one, eight and ten, and two grown-up daughters of about twenty to twenty-nine. An old

---

Source: From *The Rape of Nanking: the Forgotten Holocaust of World War II* by Iris Chang (New York; Basic Books; 1997).
Source: From *The Nuremberg Proceedings,* as quoted in Louis L. Snyder and Richard B. Morris, *They Saw It Happen* (Harrisburg, 1951).

woman with snow-white hair was holding the one-year-old child in her arms and singing to it and tickling it. The child was cooing with delight. The couple were looking on with tears in their eyes. The father was holding the hand of a boy about ten years old and speaking to him softly; the boy was fighting his tears. The father pointed to the sky, stroked his head, and seemed to explain something to him.

At that moment the S.S. man at the pit shouted something to his comrade. The latter counted off about twenty persons and instructed them to go behind the earth mound. Among them was the family which I have mentioned. I well remember a girl, slim and with black hair, who, as she passed close to me, pointed to herself and said "23." I walked around the mound and found myself confronted by a tremendous grave. People were closely wedged together and lying on top of each other so that only their heads were visible. Nearly all had blood running over their shoulders from their heads. Some of the people shot were still moving. Some were lifting their arms and turning their heads to show that they were still alive. The pit was already two-thirds full. I estimated that it already contained about 1,000 people.

I looked for the man who did the shooting. He was an S.S. man, who sat at the edge of the narrow end of the pit, his feet dangling into the pit. He had a tommy-gun on his knees and was smoking a cigarette. The people, completely naked, went down some steps which were cut in the clay wall of the pit and clambered over the heads of the people lying there, to the place to which the S.S. man directed them. They lay down in front of the dead or injured people; some caressed those who were still alive and spoke to them in a low voice.

Then I heard a series of shots. I looked into the pit and saw that the bodies were twitching or the heads lying motionless on top of the bodies which lay before them. Blood was running from their necks. I was surprised that I was not ordered away, but I saw that there were two or three postmen in uniform nearby. The next batch was approaching already. They went down into the pit, lined themselves up against the previous victims and were shot.

When I walked back round the mound, I noticed another truckload of people which had just arrived. This time it included sick and infirm persons. An old, very thin woman with terribly thin legs was undressed by others who were already naked, while two people held her up. The woman appeared to be paralyzed. The naked people carried the woman around the mound. I left with my foreman and drove in my car back to Dubno.

On the morning of the next day, when I again visited the site, I saw about thirty naked people lying near the pit—about 30 to 50 metres away from it. Some of them were still alive; they looked straight in front of them with a fixed stare and seemed to notice neither the chilliness of the morning nor the workers of my firm who stood around. A girl of about twenty spoke to me and asked me to give her clothes and help her escape. At that moment we heard a fast car approach and I noticed that it was an S.S. detail. I moved away to my site. Ten minutes later we heard shots from the vicinity of the pit. The Jews alive had been ordered to throw the corpses into the pit, then they had themselves to lie down in it to be shot in the neck.

Questions for Contemplation and Discussion

1. What does the account of the pit tell us about the Holocaust?

   It tells us the organized fashion of the genocide. People were killed in groups - in categories, one by one.

2. What does the account of the Chinese family tell us about the "Rape of Nanking"?

   They were innocent, unaware. HARMLESS. Seemed like a good family, also big.

3. What do the two accounts have in common? How are they different?

   Common: Cruel - Relentless, Ruthless - Mercilessly
   Different: The Chinese family was hit unexpectedly - rapes. The Jewish Genocide was organized.

4. There were examples of genocide before the 1930's and after the end of World War II. Why do you think genocide takes place? Is prejudice (based on race, ethnicity, religion) the only reason? Explain.

   Based on All the above. Genocide used to show intimidation and first steps of domination.

5. Some would say that those who committed such atrocities—in this case, the Nazis and the Japanese—should have been executed without a trial, because people who do not respect the dignity of others do not deserve the dignity of a fair trial. How would you respond to that?

   I Agree. Deserves execution w/out question. If you can't respect someone, one does not deserve respect in return. A genocide is unacceptable loss of 100's, thousands, possibly million lives.

6. The Japanese who brutalized Chinese during the "Rape of Nanking" sometimes justified their actions by pointing out that for centuries China had taken advantage of Japan. Japan was, accordingly, just returning the favor. How would you respond to such an argument?

   Grudges should not be held over time. Because one takes advantage of another, that does not require an ambush in return. Two wrongs don't make a right.

WHAT SHOULD BE THE RELATIONSHIP BETWEEN CHURCH AND STATE?

Pope Urban II[23]

Urban II was pope of the Roman Catholic Church from 1088 until his death in 1099. His speech launched the religious and military movement known as the Crusades.

From the confines of Jerusalem and from the city of Constantinople a grievous report has gone forth and has repeatedly been brought to our ears; namely, that a race from the kingdom of the Persians, an accursed race, a race wholly alienated from God, 'a generation that set not their heart aright, and whose spirit was not steadfast with God,' has violently invaded the lands of those Christians and has depopulated them by pillage and fire. They have led away a part of the captives into their own country, and a part they have killed by cruel tortures. They have either destroyed the churches of God or appropriated them for the rites of their own religion. They destroy the altars, after having defiled them with their uncleanness. . . . The kingdom of the Greeks is now dismembered by them and has been deprived of territory so vast in extent that it could not be traversed in two months' time.

On whom, therefore, is the labor of avenging these wrongs and of recovering this territory incumbent, if not upon you,—you, upon whom, above all other nations, God has conferred remarkable glory in arms, great courage, bodily activity, and strength to humble the heads of those who resist you? Let the deeds of your ancestors encourage you and incite your minds to manly achievements:—the glory and greatness of King Charlemagne, and of his son Louis, and of your other monarchs, who have destroyed the kingdoms of the Turks and have extended the sway of the holy Church over lands previously pagan. Let the holy sepulcher of our Lord and Saviour, which is possessed by the unclean nations, especially arouse you, and the holy places which are now treated with ignominy and irreverently polluted with the filth of the unclean. Oh, most valiant soldiers and descendants of invincible ancestors, do not degenerate, but recall the valor of your progenitors.

John Calvin[24]

John Calvin (1509–1564) was the leading Protestant reformer of Geneva, Switzerland, even though he was born and raised in France. His *Institutes of the Christian Religion* represent a rigorous, legalistic approach to Protestantism. His theology is sometimes referred to as Calvinism.

Our Lord established excommunication as a means of correction and discipline, by which those who led a disordered life unworthy of a Christian, and who despised to mend their ways and return to the strait way after they had been admonished, should be expelled from the body of the church and cut off as rotten members until they come to themselves and acknowledge their fault. . . . We have an example given by St. Paul (I Tim. i and I Cor. v), in a solemn warning that we should not keep company with one who is called a Christian but who is, none the less, a fornicator, covetous, an idolater, a railer, a drunkard, or an extortioner. So if there be in us any fear of God, this ordinance should be enforced in our Church.

To accomplish this we have determined to petition you [i.e. the town council] to establish and choose, according to your good pleasure, certain persons [namely, the elders] of upright life and good repute among all the faithful, likewise constant and not easy to corrupt, who shall be assigned and distributed in all parts of the town and have an eye on the life and conduct of every individual. If one of these see any obvious vice which is to be reprehended, he shall bring this to the attention of some one of the ministers, who shall admonish whoever it may be who is at fault and exhort him in a brotherly way to correct his ways. If it is apparent that such remonstrances do no good, he shall be warned that his obstinacy will be reported to the Church. Then if he repents, there is in that alone excellent fruit of this form of discipline. If he will not listen to warnings, it shall be time for the minister, being informed by those who have the matter in charge, to declare publicly to the congregation the efforts which have been made to bring the sinner to amend, and how all has been in vain.

Should it appear that he proposes to persevere in his hardness of heart, it shall be time to excommunicate him; that is to say, that the offender shall be regarded as cast out from the companionship of Christians and left in the power of the devil for his temporal confusion, until he shall give good proofs of penitence and amendment. In sign of his casting out he shall be excluded from the communion, and the faithful shall be forbidden to hold familiar converse with him. Nevertheless he shall not omit to attend the sermons in order to receive instruction, so that it may be seen whether it shall please the Lord to turn his heart to the right way.

Source: Speech by Pope Urban II. James Harvey Robinson, Ed.
Source: From "*Institutes of the Christian Religion*" by John Calvin. James Harvey Robinson, Ed.

Voltaire[25]

Voltaire (1694–1778) was the pen name of Francois-Marie Arouet, one of the more intriguing figures of the Enlightenment. A harsh critic of the church and what he saw as superstition, he wrote widely and often satirically.

No law made by the Church should ever have the least force unless expressly sanctioned by the government. It was owing to this precaution that Athens and Rome escaped all religious quarrels.

Such religious quarrels are the trait of barbarous nations or such as have become barbarous.

The civil magistrate alone may permit or prohibit labor on religious festivals, since it is not the function of the priest to forbid men to cultivate their fields.

Everything relating to marriage should depend entirely upon the civil magistrate. The priests should confine themselves to the august function of blessing the union.

Lending money at interest should be regulated entirely by the civil law, since trade is governed by civil law.

All ecclesiastics should be subject in every case to the government, since they are subjects of the state.

Never should the ridiculous and shameful custom be maintained of paying to a foreign priest the first year's revenue of land given to a priest by his fellow-citizens.

No priest can deprive a citizen of the least of his rights on the ground that the citizen is a sinner, since the priest—himself a sinner—should pray for other sinners, not judge them.

Officials, laborers, and priests should all alike pay the taxes of the state, since they all alike belong to the state.

There should be but one standard of weights and measures and one system of law.

Let the punishment of criminals be useful. A man when hanged is good for nothing: a man condemned to hard labor continues to serve his country and furnish a living lesson.

Every law should be clear, uniform, and precise. To interpret law is almost always to corrupt it.

Nothing should be regarded as infamous except vice.

The taxes should never be otherwise than proportional to the resources of him who pays.

Source: From *"Handy Philosophic Dictionary"* by Voltaire. James Harvey Robinson, Ed.

Questions for Contemplation and Discussion

1. What is the main message of Pope Urban? Which values are apparent in the speech?

2. Sometimes the term "theocracy" is used to describe John Calvin's vision for the city of Geneva. Look up the word in a dictionary or encyclopedia. Is that word an appropriate description of Calvin's ideas? Explain.

3. Does Voltaire believe that church and state should be separate?

4. In your opinion, what should be the proper role of church (organized religion) in government? Explain

5. What are some risks when the state dictates which religion citizens must practice? Explain

WHAT CODE SHOULD THE MILITARY FOLLOW?

Sun Tzu, Art of War[26]

Sun Tzu, (c. 544-496 B.C.E.), wrote *The Art of War*, one of the most important military writings in Chinese history. We know little about him, though he may have been a general. Until Lionel Giles translated it in the early-twentieth century, few outside of China knew of its existence.

The art of war is of vital importance to the State.

It is a matter of life and death, a road either to safety or to ruin. Hence it is a subject of inquiry which can on no account be neglected.

The art of war, then, is governed by five constant factors, to be taken into account in one's deliberations, when seeking to determine the conditions obtaining in the field. These are: (1) The Moral Law; (2) Heaven; (3) Earth; (4) The Commander; (5) Method and discipline . . .

The MORAL LAW causes the people to be in complete accord with their ruler, so that they will follow him regardless of their lives, undismayed by any danger . . .

HEAVEN signifies night and day, cold and heat, times and seasons . . .

EARTH comprises distances, great and small; danger and security; open ground and narrow passes; the chances of life and death.

The COMMANDER stands for the virtues of wisdom, sincerely, benevolence, courage and strictness . . .

By METHOD AND DISCIPLINE are to be understood the marshaling of the army in its proper subdivisions, the graduations of rank among the officers, the maintenance of roads by which supplies may reach the army, and the control of military expenditure.

These five heads should be familiar to every general: he who knows them will be victorious; he who knows them not will fail. Therefore, in your deliberations, when seeking to determine the military conditions, let them be made the basis of a comparison . . .

According as circumstances are favorable, one should Modify one's plans . . .

All warfare is based on deception. . . . Hence, when able to attack, we must seem unable; when using our forces, we must seem inactive; when we are near, we must make the enemy believe we are far away; when far away, we must make him believe we are near.

Hold out baits to entice the enemy. Feign disorder, and crush him . . . If he is secure at all points, be prepared for him. If he is in superior strength, evade him. If your opponent is [angry], seek to irritate him. Pretend to be weak, that he may grow arrogant . . .

If he is taking his ease, give him no rest . . . If his forces are united, separate them . . . Attack him where he is unprepared, appear where you are not expected.

These military devices, leading to victory, must not be divulged beforehand.

"The Truce of God"[27]

The Truce of God was first written in the late 900s by the Roman Catholic Church to cut down on the violence. This document was revised several times up through the 1200s.

Drogo, bishop of Terouanne, and count Baldwin [of Hainault] have established this peace with the cooperation of the clergy and people of the land.

Dearest brothers in the Lord, these are the conditions which you must observe during the time of the peace which is commonly called the truce of God, and which begins with sunset on Wednesday and lasts until sunrise on Monday.

1. During those four days and five nights no man or woman shall assault, wound, or slay another, or attack, seize, or destroy a castle, burg, or villa, by craft or by violence.
2. If anyone violates this peace and disobeys these commands of ours, he shall be exiled for thirty years as a penance, and before he leaves the bishopric he shall make compensation for the injury which he committed. Otherwise he shall be excommunicated by the Lord God and excluded from all Christian fellowship.
3. All who associate with him in any way, who give him advice or aid, or hold converse with him, unless it be to advise him to do penance and to leave the bishopric, shall be under excommunication until they have made satisfaction.

4. If any violator of the peace shall fall sick and die before he completes his penance, no Christian shall visit him or move his body from the place where it lay, or receive any of his possessions.
5. In addition, brethren, you should observe the peace in regard to lands and animals and all things that can be possessed. If anyone takes from another an animal, a coin, or a garment, during the days of the truce, he shall be excommunicated unless he makes satisfaction. If he desires to make satisfaction for his crime he shall first restore the thing which he stole or its value in money, and shall do penance for seven years within the bishopric. If he should die before he makes satisfaction and completes his penance, his body shall not be buried or removed from the place where it lay, unless his family shall make satisfaction for him to the person whom he injured.
6. During the days of the peace, no one shall make a hostile expedition on horseback, except when summoned by the count; and all who go with the count shall take for their support only as much as is necessary for themselves and their horses.
7. All merchants and other men who pass through your territory from other lands shall have peace from you.
8. You shall also keep this peace every day of the week from the beginning of Advent to the octave of Epiphany and from the beginning of Lent to the octave of Easter, and from the feast of Rogations [the Monday before Ascension Day] to the octave of Pentecost.
9. We command all priests on feast days and Sundays to pray for all who keep the peace, and to curse all who violate it or support its violators.
10. If anyone has been accused of violating the peace and denies the charge, he shall take the communion and undergo the ordeal of hot iron. If he is found guilty, he shall do penance within the bishopric for seven years.

Questions for Contemplation and Discussion

1. According to Sun Tzu, "All warfare is based on deception." What do you think he meant by that? Is he right? How could you apply this philosophy to life outside of war? Be specific.

2. A realist deals with life as it is, and an idealist is most interested in life as it should be. In your estimation, was Sun Tzu a realist or an idealist? Cite specific parts of the document in your response.

3. What does the Truce of God tell us about medieval warfare? What does it tell us about the Roman Catholic Church?

4. Should all participants in a war agree to some preconceived rules, or should warfare be without rules (in other words, win by any means necessary)?

WHAT IS MARRIAGE?

The Qu'ran[28]

The Qu'ran is the most important text for Muslims, as they believe that it contains the revelations from God to Muhammad (570-632 CE). Muhammad did not write it himself; his followers put it together after his death.

Sura 2:

Your wives are your field: go in, therefore, to your field as ye will; but do first some act for your souls' good: and fear ye God, and know that ye must meet Him; and bear these good tidings to the faithful.

Swear not by God, when ye make oath, that ye will be virtuous and fear God, and promote peace among men; for God is He who Heareth, Knoweth.

God will not punish you for a mistake in your oaths: but He will punish you for that which your hearts have done. God is Gracious, Merciful.

They who intend to abstain from their wives shall wait four months; but if they go back from their purpose, then verily God is Gracious, Merciful.

And if they resolve on a divorce, then verily God is He who Heareth, Knoweth.

The divorced shall wait the result, until they have had their courses thrice, nor ought they to conceal what God hath created in their wombs, if they believe in God and the last day; and it will be more just in their husbands to bring them back when in this state, if they desire what is right. And it is for the women to act as they (the husbands) act by them, in all fairness; but the men are a step above them. God is Mighty, Wise.

Ye may divorce your wives twice: Keep them honourably, or put them away with kindness. But it is not allowed you to appropriate to yourselves aught of what ye have given to them, unless both fear that they cannot keep within the bounds set up by God. And if ye fear that they cannot observe the ordinances of God, no blame shall attach to either of you for what the wife shall herself give for her redemption. These are the bounds of God: therefore overstep them not; for whoever oversteppeth the bounds of God, they are evil doers.

But if the husband divorce her a third time, it is not lawful for him to take her again, until she shall have married another husband; and if he also divorce her, then shall no blame attach to them if they return to each other, thinking that they can keep within the bounds fixed by God. And these are the bounds of God; He maketh them clear to those who have knowledge.

But when ye divorce women, and the time for sending them away is come, either retain them with generosity, or put them away with generosity: but retain them not by constraint so as to be unjust towards them. He who doth so, doth in fact injure himself. And make not the signs of God a jest; but remember God's favour toward you, and the Book and the Wisdom which He hath sent down to you for your warning, and fear God, and know that God's knowledge embraceth everything.

And when ye divorce your wives, and they have waited the prescribed time, hinder them not from marrying their husbands when they have agreed among themselves in an honourable way. This warning is for him among you who believeth in God and in the last day. This is most pure for you, and most decent. God knoweth, but ye know not.

Mothers, when divorced, shall give suck to their children two full years, if the father desire that the suckling be completed; and such maintenance and clothing as is fair for them, shall devolve on the father. No person shall be charged beyond his means. A mother shall not be pressed unfairly for her child, nor a father for his child: And the same with the father's heir. But if they choose to wean the child by consent and by bargain, it shall be no fault in them. And if ye choose to have a nurse for your children, it shall be no fault in you, in case ye pay what ye promised her according to that which is fair. Fear God, and know that God seeth what ye do.

If those of you who die leave wives, they must await their state during four months and ten days; and when this their term is expired, you shall not be answerable for the way in which they shall dispose of themselves fairly. And God is cognisant of what ye do.

And then shall no blame attach to you in making proposals of marriage to such women, or in keeping such intention to yourselves? God knoweth that ye will not forget them. But promise them not in secret, unless ye speak honourable words;

And resolve not on the marriage tie until the prescribed time be reached; and know that God knoweth what is in your minds: therefore, beware of Him; and know that God is Gracious, Mild!

It shall be no crime in you if ye divorce your wives so long as ye have not consummated the marriage, nor settled any dowry on them. And provide what is needful for them he who is in ample circumstances according to his means, and he who is straitened, according to his means—with fairness: This is binding on those who do what is right.

Source: J. M. Rodwell, translator.

But if ye divorce them before consummation, and have already settled a dowry on them, ye shall give them half of what ye have settled, unless they make a release, or he make a release in whose hand is the marriage tie. But if ye make a release, it will be nearer to piety. And forget not generosity in your relations one towards another; for God beholdeth your doings . . .

And such of you as shall die and leave wives, shall bequeath their wives a year's maintenance without causing them to quit their homes; but if they quit them of their own accord, then no blame shall attach to you for any disposition they may make of themselves in a fair way. And God is Mighty, Wise.

And for the divorced let there be a fair provision. This is a duty in those who fear God.

Thus God maketh his signs clear to you that ye may understand.

People's Republic of China: Marriage Law[29]

The People's Republic came into existence in 1949, when Mao Zedong declared China to be a communist country.

- Article 1
  This Law is the Fundamental code governing marriage and family relations.

- Article 2
  A marriage system based on the free choice of partners, on monogamy and on equality between man and woman shall be applied. The lawful rights and interests of women, children and old people shall be protected.

  Family planning shall be practised.

- Article 3
  Marriage upon arbitrary decision by any third party, mercenary marriage and any other acts of interference in the freedom of marriage shall be prohibited. The exaction of money or gifts in connection with marriage shall be prohibited.

  Bigamy shall be prohibited. Cohabitation of a married person with any third party shall be prohibited. Domestic violence shall be prohibited. Within the family maltreatment and desertion of one family member by another shall be prohibited.

- Article 4
  Husband and wife shall be faithful to and respect each other. Within the family, family members shall respect the old and cherish the young, help one another, and maintain equal, harmonious and civilized marriage and family relations.

- Article 5
  Marriage must be based upon the complete willingness of both man and woman. Neither party may use compulsion on the other party and no third party may interfere.

- Article 6
  No marriage may be contracted before the man has reached 22 years of age and the woman 20 years of age. Late marriage and late childbirth shall be encouraged . . .

- Article 10
  Marriage shall be invalid under any of the following circumstances:
  (1) if one party commits bigamy;
  (2) if the man and the woman are relatives by blood up to the third degree of kinship;
  (3) if, before marriage, one party is suffering from a disease which is regarded by medical science as rendering a person unfit for marriage and, after marriage, a cure is not effected; and
  (4) if the legally marriageable age is not attained . . .

- Article 13
  Husband and wife shall have equal status in the family.

- Article 14
  Both husband and wife shall have the right to use his or her own surname and given name.

- Article 15
  Both husband and wife shall have the freedom to engage in production and other work, to study and to participate in social activities; neither party may restrict or interfere with the other party.

Source: Ninth National People's Congress.

- Article 16
Both husband and wife shall have the duty to practise family planning . . .

- Article 21
Parents shall have the duty to bring up and educate their children; children shall have the duty to support and assist their parents.

If parents fail to perform their duty, children who are minors or who are incapable of living on their own shall have the right to demand the cost of upbringing from their parents.

If children fail to perform their duty, parents who are unable to work or have difficulties in providing for themselves shall have the right to demand support payments from their children.

Infant drowning, deserting and any other acts causing serious harm to infants and infanticide shall be prohibited.

- Article 22
Children may adopt their father's or their mother's surname.

- Article 23
Parents shall have the right and duty to subject their children who are minors to discipline and to protect them. If children who are minors cause damage to the state, the collective, or individuals, their parents shall have the duty to bear civil liability . . .

- Article 25
Children born out of wedlock shall enjoy the same rights as children born in wedlock. No one may harm or discriminate against them. The natural father or the natural mother who does not rear directly his or her child born out of wedlock shall bear the child's living and educational expenses until the child can support himself or herself.

- Article 26
The state shall protect lawful adoption. The relevant provisions of this Law governing the relationship between parents and children shall apply to the rights and duties in the relationship between foster parents and foster children. The right and duties in the relationship between a foster child and his or her natural parents shall terminate with the establishment of this adoption.

- Article 27
Maltreatment or discrimination shall not be permitted between stepparents and stepchildren.

The relevant provisions in this Law governing the relationship between parents and children shall apply to the rights and duties in the relationship between stepfathers or stepmothers and their stepchildren who receive care and education from them. . .

- Article 32
When one party alone desires a divorce, the organizations concerned may carry out mediation, or the party may appeal directly to a people's court to start divorce proceedings. In dealing with a divorce case, the people's court should carry out mediation between the parties. Divorce shall be granted if mediation fails because mutual affection no longer exists.

Divorce shall be granted if mediation fails under any of the following circumstances:
(1) bigamy or, cohabitation of a married person with any third party;
(2) domestic violence or, maltreatment and desertion of one family member by another;
(3) bad habits of gamble or drug addiction which remain incorrigible despite repeated admonition;
(4) separation caused by incompatibility, which lasts two full years; and
(5) any other circumstances causing alienation of mutual affection . . .

- Article 34
A husband may not apply for a divorce when his wife is pregnant or within one year after the birth of a child or within six months after pregnancy suspension. This restriction shall not apply in cases where the wife applies for a divorce, or when the people's court deems it necessary to accept the divorce application made by the husband . . .

- Article 36
The relationship between parents and children shall not come to an end with the parents' divorce. After divorce, whether the children are put in the custody of the father or the mother, they shall remain the children of both parents.

After divorce, both parents shall still have the right and duty to bring up and educate their children.

Questions for Contemplation and Discussion

1. What is the general message or main point of the excerpt in the Qu'ran on marriage and divorce?

2. In the Qu'ran do husbands and wives have different roles in marriage? Explain.

3. What are the similarities and differences between the Qu'ran and the Chinese marriage law on provisions for children? Explain.

4. What are the similarities and differences between the Qu'ran and the Chinese marriage law on God or gods? Explain.

5. Which provision in the Qu'ran is closest to your own values regarding marriage and commitment? Explain.

6. Which article in the Chinese marriage law is closest to your own values regarding marriage and commitment? Explain.

7. Are either of these readings on marriage at all demeaning to women? If so, which one or ones? What makes them demeaning?

8. How are children to be treated, according to the Chinese marriage law? Is this a proper way to treat them?

WHAT HAS BEEN THE IMPACT OF DISEASE IN HISTORY?

Giovanni Boccaccio, "The Decameron"[30]

Giovanni Boccaccio (1313–1375) was an Italian poet, humanist, and author. His most famous work was *The Decameron*, an entertaining and sometimes bawdy collection of 100 short stories written during the Black Death, which killed around one-third of Europeans.

I say, then, that the years of the beatific incarnation of the Son of God had reached the tale of one thousand three hundred and forty eight, when in the illustrious city of Florence, the fairest of all the cities of Italy, there made its appearance that deadly pestilence, which, whether disseminated by the influence of the celestial bodies, or sent upon us mortals by God in His just wrath by way of retribution for our iniquities, had had its origin some years before in the East, whence, after destroying an innumerable multitude of living beings, it had propagated itself without respite from place to place, and so calamitously, had spread into the West.

In Florence, despite all that human wisdom and forethought could devise to avert it, as the cleansing of the city from many impurities by officials appointed for the purpose, the refusal of entrance to all sick folk, and the adoption of many precautions for the preservation of health; despite also humble supplications addressed to God, and often repeated both in public procession and otherwise by the devout; towards the beginning of the spring of the said year the doleful effects of the pestilence began to be horribly apparent by symptoms that shewed as if miraculous.

Not such were they as in the East, where an issue [discharge] of blood from the nose was a manifest sign of inevitable death; but in men a women alike it first betrayed itself by the emergence of certain tumors in the groin or the armpits, some of which grew as large as a common apple, others as an egg, some more, some less, which the common folk called gavoccioli. From the two said parts of the body this deadly gavocciolo soon began to propagate and spread itself in all directions indifferently; after which the form of the malady began to change, black spots or livid making their appearance in many cases on the arm or the thigh or elsewhere, now few and large, then minute and numerous. And as the gavocciolo had been and still were an infallible token of approaching death, such also were these spots on whomsoever they shewed themselves.

Which maladies seemed set entirely at naught both the art of the physician and the virtue of physic [the art of medicine]; indeed, whether it was that the disorder was of a nature to defy such treatment, or that the physicians were at fault—besides the qualified there was now a multitude both of men and of women who practiced without having received the slightest tincture of medical science—and, being in ignorance of its source, failed to apply the proper remedies; in either case, not merely were those that covered few, but almost all within three days from the appearance of the said symptoms, sooner or later, died, and in most cases without any fever or other attendant malady.

Moreover, the virulence of the pest was the greater by reason the intercourse was apt to convey it from the sick to the whole, just as fire devours things dry or greasy when they are brought close to it, the evil went yet further, for not merely by speech or association with the sick was the malady communicated to the healthy with consequent peril of common death; but any that touched the clothes the sick or aught else that had been touched, or used by these seemed thereby to contract the disease.

So marvelous sounds that which I have now to relate, that, had not many, and I among them, observed it with their own eyes, I had hardly dared to credit it, much less to set it down in writing, though I had had it from the lips of a credible witness. I say, then, that such was the energy of the contagion [a contagion is a direct cause of a disease] of the said pestilence, that it was not merely propagated from man to mail, but, what is much more startling, it was frequently observed, that things which had belonged to one sick or dead of the disease, if touched by some other living creature, not of the human species, were the occasion, not merely of sickening, but of an almost instantaneous death. Whereof my own eyes (as I said a little before) had cognisance [knowledge or awareness], one day among others, by the following experience. The rags of a poor man who had died of the disease being strewn about the open street, two hogs came thither, and after, as is their wont, no little trifling with their snouts, took the rags between their teeth and tossed them to and fro about their chaps; whereupon, almost immediately, they gave a few turns, and fell down dead, as if by poison, upon the rags which in an evil hour they had disturbed.

In which circumstances, not to speak of many others of a similar or even graver complexion, divers apprehensions and imaginations were engendered in the minds of such as were left alive, inclining almost all of them to the same harsh resolution, to wit, to shun and abhor all contact with the sick and all that belonged to them, thinking thereby to make each his own health secure. Among whom there were those who thought that to live temperately and avoid all excess would count for much as a preservative against seizures of this kind. Wherefore they banded together, and dissociating themselves from all others, formed communities in houses where there were no sick, and lived a separate and secluded life, which they regulated with the utmost care, avoiding every kind of luxury, but eating and drinking moderately of the most delicate viands and the finest wines, holding converse with none but one another, lest tidings of sickness or death should reach them, and diverting their minds with music and such other delights as they could devise.

Others, the bias of whose minds was in the opposite direction, maintained, that to drink freely, frequent places of public resort, and take their pleasure with song and revel, sparing to satisfy no appetite, and to laugh and mock at no event, was the sovereign remedy for so great an evil: and that which they affirmed they also put in practice, so far as they were able, resorting day and night, now to this tavern, now to that, drinking with an entire disregard of rule or measure, and by preference making the houses of others, as it were, their inns, if they but saw in them aught that was particularly to their taste or liking; which they, were readily able to do, because the owners, seeing death imminent, had become as reckless of their property as of their lives; so that most of the houses were open to all comers, and no distinction was observed between the stranger who presented himself and the rightful lord. Thus, adhering ever to their inhuman determination to shun the sick, as far as possible, they ordered their life.

In this extremity of our city's suffering and tribulation the venerable authority of laws, human and divine, was abased and all but totally dissolved for lack of those who should have administered and enforced them, most of whom, like the rest of the citizens, were either dead or sick or so hard bested for servants that they were unable to execute any office; whereby every man was free to do what was right in his own eyes.

Not a few there were who belonged to neither of the two said parties, but kept a middle course between them, neither laying the same restraint upon their diet as the former, nor allowing themselves the same license in drinking and other dissipations as the latter, but living with a degree of freedom sufficient to satisfy their appetite and not as recluses. They therefore walked abroad, carrying in the hands flowers or fragrant herbs or divers sorts of spices, which they frequently raised to their noses, deeming it an excellent thing thus to comfort the brain with such perfumes, because the air seemed be everywhere laden and reeking with the stench emitted by the dead and the dying, and the odours of drugs.

Some again, the most sound, perhaps, in judgment, as they were also the most harsh in temper, of all, affirmed that there was no medicine for the disease superior or equal in efficacy to flight; following which prescription a multitude of men and women, negligent of all but themselves, deserted their city, their houses, their estates, their kinsfolk, their goods, and went into voluntary exile, or migrated to the country parts, as if God in visiting men with this pestilence in requital of their iniquities would not pursue them with His wrath wherever they might be, but intended the destruction of such alone as remained within the circuit of the walls of the city; or deeming perchance ["deeming perchance" can be defined as "possibly"], that it was now time for all to flee from it, and that its last hour was come.

Of the adherents of these divers opinions not all died, neither did all escape; but rather there were, of each sort and in every place many that sickened, and by those who retained their health were treated after the example which they themselves, while whole, had set, being everywhere left to languish in almost total neglect. Tedious were it to recount, how citizen avoided citizen, how among neighbors was scarce found any that shewed fellow-feeling for another, how kinsfolk held aloof, and never met, or but rarely; enough that this sore affliction entered so deep into the minds of men a women, that in the horror thereof brother was forsaken by brother nephew by uncle, brother by sister, and oftentimes husband by wife: nay, what is more, and scarcely to be believed, fathers and mothers were found to abandon their own children, untended, unvisited, to their fate, as if they had been strangers.

Wherefore the sick of both sexes, whose number could not be estimated, were left without resource but in the charity of friends (and few such there were), or the interest of servants, who were hardly to be had at high rates and on unseemly terms, and being, moreover, one and all, men and women of gross understanding, and for the most part unused to such offices, concerned themselves no further than to supply the immediate and expressed wants of the sick, and to watch them die; in which service they themselves not seldom perished with their gains . . .

Few also there were whose bodies were attended to the church by more than ten or twelve of their neighbors, and those not the honorable and respected citizens; but a sort of corpse-carriers drawn from the baser ranks, who called themselves becchini and performed such offices for hire, would shoulder the bier, and with hurried steps carry it, not to the church of the dead man's choice, but to that which was nearest at hand, with four or six priests in front and a candle or two, or, perhaps, none; nor did the priests distress themselves with too long and solemn an office, but with the aid of the becchini hastily consigned the corpse to the first tomb which they found untenanted.

The condition of the lower [poorer people], and, perhaps, in great measure of the middle ranks, of the people shewed even worse and more deplorable; for, deluded by hope or constrained by poverty, they stayed in their quarters, in their houses where they sickened by thousands a day, and, being without service or help of any kind, were, so to speak, irredeemably devoted to the death which overtook them. Many died daily or nightly in the public streets; of many others, who died at home, the departure was hardly observed by their neighbors, until the stench of their putrefying bodies carried the tidings; and what with their corpses and the corpses of others who died on every hand the whole place was a sepulchre.

It was the common practice of most of the neighbors, moved no less by fear of contamination by the putrefying bodies than by charity towards the deceased, to drag the corpses out of the houses with their own hands, aided, perhaps, by a porter, if a porter was to be had, and to lay them in front of the doors, where any one who made the round might have seen, especially in the morning, more of them than he could count; afterwards they would have biers brought up or in default, planks, whereon they laid them. Nor was it once twice only that one and the same bier carried two or three corpses at once; but quite a considerable number of such cases occurred, one bier sufficing for husband and wife, two or three brothers, father and son, and so forth. And times without number it happened, that as two priests, bearing the cross, were on their way to perform the last office for some one, three or four biers were brought up by the porters in rear of them, so that, whereas the priests supposed that they had but one corpse to bury, they discovered that there were six or eight, or sometimes more. Nor, for all their number, were their obsequies honored by either tears or lights or crowds of mourners rather, it was come to this, that a dead man was then of no more account than a dead goat would be to-day.

Daniel Defoe, "History of the Plague in London"[31]

Daniel Defoe (c. 1661–1731) was an English author, journalist, and spy. His most famous book by far was his novel Robinson Crusoe. He is regarded in the history of English literature as one of the founders of the English novel. The excerpt below is a description of the plague that struck London in the late 1660s, when Defoe was only a child, so it should not be considered a first-hand account.

The face of London was now, indeed, strangely altered: I mean the whole mass of buildings, city, liberties, suburbs, Westminster, Southwark, and altogether; for as to the particular part called the city, or within the walls, that was not yet much infected. But in the whole, the face of things, I say, was much altered. Sorrow and sadness sat upon every face, and though some part were not yet overwhelmed, yet all looked deeply concerned; and as we saw it apparently coming on, so every one looked on himself and his family as in the utmost danger.

Were it possible to represent those times exactly to those that did not see them, and give the reader due ideas of the horror that everywhere presented itself, it must make just impressions upon their minds, and fill them with surprise. London might well be said to be all in tears. The mourners did not go about the streets, indeed; for nobody put on black, or made a formal dress of mourning for their nearest friends: but the voice of mourning was truly heard in the streets. The shrieks of women and children at the windows and doors of their houses, where their nearest relations were perhaps dying, or just dead, were so frequent to be heard as we passed the streets, that it was enough to pierce the stoutest heart in the world to hear them. Tears and lamentations were seen almost in every house, especially in the first part of the visitation; for towards the latter end, men's hearts were hardened, and death was so always before their eyes that they did not so much concern themselves for the loss of their friends, expecting that themselves should be summoned the next hour.

Business led me out sometimes to the other end of the town, even when the sickness was chiefly there. And as the thing was new to me, as well as to everybody else, it was a most surprising thing to see those streets, which were usually so thronged, now grown desolate, and so few people to be seen in them, that if I had been a stranger, and at a loss for my way, I might sometimes have gone the length of a whole street, I mean of the by-streets, and see nobody to direct me, except watchmen set at the doors of such houses as were shut up; of which I shall speak presently.

One day, being at that part of the town on some special business, curiosity led me to observe things more than usually; and indeed I walked a great way where I had no business. I went up Holborn, and there the street was full of people; but they walked in the middle of the great street, neither on one side or other, because, as I suppose, they would not mingle with anybody that came out of houses, or meet with smells and scents from houses, that might be infected.

The inns of court were all shut up, nor were very many of the lawyers in the Temple, or Lincoln's Inn, or Gray's Inn, to be seen there. Everybody was at peace, there was no occasion for lawyers; besides, it being in the time of the vacation too, they were generally gone into the country. Whole rows of houses in some places were shut close up, the inhabitants all fled, and only a watchman or two left.

When I speak of rows of houses being shut up, I do not mean shut up by the magistrates, but that great numbers of persons followed the court, by the necessity of their employments, and other dependencies; and as others retired, really frighted with the distemper, it was a mere desolating of some of the streets. But the fright was not yet near so great in the city, abstractedly so called, and particularly because, though they were at first in a most inexpressible consternation, yet, as I have observed that the distemper intermitted often at first, so they were, as it were, alarmed and unalarmed again, and this several times, till it began to be familiar to them; and that even when it appeared violent, yet seeing it did not presently spread into the city, or the east or south parts, the people began to take courage, and to be, as I may say, a little hardened. It is true, a vast many people fled, as I have observed; yet they were chiefly from the west end of the town, and from that we call the heart of the city, that is to say, among the wealthiest of the people, and such persons as were unincumbered with trades and business. But of the rest, the generality staid, and seemed to abide the worst; so that in the place we call the liberties, and in the suburbs, in Southwark, and in the east part, such as Wapping, Ratcliff, Stepney, Rotherhithe, and the like, the people generally staid, except here and there a few wealthy families, who, as above, did not depend upon their business . . .

In the first place, a blazing star or comet appeared for several months before the plague, as there did, the year after, another a little before the fire. The old women, and the phlegmatic hypochondriac part of the other sex (whom I could almost call old women too), remarked, especially afterward, though not till both those judgments were over, that those two comets passed directly over the city, and that so very near the houses that it was plain they imported something peculiar to the city alone; that the comet before the pestilence was of a faint, dull, languid color, and its motion very heavy, solemn, and slow, but that the comet before the fire was bright and sparkling, or, as others said, flaming, and its motion swift and furious; and that, accordingly, one foretold a heavy judgment, slow but severe, terrible, and frightful, as was the plague, but the other foretold a stroke, sudden, swift, and fiery, as was the conflagration. Nay, so particular some people were, that, as they looked upon that comet preceding the fire, they fancied that they not only saw it pass swiftly and fiercely, and could perceive the motion with their eye, but even they heard it; that it made a rushing, mighty noise, fierce and terrible, though at a distance, and but just perceivable.

I saw both these stars, and, I must confess, had had so much of the common notion of such things in my head, that I was apt to look upon them as the forerunners and warnings of God's judgments, and, especially when the plague had followed the first, I yet saw another of the like kind, I could not but say, God had not yet sufficiently scourged the city.

The apprehensions of the people were likewise strangely increased by the error of the times, in which I think the people, from what principle I cannot imagine, were more addicted to prophecies, and astrological conjurations, dreams, and old wives' tales, than ever they were before or since. Whether this unhappy temper was originally raised by the follies of some people who got money by it, that is to say, by printing predictions and prognostications, I know not. But certain it is, books frighted them terribly, such as "Lilly's Almanack,""Gadbury's Astrological Predictions," "Poor Robin's Almanack," and the like; also several pretended religious books,—one entitled "Come out of Her, my People, lest ye be Partaker of her Plagues;" another called "Fair Warning;" another, "Britain's Remembrancer;" and many such,—all, or most part of which, foretold directly or covertly the ruin of the city. Nay, some were so enthusiastically bold as to run about the streets with their oral predictions, pretending they were sent to preach to the city; and one in particular, who, like Jonah to Nineveh, cried in the streets, "Yet forty days, and London shall be destroyed." I will not be positive whether he said "yet forty days," or "yet a few days." Another ran about naked, except a pair of drawers about his waist, crying day and night, like a man that Josephus mentions, who cried, "Woe to Jerusalem!" a little before the destruction of that city: so this poor naked creature cried, "Oh, the great and the dreadful God!" and said no more, but repeated those words continually, with a voice and countenance full of horror, a swift pace, and nobody could ever find him to stop, or rest, or take any sustenance, at least that ever I could hear of. I met this poor creature several times in the streets, and would have spoke to him, but he would not enter into speech with me, or any one else, but kept on his dismal cries continually.

Questions for Contemplation and Discussion

1. According to Boccaccio, what were the social effects of the Black Death on the people?

2. Although he lived in a pre-scientific age, Boccaccio attempts to come to grips with the scientific causes of the plague. How does he do it? Would a scientist or physician today agree or disagree with Boccaccio's approach? Be specific.

3. What does Daniel Defoe see as the effects of the plague in the 1660s?

4. Would you agree that both Boccaccio and Defoe emphasize the fear of the people? Explain.

IS VIOLENCE EVER JUSTIFIABLE TO ENACT POLITICAL CHANGE?

John Ponet, A Short Treatise of Politic Power[32]

John Ponet (c1514–1556) was a leading reformer in England during the reign of the boy-king Edward VI. Ponet held one of the most extreme positions on civil obedience in the sixteenth century. The excerpt below is from chapter VI, "Whether It Be Lawful To Depose An Evil Governor, And Kill A Tyrant."

As there is no better nor happier commonwealth nor no greater blessing of God, than where one rules, if he is a good, just, and godly man: so there is no worse nor none more miserable, nor greater plague of God, than where one rules, that is evil, unjust and ungodly. A good man knowing that he or those by whom he claims was to such office called for his virtue, to see the whole state well governed, and the people defended from injuries: neglecting utterly his own pleasure and profit, and bestows all his study and labor to see his office well discharged. And as a good physician earnestly seeks the health of his patient and a shipmaster the wealth and safeguard of those he has in his ship, so does a good governor seek the wealth of those he rules. And therefore the people feeling the benefit coming by good governors, used in times past to call such good governors, fathers: and gave them no less honor than children owe to their parents. An evil person coming to the government of any state, either by usurpation, or by election or by succession, utterly neglecting the cause why kings, princes, and other governors in commonwealths be made (that is, the wealth of the people) seeks only or chiefly his own profit and pleasure. And as a sow coming into a fair garden, roots up all the fair and sweet flowers and wholesome simples, leaving nothing behind, but her own filthy dirt: so does an evil governor subvert the laws and orders, or makes them to be wrenched or racked to serve his affections, that they can no longer do their office . . .

And first for the better and more plain prose of this matter, the manifold and continual examples that have been from time to time of the deposing of kings, and killing of tyrants, do most certainly confirm it to be most true, just and constant to God's judgment. The history of kings in the Old Testament is full of it . . .

Now if it is lawful for the body of the Church to depose and punish a pope, being the chief priest, anointed not on the arm or shoulder, as kings are, but on the head and hands, to declare a higher authority than kings have: nor crowned with a simple crown, as emperors or kings are, but with a triple crown, to show his regality and power above all others: how much more by the like arguments, reasons and authority, may emperors, kings, princes and other governors abusing their office, be deposed and removed out of their places and offices, by the body or state of the realm or commonwealth? . . .

But here you see the body of every state may (if it will) yea and ought to redress and correct the vices and heads of their governors. And for as much as you have already seen, whereof political power and government grows, and the end where unto it was ordained: and seeing it is before manifestly and sufficiently proved, that kings and princes have not an absolute power over their subjects: that they are and ought to be subject to the law of God, and the wholesome positive laws of their country: and that they may not lawfully take or use their subjects goods at their pleasure: the reasons, arguments, and laws that serve for the deposing and displacing of an evil governor, will do as much for the proof, that it is lawful to kill a tyrant, if they may be indifferently heard. As God has ordained magistrates to hear and determine private men's matters, and to punish their vices: so also will he, that the magistrates doings be called into account and reckoning, and their vices corrected and punished by the body of the whole congregation or commonwealth.

It is natural to cut away an incurable member, which (being suffered) would destroy the whole body.

Kings, princes, and other governors, although they are the heads of a political body, yet they are not the whole body. And though they be the chief members, yet they are but members: no others are the people ordained for them, but they are ordained for the people . . .

So that this principle that evil and evil doers ought to be punished, and rotten members to be cut away, was no peculiar law of the ethics, but it proceeds of nature, and therefore common to all men, as it is plain by the Chronicles and experience of all ages, and purposely exemplifies for our sure stay and learning as well as the Book of Judges, as in many other histories of Holy Scriptures, according to the express word and commandment (applied to this sense and meaning) which says: "Let evil be taken out of the midst of the congregation; that the rest which hear of it, may be afraid., and not enterprise to do the like." And Christ pronounces that every tree which brings not forth good fruit, shall be cut down, and cast into the fire: much more the evil tree, that brings forth evil fruit.

And although some do hold that the manner and means to punish evil and evildoers, is not all one among Christians (which be in deed that they profess in word) and ethnics, which think it lawful for every private man (without respect of order and

---

Source: John Ponet.

time) to punish evil: yet the laws of many Christian regions do permit, that private men may kill malefactors, yea though they were magistrates, in some cases: as when a governor shall solidly with his sword reign upon the innocent, or go about to shoot him through with a gun, or if he should be found in bed with a man's wife, or go about to deflower and ravish a man's daughter: much more if he goes about to betray and make away his country to foreigners, & etc.

Nevertheless, for as much as all things in every Christian commonwealth ought to be done decently and according to order and charity: I think it cannot be maintained by God's word, that nay private man may kill, except (where execution of just punishment upon tyrants, idolaters, and traitorous governors is either by the whole state utterly neglected, or the prince with the nobility and counsel conspire the subversion or alteration of their country and people) any private man have some special inward commandment or surely proved motion of God: as Moses had to kill the Egyptian, Phineas the Lecherous, and Ahud King Eglon, with such life: or be otherwise commanded or permitted by common authority upon just occasion and common necessity to kill . . .

If a prince robs and spoils his subjects, it is theft, and as a thief ought to be punished. If he kills and murders them contrary or without the laws of his country, it is murder, and a murderer he ought to be punished. If he commits adultery, he is an adulterer and ought to be punished with the same pains that others be. If he violently ravish men's wives, daughters, or maidens, the laws that are made against ravishers, ought to be executed on him. If he goes about to betray his country, and to bring the people under a foreign power: he is a traitor, and as a traitor he ought to suffer. And those that be judges in commonwealths, ought (upon complaint) to summon and cite them to answer to their crimes, and so to proceed, as they do with others. For the prophet speaking unto those that have the rule in commonwealths, and that be judges and other ministers of justice, he says: "Minister justice to the poor and orphaned, pronounce the miserable and poor to be innocent, if he be innocent: take the poor, and deliver the needy out of the hands of the wicked". When you sit to judge, you shall not have respect of persons, whether they be rich or poor, great or small: fear no man, for you execute the judgment of God, says the Holy Ghost by the mouth of Moses. Judge not after the outward appearance of man, but judge rightly, says Christ.

God Himself gave the example of punishment of evil governors. For when the children of Israel had committed idolatry, he commanded Moses to take the princes of the people, and to hang them up against the sun, that his wrath and fury might be turned from Israel . . .

And where this justice is not executed, but the prince and the people play together, and one winks and bears with the others faults, there cannot be, but a most corrupt, ungodly, and vicious state, which although it prosper for a season, yet no doubt at length they may be sure, that unto them shall come that came to Sodom, Gomorrah, Jerusalem, and such other, that were utterly destroyed.

And on the other side, where the nobility and people look diligently and earnestly upon their authorities, and do see the same executed on their heads and governors, making them to yield account of their doings: then without fail will the princes and governors be as diligent to see the people do their duty. And so shall the commonwealth be godly, and prosper, and God shall be glorified in all . . .

We read that after the Lord God had sundry times delivered his people of Israel from wicked tyrants, with whom he had plagued them for their wickedness and idolatry: at length when through abundance of wealth and quietness they fell to a certain careless security of life, not only forgetting God and His holy, sincere word, but also seeking everyone his own singular self gain with the hurt and contempt of his neighbor. God took from them their natural liege lord, the good judge Othoniel, and placed, yes (says the Scripture) he strengthened a strange prince among them, an idolatrous person and a wicked, called Eglon . . .

But what remedy? No man would make moan to his neighbor for fear of retribution, none would whisper against the king, they must bend or break, no remedy, patience perforce, all were fain to serve and please King Eglon. But at length they sent (as their yearly accustomed manner was) a present to the king by a witty messenger, called Ahud: who having access to the king, said he had to say unto his majesty secretly from God. And when the king had commanded all his servants away, so that Ahud and the king were alone in his summer parlor, Ahud thrust his dagger so hard into the king's fat paunch, that there lay King Eglon dead, and Ahud fled away.

Now, was this well done or evil? For the deed is so commended in Scripture, that the Holy Ghost reports Ahud to be a savior of Israel.

But note by the way, the text does not say that Ahud was sent of the people to kill the king, not that he told them what he intended: for by that means, one Judas or other would have betrayed him, and so should he have been drawn, hanged, and quartered for his enterprise, and all his conspirators have lost both life, lands, and goods for their conspiracy.

Only the Scripture says that Ahud (being a private person) was steered up only by the Spirit of God.

These examples need no further exposition, the Scripture is plain enough. But if neither the whole state not the minister of God's word would do their common duty, not any other lawful shift before mentioned can be had, not dare be attempted: yet are not the poor people destitute all together of remedy: but God has left unto them two weapons, able to conquer and destroy the greatest tyrant that ever was: that is, Penance and Prayer. Penance for their own sins, which provokes the anger and displeasure of God, and makes him to suffer tyrants, wars, famine, pestilence, and all plagues to reign among the people. And prayer, that he will withdraw His wrath, and show His merciful countenance.

Gandhi[33]

Mohandas K. Gandhi (1869–1948), sometimes referred to as Mahatma Gandhi, was one of twentieth-century India's most significant and beloved figures. His philosophy of civil obedience was instrumental in India's gaining of independence from Great Britain in 1947.

EDITOR: Passive resistance is a method of securing rights by personal suffering; it is the reverse of resistance by arms. When I refuse to do a thing that is repugnant to my conscience, I use soul-force. For instance, the Government of the day has passed a law which is applicable to me. I do not like it. If by using violence I force the Government to repeal the law, I am employing what may be termed body-force. If I do not obey the law and accept the penalty for its breach, I use soul-force. It involves sacrifice of self.

Everybody admits that sacrifice of self is infinitely superior to sacrifice of others. Moreover, if this kind of force is used in a cause that is unjust, only the person using it suffers. He does not make others suffer for his mistakes. Men have before now done many things which were subsequently found to have been wrong. No man can claim that he is absolutely in the right or that a particular thing is wrong because he thinks so, but it is wrong for him so long as that is his deliberate judgment. It is therefore meet that he should not do that which he knows to be wrong, and suffer the consequence whatever it may be. This is the key to the use of soul-force.

READER: You would then disregard laws—this is rank disloyalty. We have always been considered a law-abiding nation. You seem to be going even beyond the extremists. They say that we must obey the laws that have been passed, but that if the laws be bad, we must drive out the law-givers even by force.

EDITOR: Whether I go beyond them or whether I do not is a matter of no consequence to either of us. We simply want to find out what is right and to act accordingly. The real meaning of the statement that we are a law-abiding nation is that we are passive resisters. When we do not like certain laws, we do not break the heads of law-givers but we suffer and do not submit to the laws. That we should obey laws whether good or bad is a new-fangled notion. There was no such thing in former days. The people disregarded those laws they did not like and suffered the penalties for their breach. It is contrary to our manhood if we obey laws repugnant to our conscience. Such teaching is opposed to religion and means slavery. If the Government were to ask us to go about without any clothing, should we do so? If I were a passive resister, I would say to them that I would have nothing to do with their law. But we have so forgotten ourselves and become so compliant that we do not mind any degrading law.

A man who has realized his manhood, who fears only God, will fear no one else. Man-made laws are not necessarily binding on him. Even the Government does not expect any such thing from us. They do not say: "You must do such and such a thing," but they say: "If you do not do it, we will punish you." We are sunk so low that we fancy that it is our duty and our religion to do what the law lays down. If man will only realize that it is unmanly to obey laws that are unjust, no man's tyranny will enslave him. This is the key to self-rule or home-rule.

It is a superstition and ungodly thing to believe that an act of a majority binds a minority. Many examples can be given in which acts of majorities will be found to have been wrong and those of minorities to have been right. All reforms owe their origin to the initiation of minorities in opposition to majorities. If among a band of robbers a knowledge of robbing is obligatory, is a pious man to accept the obligation? So long as the superstition that men should obey unjust laws exists, so long will their slavery exist. And a passive resister alone can remove such a superstition.

Source: From Mohandas Gandhi, "*Indian Home Rule,*" (India; Ganesh & Co., 1922).

Questions for Contemplation and Discussion

1. What is the main point, or thesis, in Ponet's *Short Treatise?* What evidence does Ponet use to support his thesis?

2. In the first paragraph, Ponet compares leaders to physicians. Is this a good analogy, or are there some problems with it? Explain.

3. Do you agree with Ponet's advice on the qualities of a bad leader?

4. In Ponet's day, leaders were not elected, but they usually are today. What should be done if an elected leader breaks the laws he or she has promised to obey? Is Ponet's "Ahud the private person" solution at all applicable today? Explain.

5. Gandhi's non-violent approach was adapted by Martin Luther King, Jr., who talked about "meeting physical force with soul force." What do you think he meant by that?

6. Is non-violence always the best solution?

7. Should violence ever be used to solve problems in a civil society? Explain.

8. What advice would you give citizens who are required by a leader or leaders to do something that goes against their religion? Explain.

WHO SHOULD SET PRICES?

Diocletian, "Edict on Maximum Prices"[34]

Diocletian, emperor of Rome from 284 to 305, instituted many critical economic and military reforms. He provided stability after decades of strife and put the Roman Empire on a strong foundation.

As we recall the wars which we have successfully fought, we must be grateful to the fortune of our state, second only to the immortal gods, for a tranquil world that reclines in the embrace of the most profound calm, and for the blessings Of a peace that was won with great effort. That this fortune of our state be stabilized and suitably adorned is demanded by the law-abiding public and by the dignity and majesty of Rome. Therefore we, who by the gracious favor of the gods previously stemmed the tide of the ravages of barbarian nations by destroying them, must surround the peace which we established for eternity with the necessary defenses of justice.

If the excesses perpetrated by persons of unlimited and frenzied avarice [greed] could be checked by some self-restraint—this avarice which rushes for gain and profit with no thought for mankind . . .; or if the general welfare could endure without harm this riotous license by which, in its unfortunate state, it is being very seriously injured every day, the situation could perhaps be faced with dissembling and silence, with the hope that human forbearance might alleviate the cruel and pitiable situation.

But the only desire of these uncontrolled madmen is to have no thought for the common need. Among the unscrupulous, the immoderate, and the avaricious it is considered almost a creed . . . to desist from plundering the wealth of all only when necessity compels them. Through their extreme need, moreover, some persons have become acutely aware of their most unfortunate situation, and can no longer close their eyes to it. Therefore we, who are the protectors of the human race, are agreed, as we view the situation, that decisive legislation is necessary, so that the long-hoped-for solutions which mankind itself could not provide may, by the remedies provided by our foresight, be vouchsafed for the general betterment of all. . . .

We hasten, therefore, to apply the remedies long demanded by the situation, satisfied that no one can complain that our intervention with regulations is untimely or unnecessary, trivial or unimportant. These measures are directed against the unscrupulous, who have perceived in our silence of so many years a lesson in restraint but have been unwilling to imitate it. For who is so insensitive and so devoid of human feeling that he can be unaware or has not perceived that uncontrolled prices are widespread in the sales taking place in the markets and in the daily life of the cities? Nor is the uncurbed passion for profiteering lessened either by abundant supplies or by fruitful years. . . .

It is our pleasure, therefore, that the prices listed in the subjoined schedule be held in observance in the whole of our Empire. . . .

Therefore it is our pleasure that anyone who resists the measures of this statute shall be subject to a capital penalty for daring to do so. And let no one consider the statute harsh, since there is at hand a ready protection from danger in the observance of moderation. . . . We therefore exhort the loyalty of all, so that a regulation instituted for the public good may be observed with willing obedience and due scruple, especially as it is seen that by a statute of this kind provision has been made, not for single municipalities and peoples and provinces but for the whole world. . . .

Adam Smith, "An Inquiry into the Nature and Causes of the Wealth of Nations"[35]

Adam Smith (1723–1790) is regarded as one of the most important modern economic theorists. In his *An Inquiry into the Nature and Causes of the Wealth of Nations* first published in 1776, he defends the idea that the economy should be free of government control.

"Of the Natural and Market Price of Commodities"

There is in every society or neighborhood an ordinary or average rate both of wages and profit in every different employment of labor and stock. This rate is naturally regulated, as I shall show hereafter, partly by the general circumstances of the society, their riches or poverty, their advancing, stationary, or declining condition; and partly by the particular nature of each employment. There is likewise in every society or neighborhood an ordinary or average rate of rent, which is regulated too, as I shall show hereafter, partly by the general circumstances of the society or neighborhood in which the land is situated, and partly by the natural or improved fertility of the land.

Source: From *University of Chicago Reading in Western Civilization, Volume 2: Rome*, edited by John Boyer & Julius Kirshner. Copyright © 1986 by the University of Chicago Press. Reprinted by permission of the publisher.

These ordinary or average rates may be called the natural rates of wages, profit, and rent, at the time and place in which they commonly prevail. When the price of any commodity is neither more nor less than what is sufficient to pay the rent of the land, the wages of the labor, and the profits of the stock employed in raising, preparing, and bringing it to market, according to their natural rates, the commodity is then sold for what may be called its natural price. Though the price, therefore, which leaves him this profit is not always the lowest at which a dealer may sometimes sell his goods, it is the lowest at which he is likely to sell them for any considerable time; at least where there is perfect liberty, or where he may change his trade as often as he pleases.

The actual price at which any commodity is commonly sold is called its market price. It may either be above, or below, or exactly the same with its natural price. The market price of every particular commodity is regulated by the proportion between the quantity which is actually brought to market, and the demand of those who are willing to pay the natural price of the commodity, or the whole value of the rent, labor, and profit, which must be paid in order to bring it thither. When the quantity of any commodity which is brought to market falls short of the effectual demand, all those who are willing to pay the whole value of the rent, wages, and profit, which must be paid in order to bring it thither, cannot be supplied with the quantity which they want. Rather than want it altogether, some of them will be willing to give more. A competition will immediately begin among them, and the market price will rise more or less above the natural price, according as either the greatness of the deficiency, or the wealth and wanton luxury of the competitors, happen to animate more or less the eagerness of the competition.

When the quantity brought to market exceeds the effectual demand, it cannot be all sold to those who are willing to pay the whole value of the rent, wages, and profit, which must be paid in order to bring it thither. Some part must be sold to those who are willing to pay less, and the low price which they give for it must reduce the price of the whole. The market price will sink more or less below the natural price, according as the greatness of the excess increases more or less the competition of the sellers, or according as it happens to be more or less important to them to get immediately rid of the commodity. When the quantity brought to market is just sufficient to supply the effectual demand, and no more, the market price naturally comes to be either exactly, or as nearly as can be judged of, the same with the natural price. The whole quantity upon hand can be disposed of for this price, and cannot be disposed of for more. The competition of the different dealers obliges them all to accept of this price, but does not oblige them to accept of less.

Such fluctuations affect both the value and the rate either of wages or of profit, according as the market happens to be either overstocked or understocked with commodities or with labor; with work done, or with work to be done. But though the market price of every particular commodity is in this manner continually gravitating, if one may say so, towards the natural price, yet sometimes particular accidents, sometimes natural causes, and sometimes particular regulations of police, may, in many commodities, keep up the market price, for a long time together, a good deal above the natural price.

When by an increase in the effectual demand, the market price of some particular commodity happens to rise a good deal above the natural price, those who employ their stocks in supplying that market are generally careful to conceal this change. If it was commonly known, their great profit would tempt so many new rivals to employ their stocks in the same way that, the effectual demand being fully supplied, the market price would soon be reduced to the natural price, and perhaps for some time even below it. If the market is at a great distance from the residence of those who supply it, they may sometimes be able to keep the secret for several years together, and may so long enjoy their extraordinary profits without any new rivals. Secrets of this kind, however, it must be acknowledged, can seldom be long kept; and the extraordinary profit can last very little longer than they are kept.

A monopoly granted either to an individual or to a trading company has the same effect as a secret in trade or manufactures. The monopolists, by keeping the market constantly understocked, by never fully supplying the effectual demand, sell their commodities much above the natural price, and raise their emoluments, whether they consist in wages or profit, greatly above their natural rate. The price of monopoly is upon every occasion the highest which can be got. The natural price, or the price of free competition, on the contrary, is the lowest which can be taken, not upon every occasion, indeed, but for any considerable time together. The one is upon every occasion the highest which can be squeezed out of the buyers, or which, it is supposed, they will consent to give: the other is the lowest which the sellers can commonly afford to take, and at the same time continue their business.

The exclusive privileges of corporations, statutes of apprenticeship, and all those laws which restrain, in particular employments, the competition to a smaller number than might otherwise go into them, have the same tendency, though in a less degree. They are a sort of enlarged monopolies, and may frequently, for ages together, and in whole classes of employments, keep up the market price of particular commodities above the natural price, and maintain both the wages of the labor and the profits of the stock employed about them somewhat above their natural rate. Such enhancements of the market price may last as long as the regulations of police which give occasion to them.

Questions for Contemplation and Discussion

1. Does Diocletian use harsh language to condemn those who take advantage of others? Explain.

2. Do leaders sometimes make such laws not so much to help others but to make themselves look good? How so?

3. Diocletian said that those who break his law "shall be subject to a capital penalty." Is this overly harsh? Why? Why not? Explain your answer with evidence and reasoning.

4. What does Adam Smith say about prices? What is the difference between the "market price" and the "natural price"?

5. What do you think he meant when he wrote "The market price of every particular commodity is regulated by the proportion between the quantity which is actually brought to market, and the demand of those who are willing to pay the natural price of the commodity, or the whole value of the rent, labor, and profit, which must be paid in order to bring it thither"?

6. In the 1987 film "Wall Street," the unscrupulous character Gordon Gekko proclaims at a shareholder meeting, "Greed, for a lack of a better word, is good." What would be your reaction to that statement? What are some good effects of greed (if any)? What are some bad effects of greed (if any)?

HOW SHOULD POLITICAL LEADERS RULE?

Augustus, "Acts of the Divine Caesar"[36]

Caesar Augustus (63 B.C.E.–14 C.E.) was the first emperor of Rome, ruling for over forty years. He is regarded by many as one of the most signficant political leaders of the ancient world. His leadership helped Rome emerge from decades of civil war.

In my twentieth year [44 B.C.], acting on my own initiative and at my own charges, I raised an army wherewith I brought again liberty to the Republic [before Rome became an empire, its government was that of a republic] oppressed by the dominance of a faction. Therefore did the Senate [the leading representative body of the Roman Republic] admit me to its own order by honorary decrees, in the consulship [the highest elected position in the Senate] of Gaius Pansa and Aulus Hirtius. At the same time they gave unto me rank among the consulars in the expressing of my opinion [in the Senate]; and they gave unto me the imperium. It also voted that I, as propreetor, together with the consuls, should "see to it that the state suffered no harm." In the same year, too, when both consuls had fallen in battle, the people made me consul and triumvir for the re-establishing of the Republic.

The men who killed my father [Julius Caesar, who was not Augustus's natural father. Rather, Julius Caesar had adopted him] I drove into exile by strictly judicial process, and then, when they took up arms against the Republic, twice I overcame them in battle.

I undertook civil and foreign wars both by land and by sea; as victor therein I showed mercy to all surviving [Roman] citizens. Foreign nations, that I could safely pardon, I preferred to spare rather than to destroy. About 500,000 Roman citizens took the military oath of allegiance to me. Rather over 300,000 of these have I settled in colonies, or sent back to their home towns (municipia) when their term of service ran out; and to all of these I have given lands bought by me, or the money for farms—and this out of my private means . . .

The dictatorship which was offered me by the People and by the Senate, both when I was present and when I was absent, I did not accept. The annual and perpetual consulship I did not accept. Ten years in succession I was one of the "triumvirs for the reestablishing of the Republic." Up to the day that I wrote these words I have been princeps ["first citizen", a title given to him] of the Senate forty years. I have been pontifex maximus [another title, this one indicating being the high priest of the civic religion], augur, member of the "College of Fifteen for the Sacred Rites" . . .

In my fifth consulship, by order of the People and the Senate, I increased the number of patricians. Three times I revised the Senate list. In my sixth consulship, with my colleague, Marcus Agrippa, I made a census of the People. [By it] the number of Roman citizens was 4,063,000. Again in the consulship of Gaius Censorinus and Gaius Asinus I [took the census, when] the number of Roman citizens was 4,230,000. A third time . . . in the consulship of Sextus Pompeius and Sextus Appuleius , with Tiberius Caesar as colleague . . . the number of Roman citizens was 4,937,000. By new legislation I have restored many customs of our ancestors which had begun to fall into disuse, and I have myself also set many examples worthy of imitation by those to follow me . . .

I built the Curia [where the Senate met], and the Chalcidicum adjacent thereunto, the temple of Apollo [the Greek and Roman god, often associated with the sun] on the Palatine with its porticoes, the temple of the deified Julius [Caesar], the Lupercal, the portico to the Circus of Flaminius.

Aqueducts which have crumbled through age I have restored, and I have doubled the water [in the aqueduct] called the Marcian by turning a new stream into its course. The Forum Julium and the basilica which was between the temple of Castor and the temple of Saturn, works begun and almost completed by my father, I finished.

Three times in my own name and five times in that of my [adopted] sons or my grandsons I have given gladiator exhibitions; in these exhibitions about 10,000 men have fought . . . I have given hunts of African wild beasts in the circus, the Forum, the amphitheaters—and about 3500 wild beasts have been slain.

I gave the people the spectacle of a naval battle beyond the Tiber [a river flowing through the city of Rome] where is now the grove of the Caesars. For this purpose an excavation was made 1800 feet long and 1200 wide. In this contest thirty warships—triremes or biremes—took part, and many others smaller. About 3000 men fought on these craft beside the rowers.

I have cleared the sea from pirates. In that war with the slaves I delivered to their masters for punishment 30,000 slaves who had fled their masters and taken up arms against the Republic. The provinces of Gaul, Spain, Africa, Sicily, and Sardinia swore the same allegiance to me. I have extended the boundaries of all the provinces of the Roman People which were bordered by nations not yet subjected to our sway. My fleet has navigated the ocean from the mouth of the Rhine as far as the boundaries of the Cimbri where aforetime no Roman had ever penetrated by land or by sea. The German peoples there sent their legates, seeking my friendship, and that of the Roman people. At almost the same time, by my command and under my auspices two armies have been led into Ethiopia and into Arabia, which is called Felix and very many of the enemy of both peoples have fallen in battle, and many towns have been captured.

I added Egypt to the Empire of the Roman People. When the king of Greater Armenia was killed I could have made that country a province, but I preferred after the manner of our fathers to deliver the kingdom to Tigranes [a vassal prince]. . . . I have compelled the Parthians to give up to me the spoils and standards of three Roman armies, and as suppliants to seek the friendship of the Roman people. Those [recovered] standards, moreover, I have deposited in the sanctuary located in the temple of Mars the Avenger.

In my sixth and seventh consulships when I had put an end to the civil wars, after having obtained complete control of the government, by universal consent I transferred the Republic from my own dominion back to the authority of the Senate and Roman People. In return for this favor by me, I received by decree of the Senate the title Augustus, the door-posts of my house were publicly decked with laurels, a civic crown was fixed above my door, and in the Julian Curia was set a golden shield, which by its inscription bore witness that it was bestowed on me, by the Senate and Roman People, on account of my valor, clemency, justice, and piety. After that time I excelled all others in dignity, but of power I held no more than those who were my colleagues in any magistracy.

Machiavelli, The Prince[37]

Niccolo Machiavelli (1469–1527) lived in Florence, Italy, during the era of the Renaissance. Machiavelli wrote *The Prince* because he had serious concerns about the future of Italy. His frank, timeless observations describe political life as it is, not as it should be.

It would, doubtless, be happy for a prince to unite in himself every species of good quality; but as our nature does not allow so great a perfection, a prince should have prudence enough to avoid those defects and vices which may occasion his ruin; and as to those who can only compromise his safety and the possession of his dominions, he ought, if possible, to guard against them; but if he cannot succeed in this, he need not embarrass himself in escaping the scandal of those vices, but should devote his whole energies to avoid those which may cause his ruin. He should not shrink from encountering some blame on account of vices which are important to the support of his states; for everything well considered, there are some things having the appearance of virtues, which would prove the ruin of a prince, should he put them in practice, and others, upon which, though seemingly bad and vicious, his actual welfare and security entirely depend.

It has been sometimes asked, whether it is better to be loved than feared; to which I answer, than one should wish to be both. But as that is a hard matter to accomplish, I think, if it is necessary to make a selection, that it is safer to be feared than be loved. For it may be truly affirmed of mankind in general, that they are ungrateful, fickle, timid, dissembling, and self-interested; so long as you can serve them, they are entirely devoted to you; their wealth, their blood, their lives, and even their offspring are at your disposal, when you have no occasion for them; but in the day of need, they turn their back upon you. The prince who relies on professions courts his own destruction, because the friends whom he acquires by means of money alone, and whose attachment does not spring from a regard for personal merit, are seldom proof against reverse of fortune, but abandon their benefactor when he most requires their services. Men are generally more inclined to submit to him who makes himself dreaded, than to one who merely strives to be beloved; and the reason is obvious, for friendship of this kind, being a mere mortal tie, a species of duty resulting from a benefit, cannot endure against the calculations of interest: whereas fear carries with it the dread of punishment, which never loses its influence. A prince, however, ought to make himself feared, in such a manner, that if he cannot gain the love, he may at least avoid the hatred, of his subjects; and he may attain this object by respecting his subjects' property and the honour of their wives.

I conclude, then, with regard to the question, whether it is better to be loved than feared,—that it depends on the inclinations of the subjects themselves, whether they will love their prince or not; but the prince has it in his own power to make them fear him, and if he is wise, he will rather rely on his own resources than on the caprice of others, remembering that he should at the same time so conduct himself as to avoid being hated.

It is unquestionably very praiseworthy in princes to be faithful to their engagements; but among those of the present day, who have been distinguished for great exploits, few indeed have been remarkable for this virtue, or have scrupled to deceive others who may have relied on their good faith.

Source: "*The Prince*" by Machiavelli. Oliver Thatcher, Ed.

It is not necessary, however, for a prince to possess all the good qualities I have enumerated, but it is indispensable that he should appear to have them. I will even venture to affirm, that it is sometimes dangerous to use, though it is always useful to seem to possess them. A prince should earnestly endeavour to gain the reputation of kindness, clemency, piety, justice, and fidelity to his engagements. He ought to possess all these good qualities, but still retain such power over himself as to display their opposites whenever it may be expedient. I maintain, that a prince, and especially a new prince, cannot with impunity exercise all the virtues, because his own self-preservation will often compel him to violate the laws of charity, religion, and humanity. He should habituate himself to bend easily to the various circumstances which may from time to time surround him. In a word, it will be as useful to him to persevere in the path of rectitude, while he feels no inconvenience in doing so, as to know how to deviate from it when circumstances dictate such a course. He should make it a rule above all things, never to utter anything which does not breathe of kindness, justice, good faith, and piety: this last quality it is most important for him to appear to possess, as men in general judge more from appearances than from reality. All men have eyes, but few have the gift of penetration. Every one sees your exterior, but few can discern what you have in your heart; and those few dare not oppose the voice of the multitude, who have the majesty of their prince on their side. Now, in forming a judgment of the minds of men, and more especially of princes, as we cannot recur to any tribunal, we must attend only to results. Let it then be the prince's chief care to maintain his authority; the means he employs, be what they may, will, for this purpose, always appear honourable and meet applause; for the vulgar are ever caught by appearances, and judge only by the event. And as the world is chiefly composed of such as are called the vulgar, the voice of the few is seldom or never hear or regarded.

Questions for Contemplation and Discussion

1. What is Augustus' main point, or thesis? What evidence does he cite to back up his main point? Does he provide sufficient and convincing evidence? Explain.

2. Augustus himself made note of his accomplishments. Does this in any affect the credibility, objectivity, or accuracy of the document? Would you have been more persuaded if someone else other than Augustus, perhaps a historian, had said the same thing? Explain.

3. The Greek philosopher Plato believed that only the smartest should become rulers. People who are courageous should serve as soldiers, but never as rulers. The common people, lacking in both intelligence and courage, should not be allowed to become leaders either. How would you respond to that philosophy of government? What are some of its strengths and weaknesses?

4. Would you agree with Machiavelli that it is better as a leader to be feared rather than loved? Explain.

5. Would you agree with Machiavelli that it is more important for a leader to appear to be a good person than to actually be a good person? Explain.

6. Do you think Machiavelli's philosophy is useful today? Can you think of any leader past or present who seemed to follow after Machiavelli? Explain.

WHAT IS THE PURPOSE OF GOVERNMENT?

Thomas Hobbes, "Leviathan"[38]

Thomas Hobbes (1588–1679) was one of the most important political philosophers during the English Civil War. He was a firm believer in strong, absolute government as prevention against civil war and instability. Although his book *Leviathan* is his most famous, he wrote others on subjects other than politics.

CHAPTER XVII
OF THE CAUSES, GENERATION, AND DEFINITION OF A COMMON-WEALTH

The End Of Common-wealth, Particular Security The finall Cause, End, or Designe of men, (who naturally love Liberty, and Dominion over others,) in the introduction of that restraint upon themselves, (in which wee see them live in Common-wealths,) is the foresight of their own preservation, and of a more contented life thereby; that is to say, of getting themselves out from that miserable condition of Warre, which is necessarily consequent (as hath been shewn) to the naturall Passions of men, when there is no visible Power to keep them in awe, and tye them by feare of punishment . . . to the performance of their Covenants, and observation of these Lawes of Nature set down in the fourteenth and fifteenth Chapters.

Which Is Not To Be Had From The Law Of Nature [a "law of nature" is something that all people know because of God. It is sometimes different than a law that a political leader may set forth]: For the Lawes of Nature (as Justice, Equity, Modesty, Mercy, and (in summe) Doing To Others, As Wee Would Be Done To,) if themselves, without the terrour of some Power, to cause them to be observed, are contrary to our naturall Passions, that carry us to Partiality, Pride, Revenge, and the like.

And Covenants, without the Sword, are but Words, and of no strength to secure a man at all. Therefore notwithstanding the Lawes of Nature, (which every one hath then kept, when he has the will to keep them, when he can do it safely,) if there be no Power erected, or not great enough for our security; every man will and may lawfully rely on his own strength and art, for caution against all other men.

And in all places, where men have lived by small Families, to robbe and spoyle one another, has been a Trade, and so farre from being reputed against the Law of Nature, that the greater spoyles they gained, the greater was their honour; and men observed no other Lawes therein, but the Lawes of Honour; that is, to abstain from cruelty, leaving to men their lives, and instruments of husbandry.

And as small Familyes did then; so now do Cities and Kingdomes which are but greater Families (for their own security) enlarge their Dominions, upon all pretences of danger, and fear of Invasion, or assistance that may be given to Invaders, endeavour as much as they can, to subdue, or weaken their neighbours, by open force, and secret arts, for want of other Caution, justly; and are remembred for it in after ages with honour . . .

And be there never so great a Multitude; yet if their actions be directed according to their particular judgements, and particular appetites, they can expect thereby no defence, nor protection, neither against a Common enemy, nor against the injuries of one another.

For being distracted in opinions concerning the best use and application of their strength, they do not help, but hinder one another; and reduce their strength by mutuall opposition to nothing: whereby they are easily, not onely subdued by a very few that agree together; but also when there is no common enemy, they make warre upon each other, for their particular interests.

For if we could suppose a great Multitude of men to consent in the observation of Justice, and other Lawes of Nature, without a common Power to keep them all in awe; we might as well suppose all Man-kind to do the same; and then there neither would be nor need to be any Civill Government, or Common-wealth at all; because there would be Peace without subjection.

And That Continually Nor is it enough for the security, which men desire should last all the time of their life, that they be governed, and directed by one judgement, for a limited time; as in one Battell, or one Warre.

For though they obtain a Victory by their unanimous endeavour against a forraign enemy; yet afterwards, when either they have no common enemy, or he that by one part is held for an enemy, is by another part held for a friend, they must needs by the difference of their interests dissolve, and fall again into a Warre amongst themselves.

John Locke, Two Treatises of Government[39]

John Locke (1632–1704) is regarded as one of the great political philosophers in early modern England. He also wrote a treatise on epistemology, the study of how people obtain knowledge. His political thinking shaped the minds of Thomas Jefferson and other Founding Fathers.

THE SECOND TREATISE OF GOVERNMENT
CHAP. V.
Of Property.

Sec. 25. Whether we consider natural reason, which tells us, that men, being once born, have a right to their preservation, and consequently to meat and drink, and such other things as nature affords for their subsistence: or revelation, which gives us an account of those grants God made of the world to Adam, and to Noah, and his sons, it is very clear, that God, as king David says, Psal. Cxv [115]. 16. has given the earth to the children of men; given it to mankind in common.

But this being supposed, it seems to some a very great difficulty, how any one should ever come to have a property in any thing: I will not content myself to answer, that if it be difficult to make out property, upon a supposition that God gave the world to Adam, and his posterity in common, it is impossible that any man, but one universal monarch, should have any property upon a supposition, that God gave the world to Adam, and his heirs in succession, exclusive of all the rest of his posterity. But I shall endeavour to shew, how men might come to have a property in several parts of that which God gave to mankind in common, and that without any express compact of all the commoners.

Sec. 26. God, who hath given the world to men in common, hath also given them reason to make use of it to the best advantage of life, and convenience. The earth, and all that is therein, is given to men for the support and comfort of their being. And tho' all the fruits it naturally produces, and beasts it feeds, belong to mankind in common, as they are produced by the spontaneous hand of nature; and no body has originally a private dominion, exclusive of the rest of mankind, in any of them, as they are thus in their natural state: yet being given for the use of men, there must of necessity be a means to appropriate them some way or other, before they can be of any use, or at all beneficial to any particular man. The fruit or venison . . . must be his . . . that another can no longer have any right to it, before it can do him any good for the support of his life.

Sec. 27. Though the earth, and all inferior creatures, be common to all men, yet every man has a property in his own person: this no body has any right to but himself. The labour of his body, and the work of his hands, we may say, are properly his. Whatsoever then he removes out of the state that nature hath provided, and left it in, he hath mixed his labour with, and joined to it something that is his own, and thereby makes it his property. It being by him removed from the common state nature hath placed it in, it hath by this labour something annexed to it, that excludes the common right of other men: for this labour being the unquestionable property of the labourer, no man but he can have a right to what that is once joined to, at least where there is enough, and as good, left in common for others.

CHAP. IX.
Of the Ends of Political Society and Government.

Sec. 123. If man in the state of nature be so free, as has been said; if he be absolute lord of his own person and possessions, equal to the greatest, and subject to no body, why will he part with his freedom? Why will he give up this empire, and subject himself to the dominion and controul of any other power? To which it is obvious to answer, that though in the state of nature he hath such a right, yet the enjoyment of it is very uncertain, and constantly exposed to the invasion of others: for all being kings as much as he, every man his equal, and the greater part no strict observers of equity and justice, the enjoyment of the property he has in this state is very unsafe, very unsecure. This makes him willing to quit a condition, which, however free, is full of fears and continual dangers: and it is not without reason, that he seeks out, and is willing to join in society with others, who are already united, or have a mind to unite, for the mutual preservation of their lives, liberties and estates, which I call by the general name, property.

Sec. 124. The great and chief end, therefore, of men's uniting into commonwealths, and putting themselves under government, is the preservation of their property. To which in the state of nature there are many things wanting.

Questions for Contemplation and Discussion

1. According to Hobbes, what is the purpose of government?

2. What is the purpose of government, according to Locke?

3. In your view, what would you rather have: a strong government that places collective security over individual rights, or a government that considers the rights of the individual over national defense? In other words, is it ever right (and if so, when) for a government to limit the freedom of the citizens? Explain.

WHAT ARE CIVIL RIGHTS?

The Bill of Rights

The Bill of Rights is another name for the first ten amendments to the United States Constitution. They were passed by Congress on September 25, 1789, and ratified December 15, 1791.

1. Congress shall make no law respecting an establishment of religion, or prohibiting the free exercise thereof; or abridging the freedom of speech, or of the press; or the right of the people peaceably to assemble, and to petition the government for a redress of grievances.
2. A well regulated Militia, being necessary to the security of a free State, the right of the people to keep and bear Arms, shall not be infringed.
3. No Soldier shall, in time of peace be quartered in any house, without the consent of the Owner, nor in time of war, but in a manner to be prescribed by law.
4. The right of the people to be secure in their persons, houses, papers, and effects, against unreasonable searches and seizures, shall not be violated, and no Warrants shall issue, but upon probable cause, supported by Oath or affirmation, and particularly describing the place to be searched, and the persons or things to be seized.
5. No person shall be held to answer for a capital, or otherwise infamous crime, unless on a presentment or indictment of a Grand Jury, except in cases arising in the land or naval forces, or in the Militia, when in actual service in time of War or public danger; nor shall any person be subject for the same offence to be twice put in jeopardy of life or limb; nor shall be compelled in any criminal case to be a witness against himself, nor be deprived of life, liberty, or property, without due process of law; nor shall private property be taken for public use, without just compensation.
6. In all criminal prosecutions, the accused shall enjoy the right to a speedy and public trial, by an impartial jury of the State and district wherein the crime shall have been committed, which district shall have been previously ascertained by law, and to be informed of the nature and cause of the accusation; to be confronted with the witnesses against him; to have compulsory process for obtaining witnesses in his favor, and to have the Assistance of Counsel for his defence.
7. In Suits at common law, where the value in controversy shall exceed twenty dollars, the right of trial by jury shall be preserved, and no fact tried by a jury, shall be otherwise re-examined in any Court of the United States, than according to the rules of the common law.
8. Excessive bail shall not be required, nor excessive fines imposed, nor cruel and unusual punishments inflicted.
9. The enumeration in the Constitution, of certain rights, shall not be construed to deny or disparage others retained by the people.
10. The powers not delegated to the United States by the Constitution, nor prohibited by it to the States, are reserved to the States respectively, or to the people.

1889 Constitution of Japan[40]

This is a product of the Meiji Restoration (1868–1912), whose leaders sought to modernize Japan in order to compete more effectively with Western powers.

Chapter 1. The Emperor

ART. 1. The Empire of Japan shall be ruled over by Emperors of the dynasty which has reigned in an unbroken line of descent for ages past.

2. The succession to the throne shall devolve upon male descendants of the Imperial House, according to the provisions of the Imperial House Law.

3. The person of the Emperor is sacred and inviolable.

4. The Emperor being the Head of the Empire, the rights of sovereignty are vested in him, and he exercises them in accordance with the provisions of the present Constitution.

5. The Emperor exercises the legislative power with the consent of the Imperial Diet (highest legislature in an empire; has nothing to do with food).

Source: "1889 Constitution of Japan," James Harvey Robinson & Charles Beard, Ed.

6. The Emperor gives sanction to laws, and orders them to be promulgated and put into force.

7. The Emperor convokes the Imperial Diet, opens, closes, and prorogues it, and dissolves the House of Representatives. . . .

9. The Emperor issues, or causes to be issued, the ordinances necessary for the carrying out of the laws, or for the maintenance of the public peace and order, and for the promotion of the welfare of his subjects. . . .

10. The Emperor determines the organization of the different branches of the administration; he fixes the salaries of all civil and military officers, and appoints and dismisses the same. Exceptions specially provided for in the present Constitution or in other laws shall be in accordance with the respective provisions bearing thereon.

11. The Emperor has the supreme command of the army and navy.

12. The Emperor determines the organization and peace footing of the army and navy.

13. The Emperor declares war, makes peace, and concludes treaties.

Chapter II. Rights and Duties of Subjects

18. The conditions necessary for being a Japanese subject shall be determined by law.

19. All Japanese subjects shall be eligible equally for civil and military appointments, and any other public offices, subject only to the conditions prescribed by laws and ordinances.

20. Japanese subjects are liable to service in the army or navy, according to the provisions of law.

21. Japanese subjects are subject to taxation, according to the provisions of law.

22. Subject to the limitations imposed by law, Japanese subjects shall enjoy full liberty in regard to residence and change of abode.

23. No Japanese subject shall be arrested, detained, tried, or punished, except according to law.

24. No Japanese subject shall be deprived of his right of being tried by the judges determined by law.

25. Except in the cases provided for by law, the house of no Japanese subject shall be entered or searched without his permission.

26. Except in the cases provided for by law, the secrecy of the letters of Japanese subjects shall not be violated.

27. The rights of property of Japanese subjects shall not be violated. Such measures, however, as may be rendered necessary in the interests of the public welfare shall be taken in accordance with the provisions of the law.

28. Japanese subjects shall, within limits not prejudicial to peace and order, and not antagonistic to their duties as subjects, enjoy freedom of religious belief.

29. Japanese subjects shall, within the limits of law, enjoy liberty in regard to speech, writing, publication, public meetings, and associations. . . .

Questions for Contemplation and Discussion

1. Why do you think countries write constitutions? Explain.

2. What kind of power does the emperor hold, according to Japan's 1889 Constitution? In your opinion did the emperor hold too much power? Explain.

3. Do either or both of these documents discuss religion or religious themes? Explain.

4. Which of these declarations of civil rights would you prefer? Explain.

5. If you were to write a statement identifying human rights, what would you include? Explain.

WHAT IS SOCIETY'S OBLIGATION TO THE POOR?

Elizabeth I, "An Act for the Relief of the Poor"[41]

Elizabeth I (1533–1603) was the final monarch during the Tudor dynasty of England. The younger daughter of Henry VIII, Elizabeth set forth several statutes for the relief of the poor. The one below is from 1563, early in her reign.

An Act for the relief of the Poor

I. To the intent that idle and loitering persons and valiant beggars may be avoided, and the impotent, feeble and lame, which are the poor in very deed, should be hereafter relieved and well provided for: be it enacted . . . That the Statute made in the twenty-second year of the late King of famous memory, Henry the Eighth (Elizabeth's father; reigned 1509–1547), and also the Statute made in the third and fourth years of the reign of the famous King Edward the Sixth (Elizabeth's half brother; reigned 1547–1533), concerning beggars, vagabonds and idle persons . . . shall stand in their full force and effect, and shall be also from henceforth justly and truly put in execution . . .

II. And further be it enacted, That yearly upon the Sunday next after the feast day of the Nativity of St John Baptist, commonly called Midsummer Day, in every city, borough and town corporate, the mayor, bailiffs or other head officers for the time being, and in every other parish of the country the parson, vicar or curate and churchwardens shall have written in a register . . . as well the names of the inhabitants and householders within their city . . . or parish, as also the names of all such impotent, aged and needy persons as be within their city . . . or parish, which are not able to live of themselves nor with their own labour; and shall openly in the church and quietly after divine service call the said householders and inhabitants together, among whom the mayor or other head officers and two of the chief inhabitants in every such city [&c.] such as the mayor or other head officers shall think meet, and the parson, vicar or curate and churchwardens in every other parish, shall appoint yearly two able persons or more, to be gatherers and collectors of the charitable alms of all the residue of the people inhabiting in the parish whereof they be chosen collectors for the relief of the poor: which collectors the Sunday next after their election, or the Sunday following, if need require, when the people are at the church at divine service, shall gently ask and demand of every man and woman what they of their charity will be contented to give weekly towards the relief of the poor, and the same to be written in the said register . . . and the said gatherers . . . shall justly gather and truly distribute the same charitable alms weekly . . . to the said poor and impotent persons . . . without fraud, covin, favour or affection, and after such sort that the more impotent may have the more help, and such as can get part of their living to have the less, and by the discretion of the collectors to be put in such labour as they be fit and able to do, but none to go or sit openly a-begging upon pain limited in the aforesaid statutes . . .

Charles Dickens, "A Walk in a Workhouse"[42]

Charles Dickens (1812–1870) was one of the great novelists of the nineteenth century. Much of his work, including *Oliver Twist* and *A Christmas Carol*, pointed out society's neglect of the poor and criticized aristocratic privilege. "A Walk in a Workhouse," written in 1850, describes a real-life workhouse, where poor people came to earn their keep.

On a certain Sunday, I formed one of the congregation assembled in the chapel of a large metropolitan Workhouse. With the exception of the clergyman and clerk, and a very few officials, there were none but paupers present. The children sat in the galleries; the women in the body of the chapel, and in one of the side aisles; the men in the remaining aisle. The service was decorously performed, though the sermon might have been much better adapted to the comprehension and to the circumstances of the hearers. The usual supplications were offered, with more than the usual significancy in such a place, for the fatherless children and widows, for all sick persons and young children, for all that were desolate and oppressed, for the comforting and helping of the weak-hearted, for the raising-up of them that had fallen; for all that were in danger, necessity, and tribulation. The prayers of the congregation were desired 'for several persons in the various wards dangerously ill;' and others who were recovering returned their thanks to Heaven.

Among this congregation, were some evil-looking young women, and beetle-browed young men; but not many—perhaps that kind of characters kept away. Generally, the faces (those of the children excepted) were depressed and subdued, and wanted colour. Aged people were there, in every variety. Mumbling, blear-eyed, spectacled, stupid, deaf, lame; vacantly winking in the gleams of sun that now and then crept in through the open doors, from the paved yard; shading their listening ears, or blinking

---

Source: Excerpts from "*An Act for the Relief of the Poor,*" Elizabeth I (Tudor Dynasty).

eyes, with their withered hands; poring over their books, leering at nothing, going to sleep, crouching and drooping in corners. There were weird old women, all skeleton within, all bonnet and cloak without, continually wiping their eyes with dirty dusters of pocket-handkerchiefs; and there were ugly old crones, both male and female, with a ghastly kind of contentment upon them which was not at all comforting to see. Upon the whole, it was the dragon, Pauperism, in a very weak and impotent condition; toothless, fangless, drawing his breath heavily enough, and hardly worth chaining up.

When the service was over, I walked with the humane and conscientious gentleman whose duty it was to take that walk, that Sunday morning, through the little world of poverty enclosed within the workhouse walls. It was inhabited by a population of some fifteen hundred or two thousand paupers, ranging from the infant newly born or not yet come into the pauper world, to the old man dying on his bed.

In a room opening from a squalid yard, where a number of listless women were lounging to and fro, trying to get warm in the ineffectual sunshine of the tardy May morning—in the 'Itch Ward,' not to compromise the truth—a woman such as HOGARTH has often drawn, was hurriedly getting on her gown before a dusty fire. She was the nurse, or wardswoman, of that insalubrious department—herself a pauper—flabby, raw-boned, untidy—unpromising and coarse of aspect as need be. But, on being spoken to about the patients whom she had in charge, she turned round, with her shabby gown half on, half off, and fell a crying with all her might.

Not for show, not querulously, not in any mawkish sentiment, but in the deep grief and affliction of her heart; turning away her dishevelled head: sobbing most bitterly, wringing her hands, and letting fall abundance of great tears, that choked her utterance. What was the matter with the nurse of the itch-ward? Oh, 'the dropped child' was dead! Oh, the child that was found in the street, and she had brought up ever since, had died an hour ago, and see where the little creature lay, beneath this cloth! The dear, the pretty dear!

The dropped child seemed too small and poor a thing for Death to be in earnest with, but Death had taken it; and already its diminutive form was neatly washed, composed, and stretched as if in sleep upon a box. I thought I heard a voice from Heaven saying, It shall be well for thee, O nurse of the itch-ward, when some less gentle pauper does those offices to thy cold form, that such as the dropped child are the angels who behold my Father's face!

In another room, were several ugly old women crouching, witch-like, round a hearth, and chattering and nodding, after the manner of the monkeys. 'All well here? And enough to eat?' A general chattering and chuckling; at last an answer from a volunteer. 'Oh yes, gentleman! Bless you, gentleman! Lord bless the Parish of St. So-and-So! It feed the hungry, sir, and give drink to the thusty, and it warm them which is cold, so it do, and good luck to the parish of St. So-and-So, and thankee, gentleman!' Elsewhere, a party of pauper nurses were at dinner. 'How do YOU get on?' 'Oh pretty well, sir! We works hard, and we lives hard—like the sodgers!'

In another room, a kind of purgatory or place of transition, six or eight noisy madwomen were gathered together, under the superintendence of one sane attendant. Among them was a girl of two or three and twenty, very prettily dressed, of most respectable appearance and good manners, who had been brought in from the house where she had lived as domestic servant (having, I suppose, no friends), on account of being subject to epileptic fits, and requiring to be removed under the influence of a very bad one. She was by no means of the same stuff, or the same breeding, or the same experience, or in the same state of mind, as those by whom she was surrounded; and she pathetically complained that the daily association and the nightly noise made her worse, and was driving her mad—which was perfectly evident. The case was noted for inquiry and redress, but she said she had already been there for some weeks.

If this girl had stolen her mistress's watch, I do not hesitate to say she would have been infinitely better off. We have come to this absurd, this dangerous, this monstrous pass, that the dishonest felon is, in respect of cleanliness, order, diet, and accommodation, better provided for, and taken care of, than the honest pauper.

And this conveys no special imputation on the workhouse of the parish of St. So-and-So, where, on the contrary, I saw many things to commend. It was very agreeable, recollecting that most infamous and atrocious enormity committed at Tooting—an enormity which, a hundred years hence, will still be vividly remembered in the bye-ways of English life, and which has done more to engender a gloomy discontent and suspicion among many thousands of the people than all the Chartist leaders could have done in all their lives—to find the pauper children in this workhouse looking robust and well, and apparently the objects of very great care.

In the Infant School—a large, light, airy room at the top of the building—the little creatures, being at dinner, and eating their potatoes heartily, were not cowed by the presence of strange visitors, but stretched out their small hands to be shaken, with a very pleasant confidence. And it was comfortable to see two mangy pauper rocking-horses rampant in a corner.

In the girls' school, where the dinner was also in progress, everything bore a cheerful and healthy aspect. The meal was over, in the boys' school, by the time of our arrival there, and the room was not yet quite rearranged; but the boys were roaming unrestrained about a large and airy yard, as any other schoolboys might have done. Some of them had been drawing large ships upon the schoolroom wall; and if they had a mast with shrouds and stays set up for practice (as they have in the Middlesex House of Correction), it would be so much the better. At present, if a boy should feel a strong impulse upon him to learn the art of going aloft, he could only gratify it, I presume, as the men and women paupers gratify their aspirations after better board and lodging, by smashing as many workhouse windows as possible, and being promoted to prison.

In one place, the Newgate of the Workhouse, a company of boys and youths were locked up in a yard alone; their day-room being a kind of kennel where the casual poor used formerly to be littered down at night. Divers of them had been there some long time. 'Are they never going away?' was the natural inquiry. 'Most of them are crippled, in some form or other,' said the Wardsman, 'and not fit for anything.' They slunk about, like dispirited wolves or hyaenas; and made a pounce at their food when it was served out, much as those animals do. The big-headed idiot shuffling his feet along the pavement, in the sunlight outside, was a more agreeable object everyway.

Groves of babies in arms; groves of mothers and other sick women in bed; groves of lunatics; jungles of men in stone-paved down-stairs day-rooms, waiting for their dinners; longer and longer groves of old people, in up-stairs Infirmary wards, wearing out life, God knows how—this was the scenery through which the walk lay, for two hours. In some of these latter chambers, there were pictures stuck against the wall, and a neat display of crockery and pewter on a kind of sideboard; now and then it was a treat to see a plant or two; in almost every ward there was a cat.

In all of these Long Walks of aged and infirm, some old people were bedridden, and had been for a long time; some were sitting on their beds half-naked; some dying in their beds; some out of bed, and sitting at a table near the fire. A sullen or lethargic indifference to what was asked, a blunted sensibility to everything but warmth and food, a moody absence of complaint as being of no use, a dogged silence and resentful desire to be left alone again, I thought were generally apparent . . .

Questions for Contemplation and Discussion

1. What does "An Act for the Relief of the Poor" say about the poor? Explain.

2. What does the Act say about the government's role in dealing with the poor?

3. The Act offers different solutions for different people. How so? Is the Act a just one? Does it offer a genuine solution to poverty?

4. In your opinion, what causes poverty? Explain how your own views would help shape your reaction to the three readings on poverty.

5. Would you agree that Dickens was a talented writer who was a master of using vivid and descriptive language? Cite specific examples from the reading.

6. What exactly does he say about poverty and about life in a workhouse?

7. Should able-bodied poor people be forced by law to work in order to receive financial support, or should poor relief be given without any obligation or strings attached? Explain your position, remembering to support what you say with evidence and reasoning. Refer to specific parts of Dickens to illustrate.

HOW SHOULD THE GUILT OR INNOCENCE OF THE ACCUSED BE DETERMINED?

"Ordeal of Boiling Water"[43]

After the collapse of the Roman Empire in the West, some societies employed ordeals as a means of determining guilt or innocence. The Roman Catholic Church officially banned ordeals in 1215, but they nevertheless still continued. The author of the following is unknown.

Let the priest go to the church with the prosecutors and with him who is about to be tried. And while the rest wait in the vestibule of the church let the priest enter and put on the sacred garments except the chasuble and, taking the Gospel and the chrismarium and the relics of the saints and the chalice, let him go to the altar and speak thus to all the people standing near: Behold, brethren, the offices of the Christian religion. Behold the law in which is hope and remission of sins, the holy oil of the chrisma, the consecration of the body and blood of our Lord. Look that ye be not deprived of the heritage of such great blessing and of participation in it by implicating yourselves in the crime of another, for it is written, not only are they worthy of death who do these things, but they that have pleasure in them that do them.

Then let him thus address the one who is to undertake the ordeal: I command thee . . . in the presence of all, by the Father, the Son, and the Holy Ghost, by the tremendous day of judgment, by the ministry of baptism, by thy veneration for the saints, that, if thou art guilty of this matter charged against thee, if thou hast done it, or consented to it, or hast knowingly seen the perpetrators of this crime, thou enter not into the church nor mingle in the company of Christians unless thou wilt confess and admit thy guilt before thou are examined in public judgment.

Then he shall designate a spot in the vestibule where the fire is to be made for the water, and shall first sprinkle the place with holy water, and shall also sprinkle the kettle when it is ready to be hung and the water in it, to guard against the illusions of the devil. Then, entering the church with the others, he shall celebrate the ordeal mass. After the celebration let the priest go with the people to the place of the ordeal, the Gospel in his left hand, the cross, censer and relics of the saints being carried ahead, and let him chant seven penitential psalms with a litany.

Prayer over the boiling water: O God, just judge, firm and patient, who art the Author of peace, and judgest truly, determine what is right, O Lord, and make known Thy righteous judgment. O Omnipotent God, Thou that lookest upon the earth and makest it to tremble, Thou that by the gift of Thy Son, our Lord Jesus Christ, didst save the world and by His most holy passion didst redeem the human race, sanctify, O Lord, this water being heated by fire. Thou that didst save the three youths, Sidrac, Misac, and Abednago [from the Old Testament Book of Daniel], cast into the fiery furnace at the command of Nebuchadnezzar, and didst lead them forth unharmed by the hand of Thy angle, do Thou O clement and most holy Ruler, give aid if he shall plunge his hand into the boiling water, being innocent, and, as Thou didst liberate the three youths from the fiery furnace and didst free Susanna [Daniel 13] from the false charge, so, O Lord, bring forth his hand safe and unharmed from this water. But if he be guilty and presume to plunge in his hand, the devil hardening his heart, let Thy holy justice deign to declare it, that Thy virtue may be manifest in his body and his soul be saved by penitence and confession. And if the guilty man shall try to hide his sins by the use of herbs or any magic, let Thy right hand deign to bring it to no account. Through Thy only begotten Son, our Lord Jesus Christ, who dwelleth with Thee.

Benediction of the water: I bless thee, O creature of water, boiling above the fire, in the name of the Father, and of the Son, and of the Holy Ghost, from whom all things proceed; I adjure thee by Him who ordered thee to water the whole earth from the four rivers, and who summoned thee forth from the rock, and who changed thee into wine, that no wiles of the devil or magic of men be able to separate thee from thy virtues as a medium of judgment; but mayest thou punish the vile and the wicked, and purify the innocent. Through Him whom hidden things do not escape and who sent thee in the flood over the whole earth to destroy the wicked and who will yet come to judge the quick and the dead and the world by fire. Amen.

Prayer: Omnipotent, Eternal God, we humbly beseech Thee in behalf of this investigation which we are about to undertake here amongst us that iniquity may not overcome justice but that falsehood may be subjected to truth. And if any one seek to hinder or obscure this examination by any magic or by herbs of the earth, deign to ring it to naught by Thy right hand, O upright judge.

Then let the man who is to be tried, as well as the kettle or pot in which is the boiling water, be fumed with the incense of myrrh, and let this prayer be spoken: O God, Thou who within this substance of water hast hidden Thy most solemn sacraments, be graciously present with us who invoke Thee, and upon this element made ready by much purification pour down the virtue of Thy benediction that this creature, obedient to Thy mysteries, may be endued with Thy grace to detect diabolical and human fallacies, to confute their inventions and arguments, and to overcome their multiform arts. May all the wiles of the hidden enemy be brought to naught that we may clearly perceive the truth regarding those things which we with finite senses and simple hearts are seeking from Thy judgment through invocation of Thy holy name. Let not the innocent, we beseech Thee, be unjustly condemned, or the guilty be able to delude with safety those who seek the truth from Thee, who art the true Light, who seest in the shadowy darkness, and who makest our darkness light. O Thou who perceivest hidden things and knowest what is secret, show and declare this by Thy grace and make the knowledge of the truth manifest to us who believe in thee

Then let the hand that is to be placed in water be washed with soap and let it be carefully examined whether it be sound; and before it is thrust in let the priest say: I adjure thee, O vessel, by the Father and the Son and the Holy Ghost, and by the holy resurection and by the tremendous day of judgement, and by the four evangelists, that is this man is guilty of this crime, either by deed or by consent, let the water boil violently, and do thou O vessel, tuen and swing.

After this let the man who is to be tried plunge in his hand and afterwards let it be immediately sealed up. After the ordeal let him take a drink of holy water. Up to the time of the decision regarding the ordeal [a period of three days was allowed to elapse before the hand was examined] it is good thing to mix salt and holy water with all his food and drink

The Petition of Right (1628)

The Petition of Right was issued in England during the reign of Charles I by Parliament, the representative body in England's government. Parliament's leaders thought that Charles was violating their rights, including property rights and their rights against unlawful imprisonment.

The Petition exhibited to his Majesty by the Lords Spiritual and Temporal, and Commons, in this present Parliament assembled, concerning divers Rights and Liberties of the Subjects, with the King's Majesty's royal answer thereunto in full Parliament.

To the King's Most Excellent Majesty,

Humbly show unto our Sovereign Lord the King, the Lords Spiritual and Temporal, and Commons in Parliament assembles [a reference to the fact that Parliament contains two Houses: Lords and Commons], that whereas it is declared and enacted by a statute made in the time of the reign of King Edward I [1239–1307], commonly called Stratutum de Tellagio non Concedendo, that no tallage or aid shall be laid or levied by the king or his heirs in this realm, without the good will and assent of the archbishops, bishops, earls, barons, knights, burgesses, and other the freemen of the commonalty of this realm; and by authority of parliament holden in the five-and-twentieth year of the reign of King Edward III [reigned 1327–1377], it is declared and enacted, that from thenceforth no person should be compelled to make any loans to the king against his will, because such loans were against reason and the franchise of the land; and by other laws of this realm it is provided, that none should be charged by any charge or imposition called a benevolence, nor by such like charge; by which statutes before mentioned, and other the good laws and statutes of this realm, your subjects have inherited this freedom, that they should not be compelled to contribute to any tax, tallage, aid, or other like charge not set by common consent, in parliament.

II. Yet nevertheless of late divers commissions directed to sundry commissioners in several counties, with instructions, have issued; by means whereof your people have been in divers places assembled, and required to lend certain sums of money unto your Majesty, and many of them, upon their refusal so to do, have had an oath administered unto them not warrantable by the laws or statutes of this realm, and have been constrained to become bound and make appearance and give utterance before your Privy Council [an advisory body to the English monarchy] and in other places, and others of them have been therefore imprisoned, confined, and sundry other ways molested and disquieted; and divers other charges have been laid and levied upon your people in several counties by lord lieutenants, deputy lieutenants, commissioners for musters, justices of peace and others, by command or direction from your Majesty, or your Privy Council, against the laws and free custom of the realm.

III. And whereas also by the statute called 'The Great Charter of the Liberties of England,' [a reference to Magna Carta, a political document issued by nobles in 1215 against King John] it is declared and enacted, that no freeman may be taken or imprisoned or be disseized of his freehold or liberties, or his free customs, or be outlawed or exiled, or in any manner destroyed, but by the lawful judgment of his peers, or by the law of the land.

IV. And in the eight-and-twentieth year of the reign of King Edward III, it was declared and enacted by authority of parliament, that no man, of what estate or condition that he be, should be put out of his land or tenements, nor taken, nor imprisoned, nor disinherited nor put to death without being brought to answer by due process of law.

V. Nevertheless, against the tenor of the said statutes, and other the good laws and statutes of your realm to that end provided, divers of your subjects have of late been imprisoned without any cause showed; and when for their deliverance they were brought before your justices by your Majesty's writs of habeas corpus, there to undergo and receive as the court should order, and their keepers commanded to certify the causes of their detainer, no cause was certified, but that they were detained by your Majesty's special command, signified by the lords of your Privy Council, and yet were returned back to several prisons, without being charged with anything to which they might make answer according to the law.

VI. And whereas of late great companies of soldiers and mariners have been dispersed into divers counties of the realm, and the inhabitants against their wills have been compelled to receive them into their houses, and there to suffer them to sojourn against the laws and customs of this realm, and to the great grievance and vexation of the people.

VII. And whereas also by authority of parliament, in the five-and-twentieth year of the reign of King Edward III, it is declared and enacted, that no man shall be forejudged of life or limb against the form of the Great Charter and the law of the land; and by the said Great Charter and other the laws and statutes of this your realm, no man ought to be adjudged to death but by the laws established in this your realm, either by the customs of the same realm, or by acts of parliament: and whereas no offender of what kind soever is exempted from the proceedings to be used, and punishments to be inflicted by the laws and statutes of this your realm; nevertheless of late time divers commissions under your Majesty's great seal have issued forth, by which certain persons have been assigned and appointed commissioners with power and authority to proceed within the land, according to the justice of martial law, against such soldiers or mariners, or other dissolute persons joining with them, as should commit any murder, robbery, felony, mutiny, or other outrage or misdemeanor whatsoever, and by such summary course and order as is agreeable to martial law, and is used in armies in time of war, to proceed to the trial and condemnation of such offenders, and them to cause to be executed and put to death according to the law martial.

VIII. By pretext whereof some of your Majesty's subjects have been by some of the said commissioners put to death, when and where, if by the laws and statutes of the land they had deserved death, by the same laws and statutes also they might, and by no other ought to have been judged and executed.

IX. And also sundry grievous offenders, by color thereof claiming an exemption, have escaped the punishments due to them by the laws and statutes of this your realm, by reason that divers of your officers and ministers of justice have unjustly refused or forborne to proceed against such offenders according to the same laws and statutes, upon pretense that the said offenders were punishable only by martial law, and by authority of such commissions as aforesaid; which commissions, and all other of like nature, are wholly and directly contrary to the said laws and statutes of this your realm.

X. They do therefore humbly pray your most excellent Majesty, that no man hereafter be compelled to make or yield any gift, loan, benevolence, tax, or such like charge, without common consent by act of parliament; and that none be called to make answer, or take such oath, or to give attendance, or be confined, or otherwise molested or disquieted concerning the same or for refusal thereof; and that no freeman, in any such manner as is before mentioned, be imprisoned or detained; and that your Majesty would be pleased to remove the said soldiers and mariners, and that your people may not be so burdened in time to come; and that the aforesaid commissions, for proceeding by martial law, may be revoked and annulled; and that hereafter no commissions of like nature may issue forth to any person or persons whatsoever to be executed as aforesaid, lest by color of them any of your Majesty's subjects be destroyed or put to death contrary to the laws and franchise of the land.

XI. All which they most humbly pray of your most excellent Majesty as their rights and liberties, according to the laws and statutes of this realm; and that your Majesty would also vouchsafe to declare, that the awards, doings, and proceedings, to the prejudice of your people in any of the premises, shall not be drawn hereafter into consequence or example; and that your Majesty would be also graciously pleased, for the further comfort and safety of your people, to declare your royal will and pleasure, that in the things aforesaid all your officers and ministers shall serve you according to the laws and statutes of this realm, as they tender the honor of your Majesty, and the prosperity of this kingdom.

Questions for Contemplation and Discussion

1. How should the accused be treated, according to the Ordeal of Boiling Water?

2. What does the Petition of Right say about the rights of the accused?

3. Is the Ordeal of Boiling Water an example of superstition? How so?

4. Some say that some who are accused of a crime should not receive a trial by jury, because they do not deserve it. Do you agree with that? Why? Why not? In your answer, refer to the two documents

HOW WILL THE WORLD END?

Revelation 19–21[44]

And I saw heaven opened, and behold a white horse; and he that sat upon him was called Faithful and True, and in righteousness he doth judge and make war. His eyes were as a flame of fire, and on his head were many crowns; and he had a name written, that no man knew, but he himself. And he was clothed with a vesture dipped in blood: and his name is called The Word of God. And the armies which were in heaven followed him upon white horses, clothed in fine linen, white and clean. And out of his mouth goeth a sharp sword, that with it he should smite the nations: and he shall rule them with a rod of iron: and he treadeth the winepress of the fierceness and wrath of Almighty God. And he hath on his vesture and on his thigh a name written, KING OF KINGS, AND LORD OF LORDS.

And I saw an angel standing in the sun; and he cried with a loud voice, saying to all the fowls that fly in the midst of heaven, Come and gather yourselves together unto the supper of the great God; That ye may eat the flesh of kings, and the flesh of captains, and the flesh of mighty men, and the flesh of horses, and of them that sit on them, and the flesh of all men, both free and bond, both small and great. And I saw the beast, and the kings of the earth, and their armies, gathered together to make war against him that sat on the horse, and against his army. And the beast was taken, and with him the false prophet that wrought miracles before him, with which he deceived them that had received the mark of the beast, and them that worshipped his image. These both were cast alive into a lake of fire burning with brimstone. And the remnant were slain with the sword of him that sat upon the horse, which sword proceeded out of his mouth: and all the fowls were filled with their flesh.

And I saw an angel come down from heaven, having the key of the bottomless pit and a great chain in his hand. And he laid hold on the dragon, that old serpent, which is the Devil, and Satan, and bound him a thousand years, and cast him into the bottomless pit, and shut him up, and set a seal upon him, that he should deceive the nations no more, till the thousand years should be fulfilled: and after that he must be loosed a little season.

And I saw thrones, and they sat upon them, and judgment was given unto them: and I saw the souls of them that were beheaded for the witness of Jesus, and for the word of God, and which had not worshipped the beast, neither his image, neither had received his mark upon their foreheads, or in their hands; and they lived and reigned with Christ a thousand years. But the rest of the dead lived not again until the thousand years were finished. This is the first resurrection. Blessed and holy is he that hath part in the first resurrection: on such the second death hath no power, but they shall be priests of God and of Christ, and shall reign with him a thousand years.

And when the thousand years are expired, Satan shall be loosed out of his prison, and shall go out to deceive the nations which are in the four quarters of the earth, Gog, and Magog, to gather them together to battle: the number of whom is as the sand of the sea. And they went up on the breadth of the earth, and compassed the camp of the saints about, and the beloved city: and fire came down from God out of heaven, and devoured them. And the devil that deceived them was cast into the lake of fire and brimstone, where the beast and the false prophet are, and shall be tormented day and night for ever and ever.

And I saw a great white throne, and him that sat on it, from whose face the earth and the heaven fled away; and there was found no place for them. And I saw the dead, small and great, stand before God; and the books were opened: and another book was opened, which is the book of life: and the dead were judged out of those things which were written in the books, according to their works. And the sea gave up the dead which were in it; and death and hell delivered up the dead which were in them: and they were judged every man according to their works. And death and hell were cast into the lake of fire. This is the second death. And whosoever was not found written in the book of life was cast into the lake of fire.

And I saw a new heaven and a new earth: for the first heaven and the first earth were passed away; and there was no more sea. And I John saw the holy city, new Jerusalem, coming down from God out of heaven, prepared as a bride adorned for her husband. And I heard a great voice out of heaven saying, Behold, the tabernacle of God is with men, and he will dwell with them, and they shall be his people, and God himself shall be with them, and be their God. And God shall wipe away all tears from their eyes; and there shall be no more death, neither sorrow, nor crying, neither shall there be any more pain: for the former things are passed away. And he that sat upon the throne said, Behold, I make all things new. And he said unto me, Write: for these words are true and faithful. And he said unto me, It is done. I am Alpha and Omega, the beginning and the end. I will give unto him that is athirst of the fountain of the water of life freely. He that overcometh shall inherit all things; and I will be his God, and he shall be my son. But the fearful, and unbelieving, and the abominable, and murderers, and whoremongers, and sorcerers, and idolaters, and all liars, shall have their part in the lake which burneth with fire and brimstone: which is the second death . . .

And I saw no temple therein: for the Lord God Almighty and the Lamb are the temple of it. And the city had no need of the sun, neither of the moon, to shine in it: for the glory of God did lighten it, and the Lamb is the light thereof. And the nations of them which are saved shall walk in the light of it: and the kings of the earth do bring their glory and honour into it. And the gates of it shall not be shut at all by day: for there shall be no night there. And they shall bring the glory and honour of the nations into it. And there shall in no wise enter into it any thing that defileth, neither whatsoever worketh abomination, or maketh a lie: but they which are written in the Lamb's book of life.

And he shewed me a pure river of water of life, clear as crystal, proceeding out of the throne of God and of the Lamb. In the midst of the street of it, and on either side of the river, was there the tree of life, which bare twelve manner of fruits, and yielded her fruit every month: and the leaves of the tree were for the healing of the nations. And there shall be no more curse: but the throne of God and of the Lamb shall be in it; and his servants shall serve him: And they shall see his face; and his name shall be in their foreheads. And there shall be no night there; and they need no candle, neither light of the sun; for the Lord God giveth them light: and they shall reign for ever and ever.

And he said unto me, These sayings are faithful and true: and the Lord God of the holy prophets sent his angel to shew unto his servants the things which must shortly be done. Behold, I come quickly: blessed is he that keepeth the sayings of the prophecy of this book. And I John saw these things, and heard them. And when I had heard and seen, I fell down to worship before the feet of the angel which shewed me these things. Then saith he unto me, See thou do it not: for I am thy fellowservant, and of thy brethren the prophets, and of them which keep the sayings of this book: worship God. And he saith unto me, Seal not the sayings of the prophecy of this book: for the time is at hand. He that is unjust, let him be unjust still: and he which is filthy, let him be filthy still: and he that is righteous, let him be righteous still: and he that is holy, let him be holy still. And, behold, I come quickly; and my reward is with me, to give every man according as his work shall be. I am Alpha and Omega, the beginning and the end, the first and the last. Blessed are they that do his commandments, that they may have right to the tree of life, and may enter in through the gates into the city. For without are dogs, and sorcerers, and whoremongers, and murderers, and idolaters, and whosoever loveth and maketh a lie. I Jesus have sent mine angel to testify unto you these things in the churches. I am the root and the offspring of David, and the bright and morning star.

And the Spirit and the bride say, Come. And let him that heareth say, Come. And let him that is athirst come. And whosoever will, let him take the water of life freely. For I testify unto every man that heareth the words of the prophecy of this book, If any man shall add unto these things, God shall add unto him the plagues that are written in this book.

And if any man shall take away from the words of the book of this prophecy, God shall take away his part out of the book of life, and out of the holy city, and from the things which are written in this book. He which testifieth these things saith, Surely I come quickly. Amen. Even so, come, Lord Jesus.

The grace of our Lord Jesus Christ be with you all. Amen.

Victor F. Weisskopf, "On Nuclear Holocaust"[45]

Victor Weisskopf (1908–2002) was a physicist who later in life became active in protecting the environment from nuclear weapons. A leading researcher on quantum mechanics, he was part of the Manhattan Project, a group of scientists who created the atomic bomb during World War II.

Since 1930, physicists have penetrated the innermost parts of matter and have found forces and energies that normally are inactive here on Earth. These are "cosmic" forces in the real sense of the word: the energy of the sun is driven by these forces; the explosions of supernovas, and other cataclysmic phenomena, are caused by them.

There are, of course, natural radioactive substances, but these are not a true part of the Earth's contemporary environment. They are the leftovers of a much earlier time, the last embers of a cosmic fire in which our terrestrial matter was created 7 billion years ago. By delving into these inner nuclear energies, we are dealing with an order of magnitude much higher than in any other terrestrial form of energy. A chemical process—even the strongest chemical explosion—releases only a millionth, per atom, of the energy released in nuclear processes such as fission or fusion. So when these energies were first applied by human beings, the strength of technology immediately grew by a factor of a million.

It was only 40 years ago that we began to develop this process, and World War II exerted special pressure on this country to apply these great energies to weapons that would enable us to win the war. Many scientists, including myself, collaborated in this effort because of the danger—a clear and present danger at that time—that people like Hitler and political systems like Nazism would get hold of such weapons before we did. So, from 1940 to 1945, we developed ways to release these cosmic forces suddenly, creating the world's first nuclear bomb. (In some ways, it's easier to release these energies suddenly than continuously, as in a power reactor. But I will not discuss power reactors here, although many people are concerned about them—I want to deal with a much more serious problem.)

I was present on July 16, 1945, when the first atomic bomb was exploded in the desert in southern New Mexico. And while wearing sunglasses, I watched it: the amount of light released was 20 times more intense than midday sunlight. Two days later,

I drove a jeep to the place where the bomb was exploded. My passengers were Hans Bethe, Enrico Fermi, Robert Oppenheimer, and General Leslie Groves (the military leader of the project). We found the desert sand molten and glazed over a radius of about 200 yards. And General Groves's remark was, "Is that all?" He probably expected a hole to the center of the earth.

Three weeks later, one plane—the Enola Gay—flew over Hiroshima and dropped another such bomb on that city. Allied planes had been routinely making "fire raids" over the cities of Japan around that time, but the effect of this one bomb was worse than the damage inflicted by a thousand such planes: 100 thousand people were dead immediately, and many died soon afterward of diseases and other effects. That was only an "old-fashioned" bomb, the equivalent of 20 thousand tons of TNT. Nowadays, we have modernized A-bombs and H-bombs, fission and fusion bombs with yields up to many megatons, with effects correspondingly greater.

Thinking the Unthinkable

Let us suppose that one relatively big bomb—a 20-megaton bomb—fell on the center of Boston. The result would be no more city, but a crater about half a mile in diameter and 200 feet deep. Out to almost two miles, the fireball, which would have stopped growing at that radius, would bathe the surface in an atmosphere of incandescent air. Temperatures at ground level would be a few thousand degrees for the first 15 seconds or so until the fireball started to rise. And within a radius of four miles there would be total destruction: *everything,* even the strongest concrete building, would probably remain standing, but all frame and brick buildings would and from Everett to Dorchester, encompassing most of the city's hospitals and clinics. Farther out, to a radius of six miles, strong concrete buildings would probably remain standing, but all frame and brick buildings would be destroyed or badly damaged. That would go to Newton, Arlington, and Milton. Up to fifteen miles from the center, including Saugus, Quincy, Weston, and Lexington, frame buildings—most private homes—would be beyond repair.

There would be other destructive effects. Within the first 4 miles, everybody would be dead—about 750,000 people. People within 20 miles of the center could suffer second-degree burns. Flammable materials would instantly catch fire. At distances up to 40 miles, those who looked at the detonation could be blinded forever from the flash. The blast wave would be followed by winds of hundreds of miles per hour, fanning the fires over large distances. Fire storms much worse than those in the Second World War could develop up to 20 miles from the center. Within the fire storm, one could estimate that another 1.5 million people would die, for a total of over 2.2 million people. And the survivors would be badly burned.

These are all short-range, short-term effects; consider also the radiation effects. If you are exposed to more than 600 roentgens (R), you die. And the 600-R limit, depending on whether the bomb exploded near the ground or higher up, can extend as far as five or six miles. When the bomb explodes on the ground, materials at ground level are hurled into the air, absorb large amounts of radioactivity, and then fall down after about half an hour, covering the ground with a radioactive blanket. So if you survive the blast—if you are in a "shelter" you must remain inside for several more days. You thus cannot help other people, and the shelter's provisions, if indeed there are any, may not be adequate to sustain you.

The social fabric will break down from the effect of this one bomb: there will be no food supply, no water, no shelter, no power, no medical care. In Boston there are now 6,500 physicians; 5,000 of them would be dead or critically injured within the inner circle. There would be roughly 2,000 patients per doctor, or 10 minutes per patient over 20 days—not a realistic schedule. Add to that no beds, no equipment, and no drugs, and the chaos and suffering become inconceivable. Remember, too, that radiation sickness takes days or weeks to develop, so the sick toll would steadily mount. And imagine the problems posed by inadequate disposal of the dead.

Radioactive material spreads, but its precise pattern depends on the wind. With a bomb like this, deadly levels of radioactivity will cover an area of about 5,000 square miles. We would be "lucky" in Boston if there was a strong west wind and the radioactivity went out to sea, but east winds are common in the region.

This whole scenario is "unthinkable": it is impossible to think rationally about what would happen under such conditions. And that is only one bomb. At present, there are about 40 thousand nuclear bombs, mostly deployed by the United States and the Soviet Union. These are not all 20-megaton bombs, but if only part of the arsenals were used, you could extrapolate this description upward. An all-out war would kill about 100 million people, and that is a conservative estimate. The surviving population would be weakened, to say the least, and the structure of society would be virtually destroyed. Moreover, large parts of the soil would be contaminated, thus becoming unusable for food production, and genetic injuries would haunt us for generations.

Copyright © by Victor Weisskopf. Reprinted by permission.

Questions for Contemplation and Discussion

1. Should the Revelation passage be interpreted literally? If so, why? If not, why not? Is it possible to interpret all of the Bible, or the entire contents of any religious text, literally? Explain.

2. Does the essay on nuclear holocaust provide sufficient evidence? Is this an example of an appeal to fear? If so, why? If not, why not?

3. It has been said that some people look to the end of the world and to the future because they do not like life on earth, that they look forward to the future because they do not enjoy the present. Would you agree with this? Explain, citing evidence from personal experience or from history.

IS THERE AN AFTERLIFE?

Ancient Egypt, Book of the Dead[46]

This is a collection of charms, magical formulas, and ancient Egyptian funeral procedures. The text was written in hieroglyphics sometime around 1580 BCE.

He saith: Hail to thee mighty god, lord of Righteousness! I am come to thee, oh my Lord: I have brought myself that I may look upon thy glory. I know thee, and I know the name of the Forty-two gods who make their appearance with thee in the Hall of Righteousness; devouring those who harbour mischief, and swallowing their blood, upon the Day of the searching examination in presence of Unneferu.

Verily, 'Thou of the Pair of Eyes, Lord of Righteousness' is thy name.
Here am I; I am come to thee; I bring thee Right and have put a stop to Wrong.
I am not a doer of wrong to men.
I am not one who slayeth his kindred.
I am not one who telleth lies instead of truth.
I am not conscious of treason.
I am not a doer of mischief.
I do not exact as the first fruits of each day more work than should be done for me.
My name cometh not to the Bark of the God who is at the Helm.
I am not a transgressor against a god.
I am not a tale-bearer.
I am not a detractor.
I am not a doer of that which the gods abhor.
I hurt no servant with his master.
I cause no famine.
I cause not weeping.
I am not a murderer.
I give not orders for murder.
I cause not suffering to men.
I reduce not the offerings in the temples.
I lessen not the cakes of the gods.
I rob not the dead of their funeral food.
I am not an adulterer.
I am undefiled in the Sanctuary of the god of my domain.
I snatch not the milk from the mouth of infants.
I drive not the cattle from their pastures.
I stop not the water at its appointed time.
I divide not an arm of the water in its course.
I extinguish not the lamp during its appointed time.
I do not defraud the Divine Circle of their sacrificial joints.
I drive not away the cattle of the sacred estate.
I stop not a god when he cometh forth.
I am pure, I am pure, I am pure.

And I am one who see the fulness of the Eye in Annu, let no harm come to me in this land, in the Hall of Righteousness; because I know the names of the gods who make their appearance in it.

Qu'ran[47]

Sura 69:

So, when the Trumpet is blown with a single blast and the earth and the mountains are lifted up and crushed with a single blow, then, on that day, the Terror shall come to pass, and heaven shall be split, for upon that day it shall be very frail, and the angels shall stand upon its borders, and upon that day eight shall carry above them the Throne of thy Lord. On that day you

---

Source: Excerpts from *"Book of the Dead,"* Oliver Thatcher, Ed.

shall be exposed, not one secret of yours concealed. Then as for him who is given his book in his right hand, he shall say, "Here, take and read my book! Certainly I thought that I should encounter thy reckoning." So he shall be in a pleasing life in a lofty Garden, its clusters nigh to gather. "Eat and drink with wholesome appetite for that you did long ago, in the days gone by."

But as for him who is given his book in his left hand, he shall say, "Would that I had not been given my book and not known my reckoning! Would it had been the end! My wealth has not availed me, my authority is gone from me." Take him, and fetter him, and then roast him in Hell, then in a chain of seventy cubits' length insert him! Behold, he never believed in God the All-mighty, and he never urged the feeding of the needy; therefore he today has not here one loyal friend, neither any food saving foul pus, that none excepting the sinners eat.

Hindu Beliefs: The Laws of Manu[48]

Transmigration is an important part of Hindu belief, touching on both morality in this life and one's destiny in the next life. This passage comes from the *Laws of Manu*, the most significant code on law and morality in classical India.

I will briefly declare in due order what transmigrations in this whole (world a man) obtains through each of these qualities.

Those endowed with Goodness reach the state of gods, those endowed with Activity the state of men, and those endowed with Darkness ever sink to the condition of beasts; that is the threefold course of transmigrations.

But know this threefold course of transmigrations that depends on the (three) qualities (to be again) threefold, low, middling, and high, according to the particular nature of the acts and of the knowledge (of each man).

Immovable (beings), insects, both small and great, fishes, snakes, tortoises, cattle and wild animals, are the lowest conditions to which (the quality of) Darkness leads.

Elephants, horses . . . lions, tigers, and boars (are) the middling states, caused by (the quality of) Darkness.

Hypocrites . . . (belong to) the highest (rank of) conditions among those produced by Darkness.

Men who subsist the despicable occupations and those addicted to gambling and drinking (form) the lowest (order of) conditions caused by Activity . . .

Hermits, ascetics . . . (form) the first (and lowest rank of the) existences caused by Goodness.

Sacrifices, the sages, the gods . . . (constitute the second order of existences, caused by Goodness . . .

Thus (the result) of the threefold action, the whole system of transmigrations which (consists) of three classes, (each) with three subdivisions, and which includes all created beings, has been fully pointed out.

In consequence of attachment to (the objects of) the senses, and in consequence of the non-performance of their duties, fools, the lowest of men, reach the vilest births.

What wombs this individual soul enters this world and in consequence of what actions, learn the particulars of that at large and in due order. Those who committed mortal sins (mahapataka), having passed during large numbers of years through dreadful hells, obtain, after the expiration of (that term of punishment), the following births.

The slayer of a Brahmana [a text explaining Hindu ritual] enters the womb of a dog, a pig, an ass, a camel, a cow, a goat, a sheep, a deer, a bird . . .

A Brahmana who drinks (the spiritous liquor called) Sura shall enter (the bodies) of small and large insects, of moths, of birds, feeding on ondure, and of destructive beasts.

A Brahmana who steals (the gold of a Brahmana shall pass) a thousand times (through the bodies) of spiders, snakes, and lizards, of aquatic animals and of destructive Pisakas.

The violator of a Guru's bed (enters) a hundred times (the forms) of grasses, shrubs, and creepers, likewise of carnivorous (animals) and of (beasts) with fangs and of those doing cruel deeds.

Men who delight in doing hurt (become) carnivorous (animals); those who eat forbidden food, worms; thieves, creatures consuming their own kind; those who have intercourse with women of the lowest castes . . .

For stealing grain (a man) becomes a rat . . . for stealing honey a stinging insect, for stealing milk a crow, for stealing condiments a dog . . . for stealing meat a vulture . . . for stealing fine perfumes a muskrat, for stealing vegetables consisting of leaves a peacock, for stealing cooked food of various kinds a porcupine, for stealing uncooked food a hedgehog . . .

That man who has forcibly taken away any kind of property belonging to one another, or who has eaten sacrificial food (of) which (no portion) had been offered, inevitably becomes an animal.

Source: Excerpts from "Laws of Manu," Oliver Thatcher, Ed.

Questions for Contemplation and Discussion

1. What does the excerpt from the *Book of the Dead* reveal about ancient Egyptian mythology?

2. How do the *Laws of Manu* describe the process of transmigration, or reincarnation?

3. Would the threat of being reincarnated as a lower life-form be effective enough to encourage a person to live a better life? Explain.

CHAPTER 3

TIME-SPECIFIC QUESTIONS THROUGHOUT WORLD HISTORY: A READER

WHY DID THE ROMAN EMPIRE FALL?

Edward Gibbon, The History of the Decline and Fall of the Roman Empire[49]

Edward Gibbon (1737–1794) was one of the greatest historians in world history. First published in 1776, Gibbon's *Decline and Fall* represents the influence of the Enlightenment in the writing of the past.

As the happiness of a future life is the great object of religion, we may hear without surprise or scandal that the introduction, or at least the abuse of Christianity, had some influence on the decline and fall of the Roman Empire. The clergy successfully preached the doctrines of patience and pusillanimity; the active virtues of society were discouraged; and the last remains of military spirit were buried in the cloister: a large portion of public and private wealth was consecrated to the specious demands of charity and devotion; and the soldiers' pay was lavished on the useless multitudes of both sexes who could only plead the merits of abstinence and chastity.

Faith, zeal, curiosity, and more earthly passions of malice and ambition, kindled the flame of theological discord; the church, and even the state, were distracted by religious factions, whose conflicts were sometimes bloody and always implacable; the attention of the emperors was diverted from camps to synods; the Roman world was oppressed by a new species of tyranny; and the persecuted sects became the secret enemies of their country.

Yet party-spirit, however pernicious or absurd, is a principle of union as well as of dissension. The bishops, from eighteen hundred pulpits, inculcated the duty of passive obedience to a lawful and orthodox sovereign; their frequent assemblies and perpetual correspondence maintained the communion of distant churches; and the benevolent temper of the Gospel was strengthened, though confirmed, by the spiritual alliance of the Catholics. The sacred indolence of the monks was devoutly embraced by a servile and effeminate age; but if superstition had not afforded a decent retreat, the same vices would have tempted the unworthy Romans to desert, from baser motives, the standard of the republic. Religious precepts are easily obeyed which indulge and sanctify the natural inclinations of their votaries; but the pure and genuine influence of Christianity may be traced in its beneficial, though imperfect, effects on the barbarian proselytes of the North. If the decline of the Roman Empire was hastened by the conversion of Constantine [Roman emperor, died in 337], his victorious religion broke the violence of the fall, and mollified the ferocious temper of the conquerors.

This awful revolution may be usefully applied to the instruction of the present age. It is the duty of a patriot to prefer and promote the exclusive interest and glory of his native country: but a philosopher may be permitted to enlarge his views, and to consider Europe as one great republic, whose various inhabitants have attained almost the same level of politeness and cultivation. The balance of power will continue to fluctuate, and the prosperity of our own or the neighbouring kingdoms may be alternately exalted or depressed; but these partial events cannot essentially injure our general state of happiness, the system of arts, and laws, and manners, which so advantageously distinguish, above the rest of mankind, the Europeans and their colonies.

Source: Edward Gibbon.

The savage nations of the globe are the common enemies of civilised society; and we may inquire, with anxious curiosity, whether Europe is still threatened with a repetition of those calamities which formerly oppressed the arms and institutions of Rome. Perhaps the same reflections will illustrate the fall of that mighty empire, and explain the probable causes of our actual security.

Augustine, The City of God[50]

Augustine (354–430) was a bishop in the North African city of Hippo. He is regarded as one of the most original thinkers in the history of Christianity.

Let these and similar answers (if any fuller and fitter answers can be found) be given to their enemies by the redeemed family of the Lord Christ, and by the pilgrim city of King Christ. But let this city bear in mind, that among her enemies lie hid those who are destined to be fellow-citizens, that she may not think it a fruitless labor to bear what they inflict as enemies until they become confessors of the faith. So, too, as long as she is a stranger in the world, the city of God has in her communion, and bound to her by the sacraments, some who shall not eternally dwell in the lot of the saints. Of these, some are not now recognized; others declare themselves, and do not hesitate to make common cause with our enemies in murmuring against God, whose sacramental badge they wear. These men you may to-day see thronging the churches with us, to-morrow crowding the theatres with the godless. But we have the less reason to despair of the reclamation even of such persons, if among our most declared enemies there are now some, unknown to themselves, who are destined to become our friends. In truth, these two cities are entangled together in this world, and intermixed until the last judgment effects their separation.

I now proceed to speak, as God shall help me, of the rise, progress, and end of these two cities; and what I write, I write for the glory of the city of God, that, being placed in comparison with the other, it may shine with a brighter lustre . . .

But remember that, in recounting these things, I have still to address myself to ignorant men; so ignorant, indeed, as to give birth to the common saying, "Drought and Christianity go hand in hand." There are indeed some among them who are thoroughly well-educated men, and have a taste for history, in which the things I speak of are open to their observation; but in order to irritate the uneducated masses against us, they feign ignorance of these events, and do what they can to make the vulgar believe that those disasters, which in certain places and at certain times uniformly befall mankind, are the result of Christianity, which is being everywhere diffused, and is possessed of a renown and brilliancy which quite eclipse their own gods. Let them then, along with us, call to mind with what various and repeated disasters the prosperity of Rome was blighted, before ever Christ had come in the flesh, and before His name had been blazoned among the nations with that glory which they vainly grudge. Let them, if they can, defend their gods in this article, since they maintain that they worship them in order to be preserved from these disasters, which they now impute to us if they suffer in the least degree. For why did these gods permit the disasters I am to speak of to fall on their worshippers before the preaching of Christ's name offended them, and put an end to their sacrifices? . . .

Questions for Contemplation and Discussion

1. What is the thesis, or main point, of Gibbon? What is the thesis, or main point, of Augustine?

   How the Roman Empire fell

   Gibbon → —Tyrannical Monarchies —Disagreements among leaders in religion
   —Issues with the ministers

2. In what ways do Gibbon and Augustine disagree about the role religion played in creating Rome's problems?

   Religious leaders conflicts with the empire.

3. Gibbon wrote well over one thousand years after Augustine, yet Augustine's account is what historians call a primary source, since he was actually observing what he was writing about. Who do you think is the more credible source? Is Gibbon's account less reliable because he was not alive during the time of the Roman Empire? Is Augustine's analysis less reliable because he would find it hard to be objective, since he had more personal contact with Rome itself?

   Gibbon credible source   Gibbon is more reliable
   Augustine's reliable of experience
   more poetic

4. Some would say that Gibbon is guilty of the fallacy of false cause. Do you agree? Explain.

   mislead
   No he is not
   perhaps over Exaggerated

5. Which of these accounts was more persuasive to you? Why?

   Gibbon's was more persuasive understanding

WHAT WAS AFRICA LIKE BEFORE 1500?

Procopius[51]

Procopius (died c. 565) was an ancient historian who lived in the Eastern Roman Empire, sometimes called the Byzantine Empire.

At that time the idea occurred to the Emperor Justinian [Byzantine emperor, lived 483–565) to ally with himself the Aethiopians and the Homeritae, in order to injure the Persians. I shall now first explain what part of the earth these nations occupy, and then I shall point out in what manner the emperor hoped that they would be of help to the Romans. The boundaries of Palestine extend toward the east to the sea which is called the Red Sea. Now this sea, beginning at India, comes to an end at this point in the Roman domain. And there is a city called Aelas on its shore, where the sea comes to an end, as I have said, and becomes a very narrow gulf.

And as one sails into the sea from there, the Egyptian mountains lie on the right, extending toward the south; on the other side a country deserted by men extends northward to an indefinite distance; and the land on both sides is visible as one sails in as far as the island called Iotabe, not less than one thousand stades distant from the city of Aelas. On this island Hebrews had lived from of old in autonomy, but in the reign of this Justinian they have become subject to the Romans. From there on there comes a great open sea. And those who sail into this part of it no longer see the land on the right, but they always anchor along the left coast when night comes on. For it is impossible to navigate in the darkness on this sea, since it is everywhere full of shoals. But there are harbours there and great numbers of them, not made by the hand of man, but by the natural contour of the land, and for this reason it is not difficult for mariners to find anchorage wherever they happen to be.

This coast immediately beyond the boundaries of Palestine is held by Saracens ["Arabs", later used as a term for Muslims], who have been settled from of old in the Palm Groves. These groves are in the interior, extending over a great tract of land, and there absolutely nothing else grows except palm trees. The Emperor Justinian had received these palm groves as a present from Abochorabus, the ruler of the Saracens there, and he was appointed by the emperor captain over the Saracens in Palestine. And he guarded the land from plunder constantly, for both to the barbarians over whom he ruled and no less to the enemy, Abochorabus always seemed a man to be feared and an exceptionally energetic fellow. Formally, therefore, the emperor holds the Palm Groves, but for him really to possess himself of any of the country there is utterly impossible.

For a land completely destitute of human habitation and extremely dry lies between, extending to the distance of a ten days' journey; moreover the Palm Groves themselves are by no means worth anything, and Abochorabus only gave the form of a gift, and the emperor accepted it with full knowledge of the fact. So much then for the Palm Groves. Adjoining this people there are other Saracens in possession of the coast, who are called Maddeni and who are subjects of the Homeritae. These Homeritae dwell in the land on the farther side of them on the shore of the sea. And beyond them many other nations are said to be settled as far as the man-eating Saracens. Beyond these are the nations of India. But regarding these matters let each one speak as he may wish.

About opposite the Homeritae on the opposite mainland dwell the Aethiopians who are called Auxomitae, because their king resides in the city of Auxomis. And the expanse of sea which lies between is crossed in a voyage of five days and nights, when a moderately favouring wind blows. For here they are accustomed to navigate by night also, since there are no shoals at all in these parts; this portion of the sea has been called the Red Sea by some. For the sea which one traverses beyond this point as far as the shore and the city of Aelas has received the name of the Arabian Gulf, inasmuch as the country which extends from here to the limits of the city of Gaza used to be called in olden times Arabia, since the king of the Arabs had his palace in early times in the city of Petrae. Now the harbour of the Homeritae from which they are accustomed to put to sea for the voyage to Aethiopia is called Bulicas; and at the end of the sail across the sea they always put in at the harbour of the Adulitae. But the city of Adulis is removed from the harbour a distance of twenty stades (for it lacks only so much of being on the sea), while from the city of Auxomis it is a journey of twelve days.

All the boats which are found in India and on this sea are not made in the same manner as are other ships. For neither are they smeared with pitch, nor with any other substance, nor indeed are the planks fastened together by iron nails going through and through, but they are bound together with a kind of cording. The reason is not as most persons suppose, that there are certain rocks there which draw the iron to themselves (for witness the fact that when the Roman vessels sail from Aelas into this sea, although they are fitted with much iron, no such thing has ever happened to them), but rather because the Indians and the Aethiopians possess neither iron nor any other thing suitable for such purposes. Furthermore, they are not even able to buy any of these things from the Romans since this is explicitly forbidden to all by law; for death is the punishment for one who is caught. Such then is the description of the so-called Red Sea and of the land which lies on either side of it.

From the city of Auxomis to the Aegyptian boundaries of the Roman domain, where the city called Elephantine is situated, is a journey of thirty days for an unencumbered traveller. Within that space many nations are settled, and among them the Blemyes and the Nobatae, who are very large nations. But the Blemyes dwell in the central portion of the country, while the Nobatae possess the territory about the River Nile.

Formerly this was not the limit of the Roman empire, but it lay beyond there as far as one would advance in a seven days' journey; but the Roman Emperor Diocletian came there, and observed that the tribute from these places was of the smallest possible account, since the land is at that point extremely narrow (for rocks rise to an exceedingly great height at no great distance from the Nile and spread over the rest of the country), while a very large body of soldiers had been stationed there from of old, the maintenance of which was an excessive burden upon the public; and at the same time the Nobatae who formerly dwelt about the city of Oasis used to plunder the whole region; so he persuaded these barbarians to move from their own habitations, and to settle along the River Nile, promising to bestow upon them great cities and land both extensive and incomparably better than that which they had previously occupied. For in this way he thought that they would no longer harass the country about Oasis at least, and that they would possess themselves of the land given them, as being their own, and would probably beat off the Blemyes and the other barbarians.

And since this pleased the Nobatae, they made the migration immediately, just as Diocletian directed them, and took possession of all the Roman cities and the land on both sides of the river beyond the city of Elephantine. Then it was that this emperor decreed that to them and to the Blemyes a fixed sum of gold should be given every year with the stipulation that they should no longer plunder the land of the Romans. And they receive this gold even up to my time, but none the less they overrun the country there. Thus it seems that with all barbarians there is no means of compelling them to keep faith with the Romans except through the fear of soldiers to hold them in check. And yet this emperor went so far as to select a certain island in the River Nile close to the city of Elephantine and there construct a very strong fortress in which he established certain temples and altars for the Romans and these barbarians in common, and he settled priests of both nations in this fortress, thinking that the friendship between them would be secure by reason of their sharing the things sacred to them.

And for this reason he named the place Philae. Now both these nations, the Blemyes and the Nobatae, believe in all the gods in which the Greeks believe, and they also reverence Isis and Osiris, and not least of all Priapus. But the Blemyes are accustomed also to sacrifice human beings to the sun. These sanctuaries in Philae were kept by these barbarians even up to my time, but the Emperor Justinian decided to tear them down. Accordingly Narses, a Persarmenian by birth, whom I have mentioned before as having deserted to the Romans, being commander of the troops there, tore down the sanctuaries at the emperor's order, and put the priests under guard and sent the statues to Byzantium. But I shall return to the previous narrative.

Questions for Contemplation and Discussion

1. How does Procopius describe the Africans he encountered?

2. Ethnocentrism is the belief that one's own culture is better than those of others. Those who are ethnocentric tend to look down condescendingly toward other cultures. Did Procopius hold this attitude? Or did he, in your estimation, fairly describe African people? Explain, citing from the writings of Procopius.

Who "Discovered" America?

Leif Erikson[52]

Leif Erikson (c. 980–c. 1020) did not write the following historical document, but he is the subject of this anonymous account from the eleventh century.

SAGA OF ERIC THE RED [the father of Leif Erikson]

Concerning Leif the Lucky and the Introduction of Christianity into Greenland.—Eric was married to a woman named Thorhild, and had two sons; one of these was named Thorstein, and the other Leif. They were both promising men. Thorstein lived at home with his father, and there was not at that time a man in Greenland who was accounted of so great promise as he. Leif had sailed to Norway, where he was at the court of King Olaf Tryggvason. When Leif sailed from Greenland, in the summer, they were driven out of their course to the Hebrides. It was late before they got fair winds thence, and they remained there far into the summer. Leif became enamored of a certain woman, whose name was Thorgunna. She was a woman of fine family, and Leif observed that she was possessed of rare intelligence.

When Leif was preparing for his departure Thorgunna asked to be permitted to accompany him. Leif inquired whether she had in this the approval of her kinsmen. She replied that she did not care for it. Leif responded that he did not deem it the part of wisdom to abduct so high-born a woman in a strange country, "and we so few in number." "It is by no means certain that thou shalt find this to be the better decision," said Thorgunna. "I shall put it to the proof, notwithstanding," said Leif. "Then I tell thee," said Thorgunna, "that I am no longer a lone woman, for I am pregnant, and upon thee I charge it. I foresee that I shall give birth to a male child. And though thou give this no heed, yet will I rear the boy, and send him to thee in Greenland, when he shall be fit to take his place with other men. And I foresee that thou wilt get as much profit of this son as is thy due from this our parting; moreover, I mean to come to Greenland myself before the end comes." Leif gave her a gold finger-ring, a Greenland wadmal mantle, and a belt of walrus-tusk. This boy came to Greenland, and was called Thorgils. Leif acknowledged his paternity, and some men will have it that this Thorgils came to Iceland in the summer before the Froda-wonder. However, this Thorgils was afterwards in Greenland, and there seemed to be something not altogether natural about him before the end came. Leif and his companions sailed away from the Hebrides, and arrived in Norway in the autumn.

Leif went to the court of King Olaf Tryggvason. He was well received by the king, who felt that he could see that Leif was a man of great accomplishments. Upon one occasion the king came to speech with Leif, and asks him, "Is it thy purpose to sail to Greenland in the summer?" "It is my purpose," said Leif, "if it be your will." "I believe it will be well," answers the king, "and thither thou shalt go upon my errand, to proclaim Christianity there."

Leif replied that the king should decide, but gave it as his belief that it would be difficult to carry this mission to a successful issue in Greenland. The king replied that he knew of no man who would be better fitted for this undertaking, "and in thy hands the cause will surely prosper." "This can only be," said Leif, "if I enjoy the grace of your protection." Leif put to sea when his ship was ready for the voyage. For a long time he was tossed about upon the ocean, and came upon lands of which he had previously had no knowledge. There were self-sown wheat fields and vines growing there. There were also those trees there which are called "mausur," and of all these they took specimens. Some of the timbers were so large that they were used in building. Leif found men upon a wreck, and took them home with him, and procured quarters for them all during the winter.

In this wise he showed his nobleness and goodness, since he introduced Christianity into the country, and saved the men from the wreck; and he was called Leif the Lucky ever after. Leif landed in Ericsfirth, and then went home to Brattahlid; he was well received by every one. He soon proclaimed Christianity throughout the land, and the Catholic faith, and announced King Olaf Tryggvason's messages to the people, telling them how much excellence and how great glory accompanied this faith. Eric was slow in forming the determination to forsake his old belief, but Thiodhild embraced the faith promptly, and caused a church to be built at some distance from the house. This building was called Thiodhild's Church, and there she and those persons who had accepted Christianity, and they were many, were wont to offer their prayers. Thiodhild would not have intercourse with Eric after that she had received the faith, whereat he was sorely vexed.

At this time there began to be much talk about a voyage of exploration to that country which Leif had discovered. The leader of this expedition was Thorstein Ericsson, who was a good man and an intelligent, and blessed with many friends. Eric was likewise invited to join them, for the men believed that his luck and foresight would be of great furtherance. He was slow in deciding, but did not say nay, when his friends besought him to go.

They thereupon equipped that ship in which Thorbiorn had come out, and twenty men were selected for the expedition. They took little cargo with them, nought else save their weapons and provisions. On that morning when Eric set out from his home he took with him a little chest containing gold and silver; he hid this treasure, and then went his way. He had proceeded but a short distance, however, when he fell from his horse and broke his ribs and dislocated his shoulder, whereat he cried "Ai, ai!" By reason of this accident he sent his wife word that she should procure the treasure which he had concealed, for to the hiding of the treasure he attributed his misfortune. Thereafter they sailed cheerily out of Ericsfirth in high spirits over their plan. They were long tossed about upon the ocean, and could not lay the course they wished.

They came in sight of Iceland, and likewise saw birds from the Irish coast. Their ship was, in sooth, driven hither and thither over the sea. In the autumn they turned back, worn out by toil, and exposure to the elements, and exhausted by their labors, and arrived at Ericsfirth at the very beginning of winter. Then said Eric, "More cheerful were we in the summer, when we put out of the firth, but we still live, and it might have been much worse." Thorstein answers, "It will be a princely deed to endeavor to look well after the wants of all these men who are now in need, and to make provision for them during the winter." Eric answers, "It is ever true, as it is said, that 'it is never clear ere the answer comes,' and so it must be here. We will act now upon thy counsel in this matter." All of the men, who were not otherwise provided for, accompanied the father and son. They landed thereupon, and went home to Brattahlid, where they remained throughout the winter.

Christopher Columbus[53]

Christopher Columbus (1451–1506) was an Italian explorer in the service of Spanish monarchs Ferdinand and Isabella. He is given credit for being the first European in the Americas since at least the voyage of Leif Erikson. Unlike Erikson's trip, the voyage of Columbus led to the permanent European settlement of the New World. The following comes from his log.

Saturday, 13th of October [from the year 1492]

"As soon as dawn broke many of these people came to the beach, all youths, as I have said, and all of good stature, a very handsome people. Their hair is not curly, but loose and coarse, like horse hair. In all the forehead is broad, more so than in any other people I have hitherto seen. Their eyes are very beautiful and not small, and themselves far from black, but the color of the Canarians [inhabitants of the Canary Islands, which are off the northwest coast of Africa]. Nor should anything else be expected, as this island is in a line east and west from the island of Hierro in the Canaries. Their legs are very straight, all in one line, and no belly, but very well formed. They came to the ship in small canoes, made out of the trunk of a tree like a long boat, and all of one piece, and wonderfully worked, considering the country. They are large, some of them holding 40 to 45 men, others smaller, and some only large enough to hold one man. They are propelled with a paddle like a baker's shovel, and go at a marvellous rate. If the canoe capsizes, they all promptly begin to swim, and to bale it out with calabashes that they take with them.

"They brought skeins of cotton thread, parrots, darts, and other small things which it would be tedious to recount, and they give all in exchange for anything that may be given to them. I was attentive, and took trouble to ascertain if there was gold. I saw that some of them had a small piece fastened in a hole they have in the nose, and by signs I was able to make out that to the south, or going from the island to the south, there was a king who had great cups full, and who possessed a great quantity. I tried to get them to go there, but afterwards I saw that they had no inclination. I resolved to wait until to-morrow in the afternoon and then to depart, shaping a course to the S.W., for, according to what many of them told me, there was land to the S., to the S.W., and N.W., and that the natives from the N.W. often came to attack them, and went on to the S.W. in search of gold and precious stones.

"This island is rather large and very flat, with bright green trees, much water, and a very large lake in the centre, without any mountain, and the whole land so green that it is a pleasure to look on it. The people are very docile, and for the longing to possess our things, and not having anything to give in return, they take what they can get, and presently swim away. Still, they give away all they have got, for whatever may be given to them, down to broken bits of crockery and glass. I saw one give 16 skeins of cotton for three ceotis of Portugal, equal to one blanca of Spain, the skeins being as much as an arroba of cotton thread. I shall keep it, and shall allow no one to take it, preserving it all for your Highnesses, for it may be obtained in abundance. It is grown in this island, though the short time did not admit of my ascertaining this for a certainty. Here also is found the gold they wear fastened in their noses. But, in order not to lose time, I intend to go and see if I can find the island of Cipango. Now, as it is night, all the natives have gone on shore with their canoes."

Tuesday, 30th of October

He left the Rio de Mares and steered N.W., seeing a cape covered with palm trees, to which he gave the name of Cabo de Palmas, after having made good 15 leagues. The Indians on board the caravel Pinta said that beyond that cape there was a river, and that from the river to Cuba it was four days' journey. The captain of the Pinta reported that he understood from that, that this Cuba was a city, and that the land was a great continent trending far to the north. The king of that country, he gathered, was at war with the Gran Can, whom they called Cami, and his land or city Fava, with many other names.

"The Admiral resolved to proceed to that river, and to send a present, with the letter of the Sovereigns, to the king of that land. For this service there was a sailor who had been to Guinea, and some of the Indians of Guanahani wished to go with him, and afterwards to return to their homes. The Admiral calculated that he was forty-two degrees to the north of the equinoctial line (but the handwriting is here illegible). He says that he must attempt to reach the Gran Can, who he thought was here or at the city of Cathay, which belongs to him, and is very grand, as he was informed before leaving Spain. All this land, he adds, is low and beautiful, and the sea deep.

Tuesday, 6th of November

"Yesterday, at night, says the Admiral, the two men came back who had been sent to explore the interior. They said that after walking 12 leagues they came to a village of 50 houses, where there were a thousand inhabitants, for many live in one house. These houses are like very large booths. They said that they were received with great solemnity, according to custom, and all, both men and women, came out to see them. They were lodged in the best houses, and the people touched them, kissing their hands and feet, marveling and believing that they came from heaven, and so they gave them to understand. They gave them to eat of what they had.

"When they arrived, the chief people conducted them by the arms to the principal house, gave them two chairs on which to sit, and all the natives sat round them on the ground. The Indian who came with them described the manner of living of the Christians, and said that they were good people. Presently the men went out, and the women came sitting round them in the same way, kissing their hands and feet, and looking to see if they were of flesh and bones like themselves. They begged the Spaniards to remain with them at least five days. The Spaniards showed the natives specimens of cinnamon, pepper and other spices which the Admiral had given them, and they said, by signs, that there was plenty at a short distance from thence to S.E., but that there they did not know whether there was any. Finding that they had no information respecting cities, the Spaniards returned; and if they had desired to take those who wished to accompany them, more than 500 men and women would have come, because they thought the Spaniards were returning to heaven.

"There came, however, a principal man of the village and his son, with a servant. The Admiral conversed with them, and showed them much honor. They made signs respecting many lands and islands in those parts. The Admiral thought of bringing them to the Sovereigns. He says that he knew not what fancy took them; either from fear, or owing to the dark night, they wanted to land. The ship was at the time high and dry, but, not wishing to make them angry, he let them go on their saying that they would return at dawn, but they never came back. The two Christians met with many people on the road going home, men and women with a half-burnt weed in their hands, being the herbs they are accustomed to smoke. They did not find villages on the road of more than five houses all receiving them with the same reverence. They saw many kinds of trees, herbs, and sweet-smelling flowers; and birds of many different kinds, unlike those of Spain, except the partridges, geese, of which there are many, and singing nightingales. They saw no quadrupeds except the dogs that do not bark.

"The land is very fertile, and is cultivated with yams and several kinds of beans different from ours, as well as corn. There were great quantities of cotton gathered, spun, and worked up. In a single house they saw more than 500 arrobas, and as much as 4000 quintals could be yielded every year. The Admiral said that "it did not appear to be cultivated, and that it bore all the year round. It is very fine, and has a large boll. All that was possessed by these people they gave at a very low price, and a great bundle of cotton was exchanged for the point of a needle or other trifle. They are a people," says the Admiral, "guileless and unwarlike. Men and women go as naked as when their mothers bore them. It is true that the women wear a very small piece of cotton-cloth which covers their private parts and no more, and they are of very good appearance, not very dark, less so than the Canarians.

"I hold, most serene Princes, that if devout religious persons were here, knowing the language, they would all turn Christians. I trust in our Lord that your Highnesses will resolve upon this with much diligence, to bring so many great nations within the Church, and to convert them; as you have destroyed those who would not confess the Father, the Son, and the Holy Ghost. And after your days, all of us being mortal, may your kingdoms remain in peace, and free from heresy and evil, and may you be well received before the eternal Creator, to whom I pray that you may have long life and great increase of kingdoms and lordships, with the will and disposition to increase the holy Christian religion as you have done hitherto. Amen!"

"To-day I got the ship afloat, and prepared to depart on Thursday, in the name of God, and to steer S.E. in search of gold and spices, and to discover land."

These are the words of the Admiral, who intended to depart on Thursday, but, the wind being contrary, he could not go until the 12th of November.

Thursday, 14th of February

"This night the wind increased, and the waves were terrible, rising against each other, and so shaking and straining the vessel that she could make no headway, and was in danger of being stove in. They carried the mainsail very closely reefed, so as just to give her steerage-way, and proceeded thus for three hours, making 20 miles. Meanwhile, the wind and sea increased, and, seeing the great danger, the Admiral began to run before it, there being nothing else to be done. The caravel Pinta began to run before the wind at the same time, and Martin Alonso ran her out of sight, although the Admiral kept showing lanterns all night, and the other answered. It would seem that she could do no more, owing to the force of the tempest, and she was taken far from the route of the Admiral. He steered that night E.N.E., and made 54 miles, equal to 13 leagues.

"At sunrise the wind blew still harder, and the cross sea was terrific. They continued to show the closely-reefed mainsail, to enable her to rise from between the waves, or she would otherwise have been swamped. An E.N.E. course was steered, and afterwards N.E. by E. for six hours, making 7½ leagues. The Admiral ordered that a pilgrimage should be made to Our Lady of Guadalupe, carrying a candle of 6 lbs. of weight in wax, and that all the crew should take an oath that the pilgrimage should be made by the man on whom the lot fell. As many chick-peas were got as there were persons on board, and on one a cross was cut with a knife. They were then put into a cap and shaken up. The first who put in his hand was the Admiral, and he drew out the chick-pea with a cross, so the lot fell on him; and he was bound to go on the pilgrimage and fulfil the vow. Another lot was drawn, to go on pilgrimage to Our Lady of Loreto, which is in the march of Ancona, in the Papal territory, a house where Our Lady works many and great miracles. The lot fell on a sailor of the port of Santa Maria, named Pedro de Villa, and the Admiral promised to pay his travelling expenses. Another pilgrimage was agreed upon, to watch for one night in Santa Clara at Moguer, and have a mass said, for which they again used the chick-peas, including the one with a cross. The lot again fell on the Admiral. After this the Admiral and all the crew made a vow that, on arriving at the first land, they would all go in procession, in their shirts, to say their prayers in a church dedicated to Our Lady.

"Besides these general vows made in common, each sailor made a special vow; for no one expected to escape, holding themselves for lost, owing to the fearful weather from which they were suffering. The want of ballast increased the danger of the ship, which had become light, owing to the consumption of the provisions and water. On account of the favorable weather enjoyed among the islands, the Admiral had omitted to make provision for this need, thinking that ballast might be taken on board at the island inhabited by women, which he had intended to visit. The only thing to do was to fill the barrels that had contained wine or fresh water with water from the sea, and this supplied a remedy.

"Here the Admiral writes of the causes which made him fear that he would perish, and of others that gave him hope that God would work his salvation, in order that such news as he was bringing to the Sovereigns might not be lost. It seemed to him that the strong desire he felt to bring such great news, and to show that all he had said and offered to discover had turned out true, suggested the fear that he would not be able to do so, and that each stinging insect would be able to thwart and impede the work. He attributes this fear to his little faith, and to his want of confidence in Divine Providence.

"He was comforted, on the other hand, by the mercies of God in having vouchsafed him such a victory, in the discoveries he had made, and in that God had complied with all his desires in Castile [a region in Spain that was once an autonomous kingdom], after much adversity and many misfortunes. As he had before put all his trust in God, who had heard him and granted all he sought, he ought now to believe that God would permit the completion of what had been begun, and ordain that he should be saved. Especially as he had freed him on the voyage out, when he had still greater reason to fear, from the trouble caused by the sailors and people of his company, who all with one voice declared their intention to return, and protested that they would rise against him.

"But the eternal God gave him force and valor to withstand them all, and in many other marvellous ways had God shown his will in this voyage besides those known to their Highnesses. Thus he ought not to fear the present tempest, though his weakness and anxiety prevent him from giving tranquillity to his mind. He says further that it gave him great sorrow to think of the two sons he left at their studies in Cordova [a city in Spain], who would be left orphans, without father or mother, in a strange land; while the Sovereigns would not know of the services he had performed in this voyage, nor would they receive the prosperous news which would move them to help the orphans.

"To remedy this, and that their Highnesses might know how our Lord had granted a victory in all that could be desired respecting the Indies, and that they might understand that there were no storms in those parts, which may be known by the herbs and trees which grow even within the sea; also that the Sovereigns might still have information, even if he perished in the storm, he took a parchment and wrote on it as good an account as he could of all he had discovered, entreating any one who might pick it up to deliver it to the Sovereigns. He rolled this parchment up in waxed cloth, fastened it very securely, ordered a large wooden barrel to be brought, and put it inside, so that no one else knew what it was. They thought that it was some act of devotion, and so he ordered the barrel to be thrown into the sea. Afterwards, in the showers and squalls, the wind veered to the west, and they went before it, only with the foresail, in a very confused sea, for five hours. They made 2½ leagues N.E. They had taken in the reefed mainsail, for fear some wave of the sea should carry all away."

Questions for Contemplation and Discussion

1. How is Leif Erikson described in the document? Is he portrayed heroically?

2. What does Christopher Columbus's log tell us about him?

3. How does Columbus describe the natives he encountered? Did he look down on them, as if he believed that he was better than them? Explain, citing from Columbus's log?

4. Do these documents, in your estimation, depict Erikson and Columbus as heroes? Explain.

WAS CHRISTOPHER COLUMBUS A HERO?

Pope Leo XIII[54]

Born Gioacchino Pecci, Leo XIII served as pope from 1878 to his death in 1903 at the age of 92.

On the Columbus Quadricentennial

Quatro Abeunte Saeculo Encyclical of Pope Leo XIII promulgated on July 16, 1892.

To Our Venerable Brethren, the Archbishops and Bishops of Spain, Italy, and the two Americas.

Now that four centuries have sped since a Ligurian [Part of Italy] first, under God's guidance, touched shores unknown beyond the Atlantic, the whole world is eager to celebrate the memory of the event, and glorify its author. Nor could a worthier reason be found where through zeal should be kindled. For the exploit is in itself the highest and grandest which any age has ever seen accomplished by man; and he who achieved it, for the greatness of his mind and heart, can be compared to but few in the history of humanity. By his toil another world emerged from the unsearched bosom of the ocean: hundreds of thousands of mortals have, from a state of blindness, been raised to the common level of the human race, reclaimed from savagery to gentleness and humanity; and, greatest of all, by the acquisition of those blessings of which Jesus Christ is the author, they have been recalled from destruction to eternal life. Europe, indeed, overpowered at the time by the novelty and strangeness of the discovery, presently came to recognize what was due to Columbus, when, through the numerous colonies shipped to America, through the constant intercourse and interchange of business and the ocean-trade, an incredible addition was made to our knowledge of nature, and to the commonwealth; whilst at the same time the prestige of the European name was marvelously increased. Therefore, amidst so lavish a display of honor, so unanimous a tribute of congratulations, it is fitting that the Church should not be altogether silent; since she, by custom and precedent, willingly approves and endeavors to forward whatsoever she see, and wherever she see it, that is honorable and praiseworthy. It is true she reserves her special and greatest honors for virtues that most signally proclaim a high morality, for these are directly associated with the salvation of souls; but she does not, therefore, despise or lightly estimate virtues of other kinds. On the contrary, she has ever highly favored and held in honor those who have deserved well of men in civil society, and have thus attained a lasting name among posterity. For God, indeed, is especially wonderful in his Saints—"mirabilis in Sanctis suis;" but the impress of His Divine virtue also appears in those who shine with excellent power of mind and spirit, since high intellect and greatness of spirit can be the property of men only through their parent and creator, God . . .

For Columbus is ours . . . it is indubitable that the Catholic faith was the strongest motive for the inception and prosecution of the design; so that for this reason also the whole human race owes not a little to the Church . . .

Columbus certainly had joined to the study of nature the study of religion, and had trained his mind on the teachings that well up from the most intimate depths of the Catholic faith. For this reason, when he learned from the lessons of astronomy and the record of the ancients, that there were great tracts of land lying towards the West, beyond the limits of the known world, lands hitherto explored by no man, he saw in spirit a mighty multitude, cloaked in miserable darkness, given over to evil rites, and the superstitious worship of vain gods. Miserable it is to live in a barbarous state and with savage manners: but more miserable to lack the knowledge of that which is highest, and to dwell in ignorance of the one true God. Considering these things, therefore, in his mind, he sought first of all to extend the Christian name and the benefits of Christian charity to the West, as is abundantly proved by the history of the whole undertaking. For when he first petitioned Ferdinand and Isabella, the Sovereigns of Spain, for fear lest they should be reluctant to encourage the undertaking, he clearly explained its object: "That their glory would grow to immortality, if they resolved to carry the name and doctrine of Jesus Christ into regions so distant." And in no long time having obtained his desires, he bears witness: "That he implores of God that, through His Divine aid and grace, the Sovereigns may continue steadfast in their desire to fill these new missionary shores with the truths of the Gospel." He hastens to seek missionaries from Pope Alexander VI, through a letter in which this sentence occurs: "I trust that, by God's help, I may spread the Holy Name and Gospel of Jesus Christ as widely as may be." He was carried away, as we think, with joy, when on his first return from the Indies he wrote to Raphael Sanchez: "That to God should be rendered immortal thanks, Who had brought his labors such prosperous issues; that Jesus Christ rejoices and triumphs on earth no less than in Heaven, at the approaching salvation of nations innumerable, who were before hastening to destruction." And if he moved Ferdinand and Isabella to decree that only Catholic Christians should be suffered to approach the New World and trade with the natives, he brought forward as reason, "that he sought nothing from his enterprise and endeavor but the increase and

---

Source: Pope Leo XII, "Quarto Abeunte Saeculo, Encyclical Promulgated on July 16, 1892."

glory of the Christian religion." And this was well known to Isabella, who better than any had understood the great man's mind; indeed it is evident that it had been clearly laid before that most pious, masculine-minded, and great-souled woman. For she had declared of Columbus that he would boldly thrust himself upon the vast ocean, "to achieve a most signal thing, for the sake of the Divine glory." And to Columbus himself, on his second return, she writes: "That the expenses she had incurred, and was about to incur, for the Indian expeditions, had been well bestowed; for thence would ensure a spreading of Catholicism." . . .

Then in addition were fights with savages, the infidelity of friends and companions, criminal conspiracies, the perfidy of the envious, and the calumnies of detractors. He must needs have succumbed under labors so vast and overwhelming if he had not been sustained by the consciousness of a nobler aim, which he knew would bring much glory to the Christian name, and salvation to an infinite multitude. And in contrast with his achievement the circumstances of the time show with wonderful effect. Columbus threw open America at the time when a great storm was about to break over the Church. As far, therefore, as it is lawful for man to divine from events the ways of Divine Providence, he seemed to have truly been born, by a singular provision of God, to remedy those losses which were awaiting the Catholic Church on the side of Europe . . .

This, then, was the object, this the end Columbus had in view in traversing such a vast extent of land and water to discover those countries hitherto uncultivated and inaccessible, but which, afterwards, as we have seen, have made such rapid strides in civilization and wealth and fame. And in truth the magnitude of the undertaking, as well as the importance and variety of the benefits that arose from it, call for some fitting and honorable commemoration of it among men. And, above all, it is fitting that we should confess and celebrate in an especial manner the will and designs of the Eternal Wisdom, under whose guidance the discoverer of the New World placed himself with a devotion so touching.

In order, therefore, that the commemoration of Columbus may be worthily observed, religion must give her assistance to the secular ceremonies. And as at the time of the first news of the discovery public thanksgiving was offered by the command of the Sovereign Pontiff to Almighty God, so now we have resolved to act in like manner in celebrating the anniversary of this auspicious event . . .

Given at Rome, from St. Peter's, on the 16th day of July, 1892, in the fifteenth year of Our Pontificate.

Justin Winsor[55]

Justin Winsor (1831–1897) was one of the nineteenth century's greatest scholars. He was a founding member of the American Historical Association and the American Library Association.

The very domination of this man in the history of two hemispheres warrants us in estimating hum by an austere sense of occasions lost and of opportunities embraced. The really great man is superior to his age, and anticipates the future; not as a sudden apparition, but as the embodiment of a long growth of ideas of which he is the inheritor and the capable exemplar . . . It is extremely doubtful if any instance can be found of a great idea changing the world's history, which has been created by any single man. None such was created by Columbus . . . If he had reached the opulent and powerful kings of the Orient, his little cockboats and their brave souls might have fared hard for their intrusion. His blunder in geography very likely saved them from annihilation . . .

That Columbus was a devout Catholic, according to the Catholicism of his epoch, does not admit of question, but when tried by any test that finds the perennial in holy acts, Columbus fails to bear the examination. He has nothing of the generous and noble spirit of a conjoint lover of man and of God, as the higher spirits of all times have developed it. There was no all-loving Deity in his conception. His Lord was one in whose name it was convenient to practice enormities . . . The people he went to save for Christ were easy to exterminate. He mourned bitterly that his own efforts were ill-requited. He had no pity for the misery of others, except they be his dependents and co-sharers of his purposes. He found a policy worth commemorating in slitting the noses and tearing off the ears of a naked heathen . . . He talked a great deal about making converts of the poor souls, while the very first sight which he had of them prompted him to consign them to the slave-mart . . . It is to Columbus, also, that we trace the beginning of that monstrous guilt which Spanish law sanctioned under the name of repartimientos [Spain's often abusive system of forcing natives to work in the new world], and by which to every colonist, and even to the vilest, absolute power was given over as many natives as his means and rank entitled him to hold. Las Casas tells us that Ferdinand could hardly have had a conception of the enormities of the system. If so, it was because he winked out of sight the testimony of observers, while he listened to the tales prompted of greed, rapine, and cruelty. The value of the system to force heathen out of hell, and at the same time to replenish his treasury, was the side of it presented to Ferdinand's mind by such as had access to his person . . .

Source: Justin Winsor.

The downfall of Columbus began when he wrested from his reluctant monarchs what he called his privileges, and when he insisted upon riches as the accompaniment of such state and consequence as those privileges might entail . . . If Columbus had found riches in the New World as easily as he anticipated, it is possible that such affluence would have moulded his character in other ways for good or for evil. He soon found confronting a difficult task, to satisfy with insufficient means a craving which his exaggerations had established. This led him to spare no device, at whatever sacrifice of the natives, to produce the coveted gold, and it was an ingenious mockery that induced him to deck his captives with golden chains and parade them through the Spanish towns . . . A second instance of Columbus's luckless impotence, at a time when an honorable man would have relied upon his character, was the attempt to make it appear that he had reached the coast of Asia by imposing an oath on his men to that effect, in penalty of having their tongues wrenched out if they had recanted. One can hardly conceive a more debasing exercise of power.

We have seen a pitiable man meet a pitiable death. Hardly a name in profane history is more august than his. Hardly another character in the world's record has made so little of its opportunities. His discovery was a blunder; his blunder was a new world; the New World is his monument! Its discoverer might have been its father; he proved to be its despoiler. He might have given its young days such a benignity as the world likes to associate with a maker; he left it a legacy of devastation and crime. He might have been an unselfish promoter of geographical science; he proved a rapid seeker for gold and a viceroyalty. He might have won converts to the fold of Christ by the kindness of his spirit; he gained the execrations of the good angels. He might, like Las Casas [Spanish priest who criticized Spanish abuse of natives], have rebuked the fiendishness of his contemporaries; he set them an example of perverted belief. The triumph of Barcelona led down to the ignominy of Valladolid [Valladolid is a Spanish city where Columbus died], with every step in the degradation palpable and resultant.

Questions for Contemplation and Discussion

1. Which qualities of Columbus does the pope praise? Explain.

2. Is the pope guilty of "stacking the deck," of focusing on Columbus's positive traits while ignoring his negative ones? Explain.

3. Which qualities of Columbus does Justin Winsor condemn? Explain.

4. What does Winsor mean when he refers to Columbus as "pitiable"?

5. Is Winsor being fair with Columbus?

6. Some might say that it is not appropriate to criticize heroes from the past—Columbus, a former president, or the founding fathers. What is your reaction to that? Do leaders or important historical figures deserve not to have their reputations challenged?

WHAT WAS SLAVERY LIKE?

Gomes (Gil) Eannes de Azurara, The Chronicle of the Discovery and Conquest of Guinea[56]

Gomes Eannes (1410–1474) was a leading Portuguese explorer who worked for Prince Henry (the Navigator). His account of slavery is one of the earliest in existence.

On the next day, which was the 8th of the month of August, very early in the morning, by reason of the heat, the seamen began to make ready their boats, and to take out their captives and carry them on shore, as they were commanded . . . But what heart could be so hard as not to be pierced with piteous feeling to see that company? For some kept their heads low and their faces bathed in tears, looking up one upon another; others stood groaning very grievously, looking up to the height of heaven, fixing their eyes upon it, crying out loudly, as if asking help of the Father of Nature; others struck their faces with the palms of their hands, throwing themselves at full length upon the ground; others made their lamentations in the matter of a dirge, after the custom of their country. And though we could not understand the words of their language, the sound of it right well accorded with the measure of their sadness.

But to increase their sufferings still more, there now arrived those who had charge of the division of the captives and who began to separate one from another in order to make an equal partition of the fifths; and then it was needful to part fathers from sons, husbands from wives, brothers from brothers. No respect was shewn either to friends or relations, but each fell where his lot took him.

And who could finish that partition without very great toil, for as often as they had placed them in one part, the sons, seeing their fathers in another, rose with great energy and rushed over to them; the mothers clasped their other children in their arms, and threw themselves flat on the ground with them, receiving blows with little pity for their own flesh, if only they might not be torn from them.

The Infant was there, mounted upon a powerful steed, and accompanied by his retinue, making distribution of his favours, as a man who sought to gain but small treasure from his share: for he made a very speedy partition of the forty-six souls that fell to him as his fifth. His chief riches lay in his purpose, and he reflected with great pleasure upon the salvation of those souls that before were lost. And certainly his expectation was not in vain, since, as we said before, as soon as they understood our language, they turned Christians with very little ado; and I who put together this history into the present volume, saw in the town of Lagos [today, capital of Nigeria] boys and girls (the children and grandchildren of those first captives) born in this land, as good and true Christians as if they had directly descended, from the beginning of the dispensation of Christ, from those who were first baptised.

The Autobiography of Olaudah Equiano[57]

Olaudah Equiano (1745–1797) was a former slave who published his autobiography in 1789. The book became a best seller and helped galvanize the cause to abolish slavery.

When I looked round the ship too, and saw a large furnace of copper boiling, and a multitude of black people of every description chained together, every one of their countenances expressing dejection and sorrow, I no longer doubted of my fate; and, quite overpowered with horror and anguish, I fell motionless on the deck and fainted. I asked them if we were not to be eaten by those white men with horrible looks, red faces, and long hair. They told me I was not: and one of the crew brought me a small portion of spirituous liquor in a wine glass, but, being afraid of him, I would not take it out of his hand. One of the blacks, therefore, took it from him and gave it to me, and I took a little down my palate, which, instead of reviving me, as they thought it would, throw me into the greatest consternation at the strange feeling it produced, having never tasted any such liquor before. Soon after this, the blacks who brought me on board went off, and left me abandoned to despair.

I now saw myself deprived of all chance of returning to my native country, or even the least glimpse of hope of gaining the shore, which I now considered as friendly; and I even wished for my former slavery in preference to my present situation, which was filled with horrors of every kind, still heightened by my ignorance of what I was to undergo. I was not long suffered to indulge my grief; I was soon put down under the decks, and there I received such a salutation in my nostrils as I had never experienced in my life: so that, with the loathsomeness of the stench, and crying together, I became so sick and low that I was not able to eat, nor had I the least desire to taste any thing. I now wished for the last friend, death, to relieve me; but soon, to

---

Source: Gomez Eannes de Azurara, translated by C. R. Beazley and Edgar Prestage.
Source: Olaudah Equiano.

my grief, two of the white men offered me eatables; and, on my refusing to eat, one of them held me fast by the hands, and laid me across, I think the windlass, and tied my feet, while the other flogged me severely . . .

One day they had taken a number of fishes; and when they had killed and satisfied themselves with as many as they thought fit, to our astonishment who were on deck, rather than give any of them to us to eat, as we expected, they tossed the remaining fish into the sea again, although we begged and prayed for some as well as we could, but in vain; and some of my countrymen, being pressed by hunger, took an opportunity, when they thought no one saw them, of trying to get a little privately; but they were discovered, and the attempt procured them some very severe floggings.

One day, when we had a smooth sea and moderate wind, two of my wearied countrymen who were chained together, (I was near them at the time,) preferring death to such a life of misery, somehow made through the nettings and jumped into the sea: immediately, another quite dejected fellow, who, on account of his illness, was suffered to be out of irons, also followed their example; and I believe many more would very soon have done the same, if they had not been prevented by the ship's crew, who were instantly alarmed. Those of us that were the most active, were in a moment put down under the deck, and there was such a noise and confusion amongst the people of the ship as I never heard before, to stop her, and get the boat out to go after the slaves. However, two of the wretches were drowned, but they got the other, and afterwards flogged him unmercifully, for thus attempting to prefer death to slavery. In this manner we continued to undergo more hardships than I can now relate, hardships which are inseparable from this accursed trade. Many a time we were near suffocation from the want of fresh air, which we were often without for whole days together. This, and the stench of the necessary tubs, carried off many.

During our passage, I first saw flying fishes, which surprised me very much; they used frequently to fly across the ship, and many of them fell on the deck. I also now first saw the use of the quadrant; I had often with astonishment seen the mariners make observations with it, and I could not think what it meant. They at last took notice of my surprise; and one of them, willing to increase it, as well as to gratify my curiosity, made me one day look through it. The clouds appeared to me to be land, which disappeared as they passed along. This heightened my wonder; and I was now more persuaded than ever, that I was in another world, and that every thing about me was magic.

At last, we came in sight of the island of Barbadoes, at which the whites on board gave a great shout, and made many signs of joy to us. We did not know what to think of this; but as the vessel drew nearer, we plainly saw the harbor, and other ships of different kinds and sizes, and we soon anchored amongst them, off Bridgetown. Many merchants and planters now came on board, though it was in the evening. They put us in separate parcels, and examined us attentively. They also made us jump, and pointed to the land, signifying we were to go there. We thought by this, we should be eaten by these ugly men, as they appeared to us; and, when soon after we were all put down under the deck again, there was much dread and trembling among us, and nothing but bitter cries to be heard all the night from these apprehensions, insomuch, that at last the white people got some old slaves from the land to pacify us. They told us we were not to be eaten, but to work, and were soon to go on land, where we should see many of our country people. This report eased us much. And sure enough, soon after we were landed, there came to us Africans of all languages.

We were conducted immediately to the merchant's yard, where we were all pent up together, like so many sheep in a fold, without regard to sex or age. As every object was new to me, every thing I saw filled me with surprise. What struck me first, was, that the houses were built with bricks and stories, and in every other respect different from those I had seen in Africa; but I was still more astonished on seeing people on horseback. I did not know what this could mean; and, indeed, I thought these people were full of nothing but magical arts. While I was in this astonishment, one of my fellow-prisoners spoke to a countryman of his, about the horses, who said they were the same kind they had in their country. I understood them, though they were from a distant part of Africa; and I thought it odd I had not seen any horses there; but afterwards, when I came to converse with different Africans, I found they had many horses amongst them, and much larger than those I then saw.

We were not many days in the merchant's custody, before we were sold after their usual manner, which is this: On a signal given, (as the beat of a drum) the buyers rush at once into the yard where the slaves are confined, and make choice of that parcel they like best. The noise and clamor with which this is attended, and the eagerness visible in the countenances of the buyers, serve not a little to increase the apprehension of terrified Africans, who may well be supposed to consider them as the ministers of that destruction to which they think themselves devoted. In this manner, without scruple, are relations and friends separated, most of them never to see each other again. I remember, in the vessel in which I was brought over, in the men's apartment, there were several brothers, who, in the sale, were sold in different lots; and it was very moving on this occasion, to see and hear their cries at parting.

O, ye nominal Christians! Might not an African ask, you learned you this from your God, who says unto you, Do unto all men as you would men should do unto you? Is it not enough that we are torn from our country and friends, to toil for your luxury and lust of gain? Must every tender feeling be likewise sacrificed to your avarice. Are the dearest friends and relations, now rendered more dear by their separation from their kindred, still to be parted from each other, and thus prevented from cheering the gloom of slavery, with the small comfort of being together; and mingling their sufferings and sorrows? Why are parents to lose their children, brothers their sisters, husbands their wives? Surely, this is a new refinement in cruelty, which, while it has no advantage to atone for it, thus aggravates distress; and adds fresh horrors even to the wretchedness of slavery.

Questions for Contemplation and Discussion

1. Do the two readings present a similar picture of slavery? How so? Explain.

2. What do the readings reveal about the effects of slavery on families? Explain.

3. What do the readings reveal about the psychological effects of slavery? Explain.

4. Does the fact that Equiano was writing from the perspective of a former slave make his account more compelling? Are there ever any disadvantages to being an eyewitness to history? Explain.

5. What do you think Equiano meant when he wrote of "nominal Christians?

WAS MARTIN LUTHER RIGHT?

Martin Luther, "The Smalcald Articles" (1537)[58]

Martin Luther (1483–1546) was a German monk and professor whose questioning of Roman Catholic Church teaching launched the Protestant Reformation. Luther believed that the Bible demonstrated that some Catholic teachings were in error.

First, purgatory. Here they carried their trade into purgatory by masses for souls, and vigils, and weekly, monthly, and yearly celebrations of obsequies, and finally by the Common Week and All Souls Day, by soul-baths so that the Mass [Protestants call this the Lord's Supper] is used almost alone for the dead, although Christ has instituted the Sacrament alone for the living. Therefore purgatory, and every solemnity, rite, and commerce connected with it, is to be regarded as nothing but a specter of the devil. For it conflicts with the chief article [which teaches] that only Christ, and not the works of men, are to help [set free] souls. Not to mention the fact that nothing has been [divinely] commanded or enjoined upon us concerning the dead. Therefore all this may be safely omitted, even if it were no error and idolatry.

The Papists quote here Augustine [Christian theologian from the 400's] and some of the Fathers who are said to have written concerning purgatory, and they think that we do not understand for what purpose and to what end they spoke as they did. St. Augustine does not write that there is a purgatory nor has he a testimony of Scripture to constrain him thereto, but he leaves it in doubt whether there is one, and says that his mother asked to be remembered at the altar or Sacrament . . .

Our Papists, however, cite such statements [opinions] of men in order that men should believe in their horrible, blasphemous, and cursed traffic in masses for souls in purgatory [or in sacrifices for the dead and oblations], etc. But they will never prove these things from Augustine . . .

The Word of God shall establish articles of faith, and no one else, not even an angel . . .

The relics, in which there are found so many falsehoods and tomfooleries concerning the bones of dogs and horses, that even the devil has laughed at such rascalities, ought long ago to have been condemned, even though there were some good in them; and so much the more because they are without the Word of God; being neither commanded nor counseled, they are an entirely unnecessary and useless thing. But the worst is that [they have imagined that] these relics had to work indulgence and the forgiveness of sins [and have revered them] as a good work and service of God, like the Mass, etc . . .

The invocation of saints is also one of the abuses of Antichrist conflicting with the chief article, and destroys the knowledge of Christ. Neither is it commanded nor counseled, nor has it any example [or testimony] in Scripture, and even though it were a precious thing, as it is not [while, on the contrary, it is a most harmful thing], in Christ we have everything a thousandfold better [and surer, so that we are not in need of calling upon the saints].

And although the angels in heaven pray for us (as Christ Himself also does), as also do the saints on earth, and perhaps also in heaven, yet it does not follow thence that we should invoke and adore the angels and saints, and fast, hold festivals, celebrate Mass in their honor, make offerings, and establish churches, altars, divine worship, and in still other ways serve them, and regard them as helpers in need [as patrons and intercessors], and divide among them all kinds of help, and ascribe to each one a particular form of assistance, as the Papists teach and do. For this is idolatry, and such honor belongs alone to God. For as a Christian and saint upon earth you can pray for me, not only in one, but in many necessities. But for this reason I am not obliged to adore and invoke you, and celebrate festivals, fast, make oblations, hold masses for your honor [and worship], and put my faith in you for my salvation. I can in other ways indeed honor, love, and thank you in Christ . . .

That the Pope is not, according to divine law or according to the Word of God, the head of all Christendom (for this [name] belongs to One only, whose name is Jesus Christ), but is only the bishop and pastor of the Church at Rome, and of those who voluntarily or through a human creature (that is, a political magistrate) have attached themselves to him, to be Christians, not under him as a lord, but with him as brethren [colleagues] and comrades, as the ancient councils and the age of St. Cyprian show.

But to-day none of the bishops dare to address the Pope as brother as was done at that time [in the age of Cyprian]; but they must call him most gracious lord, even though they be kings or emperors. This [Such arrogance] we will not, cannot, must not take upon our conscience [with a good conscience approve]. Let him, however, who will do it, do so without us [at his own risk] . . .

For all his bulls and books are extant, in which he roars like a lion (as the angel in Rev. 12 depicts him, [crying out] that no Christian can be saved unless he obeys him and is subject to him in all things that he wishes, that he says, and that he does. All of which amounts to nothing less than saying: Although you believe in Christ, and have in Him [alone] everything that is necessary to salvation, yet it is nothing and all in vain unless you regard [have and worship] me as your god, and be subject and obedient to me.

And yet it is manifest that the holy Church has been without the Pope for at least more than five hundred years, and that even to the present day the churches of the Greeks and of many other languages neither have been nor are yet under the Pope. Besides, as often remarked, it is a human figment which is not commanded, and is unnecessary and useless; for the holy Christian [or catholic] Church can exist very well without such a head, and it would certainly have remained better [purer, and its career would have been more prosperous] if such a head had not been raised up by the devil.

And the Papacy is also of no use in the Church, because it exercises no Christian office; and therefore it is necessary for the Church to continue and to exist without the Pope . . .

Therefore the Church can never be better governed and preserved than if we all live under one head, Christ, and all the bishops equal in office (although they be unequal in gifts), be diligently joined in unity of doctrine, faith, Sacraments, prayer, and works of love, etc., as St. Jerome writes that the priests at Alexandria together and in common governed the churches, as did also the apostles, and afterwards all bishops throughout all Christendom, until the Pope raised his head above all.

This teaching shows forcefully that the Pope is the very Antichrist, who has exalted himself above, and opposed himself against Christ because he will not permit Christians to be saved without his power, which, nevertheless, is nothing, and is neither ordained nor commanded by God . . .

Accordingly he had to make himself equal and superior to Christ, and had to cause himself to be proclaimed the head and then the lord of the Church, and finally of the whole world, and simply God on earth, until he has dared to issue commands even to the angels in heaven. And when we distinguish the Pope's teaching from, or measure and hold it against, Holy Scripture, it is found [it appears plainly] that the Pope's teaching, where it is best, has been taken from the imperial and heathen law and treats of political matters and decisions or rights . . . but in all these things nothing at all of Christ, faith, and the commandments of God.

Lastly, it is nothing else than the devil himself, because above and against God he urges [and disseminates] his [papal] falsehoods concerning masses, purgatory, the monastic life, one's own works and [fictitious] divine worship (for this is the very Papacy [upon each of which the Papacy is altogether founded and is standing]), and condemns, murders and tortures all Christians who do not exalt and honor these abominations [of the Pope] above all things. Therefore, just as little as we can worship the devil himself as Lord and God, we can endure his apostle, the Pope, or Antichrist, in his rule as head or lord. For to lie and to kill, and to destroy body and soul eternally, that is wherein his papal government really consists, as I have very clearly shown in many books.

The Council of Trent.[59]

The Council of Trent consisted of a series of meetings from between 1545–1563. The Roman Catholic Church called these meetings to respond to the threat of Protestantism, and to defend Catholic doctrine from the criticisms of Protestants like Luther.

Begun on the third, and terminated on the fourth, day of December, MDLXIII. [1563], being the ninth and last under the Sovereign Pontiff [Pope], Pius IV.

DECREE CONCERNING PURGATORY.

Whereas the Catholic Church, instructed by the Holy Ghost, has, from the sacred writings and the ancient tradition of the Fathers, taught, in sacred councils, and very recently in this oecumenical Synod, that there is a Purgatory, and that the souls there detained are helped by the suffrages of the faithful, but principally by the acceptable sacrifice of the altar; the holy Synod enjoins on bishops that they diligently endeavour that the sound doctrine concerning Purgatory, transmitted by the holy Fathers and sacred councils, be believed, maintained, taught, and every where proclaimed by the faithful of Christ.

But let the more difficult and subtle questions, and which tend not to edification, and from which for the most part there is no increase of piety, be excluded from popular discourses before the uneducated multitude. In like manner, such things as are uncertain, or which labour under an appearance of error, let them not allow to be made public and treated of. While those things which tend to a certain kind of curiosity or superstition, or which savour of filthy lucre, let them prohibit as scandals and stumbling-blocks of the faithful. But let the bishops take care, that the suffrages of the faithful who are living, to wit the sacrifices of masses, prayers, alms, and other works of piety, which have been wont to be performed by the faithful for the other faithful departed, be piously and devoutly performed, in accordance with the institutes of the church; and that whatsoever is due on their behalf, from the endowments of testators, or in other way, be discharged, not in a perfunctory manner, but diligently and accurately, by the priests and ministers of the church, and others who are bound to render this (service).

ON THE INVOCATION, VENERATION, AND RELICS, OF SAINTS, AND ON SACRED IMAGES.

The holy Synod enjoins on all bishops, and others who sustain the office and charge of teaching, that, agreeably to the usage of the Catholic and Apostolic Church, received from the primitive times of the Christian religion, and agreeably to the consent of the holy Fathers, and to the decrees of sacred Councils, they especially instruct the faithful diligently concerning the intercession and invocation of saints; the honour (paid) to relics; and the legitimate use of images: teaching them, that the saints, who reign together with Christ, offer up their own prayers to God for men; that it is good and useful suppliantly to invoke them, and to have recourse to their prayers, aid, (and) help for obtaining benefits from God, through His Son, Jesus Christ our Lord, who is our alone Redeemer and Saviour; but that they think impiously, who deny that the saints, who enjoy eternal happiness in heaven, are to be invocated; or who assert either that they do not pray for men; or, that the invocation of them to pray for each of us even in particular, is idolatry; or, that it is repugnant to the word of God; and is opposed to the honour of the one mediator of God and men, Christ Jesus; or, that it is foolish to supplicate, vocally, or mentally, those who reign in heaven. Also, that the holy bodies of holy martyrs, and of others now living with Christ,—which bodies were the living members of Christ, and the temple of the Holy Ghost, and which are by Him to be raised unto eternal life, and to be glorified,—are to be venerated by the faithful; through which (bodies) many benefits are bestowed by God on men; so that they who affirm that veneration and honour are not due to the relics of saints; or, that these, and other sacred monuments, are uselessly honoured by the faithful; and that the places dedicated to the memories of the saints are in vain visited with the view of obtaining their aid; are wholly to be condemned, as the Church has already long since condemned, and now also condemns them.

Moreover, that the images of Christ, of the Virgin Mother of God, and of the other saints, are to be had and retained particularly in temples, and that due honour and veneration are to be given them; not that any divinity, or virtue, is believed to be in them, on account of which they are to be worshipped; or that anything is to be asked of them; or, that trust is to be reposed in images, as was of old done by the Gentiles who placed their hope in idols; but because the honour which is shown them is referred to the prototypes which those images represent; in such wise that by the images which we kiss, and before which we uncover the head, and prostrate ourselves, we adore Christ; and we venerate the saints, whose similitude they bear: as, by the decrees of Councils, and especially of the second Synod of Nicaea, has been defined against the opponents of images.

And the bishops shall carefully teach this,—that, by means of the histories of the mysteries of our Redemption, portrayed by paintings or other representations, the people is instructed, and confirmed in (the habit of) remembering, and continually revolving in mind the articles of faith; as also that great profit is derived from all sacred images, not only because the people are thereby admonished of the benefits and gifts bestowed upon them by Christ, but also because the miracles which God has performed by means of the saints, and their salutary examples, are set before the eyes of the faithful; that so they may give God thanks for those things; may order their own lives and manners in imitation of the saints; and may be excited to adore and love God, and to cultivate piety. But if any one shall teach, or entertain sentiments, contrary to these decrees; let him be anathema.

And if any abuses have crept in amongst these holy and salutary observances, the holy Synod ardently desires that they be utterly abolished; in such wise that no images, (suggestive) of false doctrine, and furnishing occasion of dangerous error to the uneducated, be set up. And if at times, when expedient for the unlettered people; it happen that the facts and narratives of sacred Scripture are portrayed and represented; the people shall be taught, that not thereby is the Divinity represented, as though it could be seen by the eyes of the body, or be portrayed by colours or figures.

Moreover, in the invocation of saints, the veneration of relics, and the sacred use of images, every superstition shall be removed, all filthy lucre be abolished; finally, all lasciviousness be avoided; in such wise that figures shall not be painted or adorned with a beauty exciting to lust; nor the celebration of the saints, and the visitation of relics be by any perverted into revellings and drunkenness; as if festivals are celebrated to the honour of the saints by luxury and wantonness.

In fine, let so great care and diligence be used herein by bishops, as that there be nothing seen that is disorderly, or that is unbecomingly or confusedly arranged, nothing that is profane, nothing indecorous, seeing that holiness becometh the house of God.

And that these things may be the more faithfully observed, the holy Synod ordains, that no one be allowed to place, or cause to be placed, any unusual image, in any place, or church, howsoever exempted, except that image have been approved of by the bishop: also, that no new miracles are to be acknowledged, or new relics recognised, unless the said bishop has taken cognizance and approved thereof; who, as soon as he has obtained some certain information in regard to these matters, shall, after having taken the advice of theologians, and of other pious men, act therein as he shall judge to be consonant with truth and piety. But if any doubtful, or difficult abuse has to be extirpated; or, in fine, if any more grave question shall arise touching these matters, the bishop, before deciding the controversy, shall await the sentence of the metropolitan and of the bishops of the province, in a provincial Council; yet so, that nothing new, or that previously has not been usual in the Church, shall be resolved on, without having first consulted the most holy Roman Pontiff . . .

ON THE CLOSE OF THE COUNCIL, AND ON SUING FOR CONFIRMATION FROM OUR MOST HOLY LORD.

Most illustrious lords and most reverend Fathers, doth it please you, that, to the praise of Almighty God, an end be put to this sacred oecumenical Synod? and that the confirmation of all and singular the things which have therein been decreed and defined, as well under the Roman Pontiffs, Paul III., and Julius III., of happy memory, as under our most holy lord Pius IV., be requested, in the name of this holy Synod, by the presidents, and the Legates of the Apostolic See, from the most blessed Roman Pontiff?

They answered: It pleaseth us.

Questions for Contemplation and Discussion

1. What is Martin Luther's main point?

2. Is Luther being fair and objective in describing Roman Catholicism? Explain. If you believe that he was NOT fair, what words and phrases from the document demonstrate this?

3. Some say that Martin Luther's writings demonstrate that he had a strong commitment and faith in the Bible? Based on your reading of Luther, would you agree with that assessment? Explain.

4. What is the role of the pope, according to the Council of Trent document?

5. During the Reformation, which was launched by Luther, political leaders in Europe would choose the religion and make the entire country practice it. A Protestant leader would dictate that all citizens be Protestants, and Catholic leaders would make their people remain in the Roman Catholic church. What is your opinion of this arrangement? Explain.

Why was the Transatlantic Slave Trade Abolished?

Thomas Clarkson, The History of the Rise, Progress and Accomplishment of the Abolition of the African Slave-Trade, by the British Parliament [60]

Thomas Clarkson (1760–1846) was an abolitionist who sought to end slavery in the British Empire. His views were influential in Parliament. Ultimately in Great Britain the slave trade was abolished in 1807, and slavery itself ended in 1833, partly because of Clarkson's efforts.

I scarcely know of any subject, the contemplation of which is more pleasing, than that of the correction or of the removal of any of the acknowledged evils of life; for while we rejoice to think that the sufferings of our fellow-creatures have been thus, in any instance, relieved, we must rejoice equally to think, that our own moral condition must have been necessarily improved by the change.

That evils, both physical and moral, have existed long upon earth there can be no doubt. One of the sacred writers, to whom we more immediately appeal for the early history of mankind, informs us that the state of our first parents was a state of innocence and happiness; but that, soon after their creation, sin and misery entered into the world. The poets in their fables, most of which, however extravagant they may seem, had their origin in truth, speak the same language. Some of these represent the first condition of man by the figure of the golden, and his subsequent degeneracy and subjection to suffering by that of the silver, and afterwards of the iron age. Others tell us that the first female was made of clay; that she was called Pandora, because every necessary gift, qualification, or endowment, was given to her by the gods, but that she received from Jupiter, at the same time, a box from which, when opened, a multitude of disorders sprung, and that these spread themselves immediately afterwards among all of the human race. Thus it appears, whatever authorities we consult, that those which may be termed the evils of life existed in the earliest times. And what does subsequent history, combined with our own experience, tell us, but that these have been continued, or that they have come down in different degrees through successive generations of men, in all the known countries of the universe, to the present day?

But though the inequality visible in the different conditions of life, and the passions interwoven into our nature, (both which have been allotted to us for wise purposes, and without which we could not easily afford a proof of the existence of that, which is denominated virtue,) have a tendency to produce vice and wretchedness among us, yet we see, in this our constitution, what may operate partially as preventives and corrective of them. If there be a radical propensity in our nature to do that which is wrong, there is, on the other hand, a counteracting power within it, or an impulse by means of the action of the divine Spirit upon our minds, which urges us to do that which is right . . . If the voice of temptation, clothed in musical and seducing accents, charms us one way, the voice of holiness, speaking to us from within, in a solemn and powerful manner, commands us another. Does one man obtain a victory over his corrupt affections? An immediate perception of pleasure, like the feeling of a reward divinely conferred upon him, is noticed. Does another fall prostrate beneath their power? A painful feeling, and such as pronounces to him the sentence of reproof and punishment is found to follow. If one, by suffering his heart to become hardened, oppresses a fellow-creature, the tear of sympathy starts up in the eye of another, and the latter instantly feels a desire, involuntarily generated, of flying to his relief. Thus impulses, feelings, and dispositions have been implanted in our nature, for the purpose of preventing and rectifying the evils of life. And as these have operated, so as to stimulate some men to lessen them by the exercise of an amiable charity, so they have operated to stimulate others in various other ways to the same end. Hence the philosopher has left moral precepts behind him in favour of benevolence, and the legislator has endeavoured to prevent barbarous practices by the introduction of laws.

In consequence then of these impulses and feelings, by which the pure power in our nature is thus made to act as a check upon the evil part of it, and in consequence of the influence which philosophy and legislative wisdom have had in their respective provinces, there has been always, in all times and countries, a counteracting energy, which has opposed itself, more or less, to the crimes and miseries of mankind. But it seems to have been reserved for Christianity to increase this energy, and to give it the widest possible domain. It was reserved for her, under the same divine influence, to give the best views of the nature and of the present and future condition of man; to afford the best moral precepts, to communicate the most benign stimulus to the heart, to produce the most blameless conduct, and thus to cut off many of the causes of wretchedness, and to heal it wherever it was found. At her command, wherever she has been duly acknowledged, many of the evils of life have already fled. The prisoner of war is no longer led into the amphitheatre to become a gladiator, and to imbrue his hands in the blood of his fellow-captive for the sport of a thoughtless multitude. The stern priest, cruel through fanaticism and custom, no longer leads his fellow-creature to the altar to sacrifice him to fictitious gods. The venerable martyr, courageous through faith and the sanctity of his life, is no longer hurried to the flames. The haggard witch, poring over her incantations by moon-light, no longer scatters her superstitious poison among her miserable neighbours, nor suffers for her crime.

But in whatever way Christianity may have operated towards the increase of this energy, or towards a diminution of human misery, it has operated in none more powerfully than by the new views and consequent duties, which it introduced on the subject of charity, or practical benevolence and love. Men in ancient times looked upon their talents, of whatever description, as, their own, which they might use, or cease to use at their discretion. But the Author of our religion was the first who taught that, however in a legal point of view, the talent of individuals might belong exclusively to themselves, so that no other person had a right to demand the use of it by force, yet in the Christian dispensation they were but the stewards of it for good; that so much was expected from this stewardship, that it was difficult for those who were intrusted with it to enter into his spiritual kingdom; that these had no right to conceal their talent in a napkin, but that they were bound to dispense a portion of it to the relief of their fellow-creatures; and that, in proportion to the magnitude of it, they were accountable for the extensiveness of its use. He was the first who pronounced the misapplication of it to be a crime, and to be a crime of no ordinary dimensions. He was the first who broke down the boundary between Jew and Gentile, and, therefore, the first who pointed out to men the inhabitants of other countries, for the exercise of their philanthropy and love. Hence a distinction is to be made both in the principle and practice of charity, as existing in ancient or in modern times. Though the old philosophers, historians, and poets, frequently inculcated benevolence, we have no reason to conclude from any facts they have left us, that persons in their days did anything more than occasionally relieve an unfortunate object, who might present himself before them, or that, however they might deplore the existence of public evils among them, they joined in associations for their suppression, or that they carried their charity, as bodies of men, into other kingdoms. To Christianity alone we are indebted for the new and sublime spectacle, of seeing men going beyond the bounds of individual usefulness to each other; of seeing them associate for the extirpation of private and public misery; and of seeing them carry their charity, as a united brotherhood, into distant lands. And in this wider field of benevolence it would be unjust not to confess, that no country has shone with more true lustre than our own, there being scarcely any case of acknowledged affliction, for which some of her Christian children have not united in an attempt to provide relief.

Among the evils corrected or subdued, either by the general influence of Christianity on the minds of men, or by particular associations of Christians, the African. Slave Trade appears to me to have occupied the foremost place. The abolition of it, therefore, of which it has devolved upon me to write the history, should be accounted as one of the greatest blessings, and as such should be one of the most copious sources of our joy: indeed, I know of no evil, the removal of which should excite in us a higher degree of pleasure. For, in considerations of this kind, are we not usually influenced by circumstances? Are not our feelings usually affected according to the situation, or the magnitude, or the importance of these? Are they not more or less elevated, as the evil under our contemplation has been more or less productive of misery, or more or less productive of guilt? Are they not more or less elevated again, as we have found it more or less considerable in extent? Our sensations will undoubtedly be in proportion to such circumstances, or our joy to the appreciation . . . of the evil which has been removed.

Eric Williams, Capitalism and Slavery[61]

Eric Williams (1911–1981) earned a Ph.D. from Oxford University and became a history professor at Harvard University. He later became Prime Minister of Trinidad and Tobago.

Capitalism & Slavery

BRITISH CAPITALISM AND THE WEST INDIES

Whereas before, in the eighteenth century, every important vested interest in England was lined up on the side of monopoly and the colonial system; after 1783, one by one, every one of those interests came out against monopoly and the West Indian slave system. British exports to the world were in manufactured goods which could be paid for only in raw materials—the cotton of the United States, the cotton, coffee and sugar of Brazil, the sugar of Cuba, the sugar and cotton of India. The expansion of British exports depended on the capacity of Britain to absorb the raw material as payment. The British West Indian monopoly, prohibiting the importation of non-British-plantation sugar for home consumption, stood in the way. Every important vested interest—the cotton manufacturers, the shipowners, the sugar refiners; every important industrial and commercial town—London, Manchester, Liverpool, Birmingham, Sheffield, the West Riding of Yorkshire, joined in the attack on West Indian slavery and West Indian monopoly. The abolitionists, significantly, concentrated their attack on the industrial centers.

Source: From *Capitalism and Slavery* by Eric Williams. Copyright © 1944 by the University of North Carolina Press, renewed 1972 by Eric Williams. New introduction by Colin A. Palmer © 1994 by the University of North Carolina Press. Used by permission of the publisher.

THE "SAINTS" AND SLAVERY

The humanitarians were the spearhead of the onslaught which destroyed the West Indian system and freed the Negro. But their importance has been seriously misunderstood and grossly exaggerated by men who have sacrificed scholarship to sentimentality and, like the scholastics of old, placed faith before reason and evidence.

The British humanitarians were a brilliant band. Clarkson personifies all the best in the humanitarianism of the age. One can appreciate even today his feelings when, in ruminating upon the subject of his prize-winning essay, he first awoke to the realization of the enormous injustice of slavery. Clarkson was an indefatigable worker, who conducted endless and dangerous researches into the conditions and consequences of the slave trade, a prolific pamphleteer whose history of the abolition movement is still a classic. His labors in the cause of justice to Africa were accomplished only at the cost of much personal discomfort, and imposed a severe strain on his scanty resources.

It was not until 1823 that emancipation became the avowed aim of the abolitionists. The chief reason was the persecution of the missionaries in the colonies—the death of Smith in Guiana, the expulsion of Shrewsbury in Barbados, the persecution of Knibb in Jamaica. Even then emancipation was to be gradual. "Nothing rash," warned Buxton, "nothing rapid, nothing abrupt, nothing bearing any feature of violence."

These economic changes are gradual, imperceptible, but they have an irresistible cumulative effect. Men, pursuing their interests, are rarely aware of the ultimate results of their activity. The commercial capitalism of the eighteenth century developed the wealth of Europe by means of slavery and monopoly. But in so doing it helped to create the industrial capitalism of the nineteenth century, which turned round and destroyed the power of commercial capitalism, slavery, and all its works. Without a grasp of these economic changes the history of the period is meaningless.

Questions for Contemplation and Discussion

1. How does Clarkson describe slavery? Cite details from the document in your answer.

2. In Clarkson's view, why is slavery wrong? Explain.

3. Why was slavery abolished, in Clarkson's estimation? Explain.

4. Why was slavery abolished, in Williams's view? Explain.

5. What is Williams's view of Clarkson and other "humanitarians"? What role did they have in the ending of the slave trade?

6. When studying history, in particular, the causes of events, is it more useful to examine the economic causes/background, or the religious causes/background? In other words, should religious causes and economic causes of historical events receive equal and balanced consideration? Explain.

WHAT WERE THE EFFECTS OF IMPERIALISM?

F.D. Lugard, The Rise of Our East African Empire[62]

Frederick John Dealtry Lugard (1858–1945) was a leading colonial administrator in the British Empire. He served in East Africa, West Africa, and the Far East.

There are some who say we have no right in Africa at all, that "it belongs to the natives." I hold that our right is the necessity that is upon us to provide for our ever-growing population—either by opening new fields for emigration, or by providing work and employment which the development of over-sea extension entails—and to stimulate trade by finding new markets, since we know what misery trade depression brings at home.

While thus serving our own interests as a nation, we may, by selecting men of the right stamp for the control of new territories, bring at the same time many advantages to Africa. Nor do we deprive the natives of their birthright of freedom, to place them under a foreign yoke . . . In Africa, moreover, there is among the people a natural inclination to submit to a higher authority.

Frederick Starr[63]

Professor Frederick Starr (1859–1933) was one of America's first great anthropologists.

Why should we pick out the Congo Free State [owned by Belgium's King Leopold] for our assault. Atrocities occur wherever the white man with his thirst for gold comes into contact with "a lower people." He is ever there to exploit; he believes that they were created for exploitation. If we want to find cruelty, atrocities, all kinds of frightful maltreatment, we may find them in almost every part of negro Africa. They exist in the French Congo, in German Africa, in Nigeria, even in Uganda. If we insist on finding them, we may find cruelty, dispossession, destruction of life and property, in all these areas. The only ruthless act involving the death of a black native that we really saw was in French territory. If there were any object in doing so, we could write a harrowing story of British iniquity in Africa, but it is unnecesary; every one who stops to think and who reads at all knows the facts. Wherever British trade finds native custom standing in its way, we shall find cruelty. . . .

To me the real wonder is that there are any of the Congo peoples left. Think of the constant drain due to the foreign slave trade, continued from an early date until after the middle of the last century. Think of the continuous losses due to the barbarism of native chiefs and demands of native customs,—to wars, cannabalism, execution, and ordeal. Think of the destruction caused by punitive expeditions,—towns burned, people killed. Think of the drafts made by the public works which the state has been forced to carry out. Think of the multitudes who have died from the diseases of the country and from pestilence introduced by the newcomers. Yet the population really shows signs of great vitality to-day, and the most discouraged missionary hesitates to give a real prediction for the future . . .

Returned from the Congo country and a year and more of contact with the dark natives, I find that a curious and most disagreeable sensation has taken possession of me. I had read often and heard that other peoples find the faces of white men terrifying and cruel. The Chinese, the Japanese, and other peoples of Asia tell the same story. The white man's face is fierce and terrible. His great and prominent nose suggests the beak of some bird of prey. His fierce face causes babes to cry, children to run in terror, grown folk to tremble. I had been always inclined to think that this feeling was individual and trifling; that it was solely due to strangeness and lack of contact. To-day I know better. Contrasted with the other faces of the world, the face of the fair white is terrible, fierce, and cruel. No doubt our intensity of purpose, our firmness and dislike of interference, our manner in walk and action and in speech all add to the effect. However that may be, both in Europe and our own land, after my visit to the blacks I see the cruelty and fierceness of the white man's face as I never would have believed was possible. For the first time I can appreciate fully the feelings of the natives. The white man's face is a dreadful prediction; where the white man goes, he devastates, destroys, depopulates. Witness America, Australia, and Van Dieman's Land [reference to Tasmania, an island off the coast of Australia that was a prison colony].

Source: F. D. Lugard.
Source: James Harvey Robinson & Charles Beard, Ed.

Questions for Contemplation and Discussion

1. What do you think Lugard means when he says "there is among the people (in Africa) a natural inclination to submit to a higher authority"?

2. How would you describe Lugard's value system? Which values are important to him, and which ones are not? Explain.

3. What is the main point of Professor Starr's account of imperialism?

4. Both interpretations of imperialism lack specific examples. What kinds of evidence would make both of these views more persuasive? Be creative.

5. V.I. Lenin, the leader of the Bolshevik Revolution in Russia, argued that imperialism was dangerous because it encouraged the economic exploitation of weaker nations by stronger nations. Some would say that Lenin is right that imperialism exploits, but that the process is proper and natural. What are the strengths and weaknesses of both positions? Explain.

WHAT WERE THE EFFECTS OF THE INDUSTRIAL REVOLUTION?

William Blake on Child Labor[64]

Blake (1757–1827) was an English poet who wrote on religion and politics. He wrote his two most famous collections, *Songs of Innocence* and *Songs of Experience,* in the 1790s.

The Chimney Sweeper

When my mother died I was very young,
And my father sold me while yet my tongue
Could scarcely cry "Weep! weep! weep! weep!"
So your chimneys I sweep, and in soot I sleep.
There's little Tom Dacre, who cried when his head,
That curled like a lamb's back, was shaved; so I said,
"Hush, Tom! never mind it, for, when your head's bare,
You know that the soot cannot spoil your white hair."
And so he was quiet, and that very night,
As Tom was a-sleeping, he had such a sight!—
That thousands of sweepers, Dick, Joe, Ned, and Jack,
Were all of them locked up in coffins of black.
And by came an angel, who had a bright key,
And he opened the coffins, and let them all free;
Then down a green plain, leaping, laughing, they run,
And wash in a river, and shine in the sun.
Then naked and white, all their bags left behind,
They rise upon clouds, and sport in the wind;
And the Angel told Tom, if he'd be a good boy,
He'd have God for his father, and never want joy.
And so Tom awoke, and we rose in the dark,
And got with our bags and our brushes to work.
Though the morning was cold, Tom was happy and warm:
So, if all do their duty, they need not fear harm.

George Howell on Trade Unions[65]

George Howell (1833–1910) was a bricklayer by trade who fought for better working conditions and pay for workers and wrote several books on trade unions. After several defeats, he was finally elected to Parliament in 1886.

In their essence trade unions are voluntary associations of workmen for mutual assistance in securing generally the most favorable conditions of labor. This is their primary and fundamental object and includes all efforts to raise wages or resist a reduction in wages; to diminish the hours of labor or resist attempts to increase the working hours; and to regulate all matters relating to methods of employment or discharge and mode of working. They have other aims also, some of them not less important than those embraced in the foregoing definition, and the sphere of their action extends to almost every detail connected with the labor of workmen and the well-being of their everyday lives. . . .

It must be conceded that every man has a perfect right for himself to fix the price at which he will give his labor, or to refuse to work if the terms offered him do not suit him. So equally has another man the right to accept or refuse either the work or the terms without molestation from his fellow-workmen or from his employer; and that which one has the right to do singly, two or more have the right to do in agreement so long as they both individually and in combination do not interfere by unlawful means with the free action of a third party to refuse or accept the proffered terms. An employer has an equal right to say to

---

Source: William Blake, *"The Chimney Sweeper."*
Source: James Harvey Robinson & Charles Beard, *George Howell on Trade Union.*

the workman, "I will give only a certain price, or employ you on specified conditions; if you don't like it you can go elsewhere." A good deal depends in all cases upon the manner in which these things are said and done; the right, however, remains in theory and in fact.

An individual workman has but little chance of obtaining what he deems a fair day's pay for a fair day's work, or other equitable conditions of labor. His necessities often compel him to accept terms which he feels to be inadequate and even unjust, but the question with him is how to enforce higher wages or better terms. It is true that he wants work; it is equally true that the employer wants his labor, but the latter can afford to wait until another man more needy than the first applies for employment, when perhaps he will be able to obtain the services of the last comer on his own (the employer's) terms. In any case he can but wait and see, and if he cannot procure workmen on the terms he has fixed, there is no great harm done; he can only then agree to give the higher price and secure their labor. With the journeyman it is different; he cannot wait, his means are exhausted and hunger compels him to accept any terms that may be offered.

But if the workmen who are thus seeking employment have mutually agreed not to accept work below a stated price, or only upon specified conditions, and they have with others provided a fund which will enable them to withhold their labor until a better price is offered, they are justified in so doing, and they have by this arrangement placed themselves upon something like an equality with the employer, because they have the means of waiting and bidding for better terms.

Questions for Contemplation and Discussion

1. During the Industrial Revolution, thousands and ultimately millions of people moved from the countryside to the cities. What effects do you think would such a migration have on cities? On the countryside?

2. What does the poem "The Chimney Sweeper" reveal about the role of children in industrialization? Does the poem, from what you can tell, reveal facts as well as the opinion of Blake?

3. In your opinion, is it morally right to have children work? What guidelines should be in place for child labor? Explain.

4. Some say that trade unions gave workers more power than they had by themselves. Would you agree with this, based on George Howell's description?

5. Some historians would say that although there were some social problems associated with industrialization, such as unsanitary cities and child labor, the Industrial Revolution was for the large part and in the long run good for society. From what you know about industrialization, how would you react to that assessment?

WHAT IS NATIONALISM?

Guiseppe Mazzini, An Essay On the Duties of Man Addressed to Workingmen[66]

Mazzini (1805–1872) was one of the intellectual founders of the nation of Italy. Leader of a group called New Italy, he wrote some of the most insightful defenses of nationalism in the nineteenth century.

O, my brothers, love your Country! Our country is our Home, a house God has given us, placing therein a numerous family that loves us, and whom we love; a family with whom we sympathize more readily and whom we understand more quickly than we do others; and which, from its being centred round a given spot, and from the homogeneous nature of its elements, is adapted to a special branch of activity. Our Country is our common workshop, whence the products of our activity are sent forth for the benefit of the whole world; wherein the tools and implements of labour we can most usefully employ are gathered together; nor may we reject them without disobeying the plan of the Almighty, and diminishing our own strength.

In labouring for our own country on the right principle, we labour for Humanity. Our country is the fulcrum of the lever we have to wield for the common good. If we abandon the fulcrum, we run the risk of rendering ourselves useless not only to Humanity but to our country itself. Before men can associate with the nations of which Humanity is composed, they must have a national existence. There is no true association except among equals. It is only through our country that we can have a recognized collective existence. Humanity is a vast army advancing to the conquest of lands unknown, against enemies both powerful and astute. The peoples are the different corps, the divisions of that army. Each of them has its post assigned to it, and its special operation to execute; and the common victory depends upon the exactitude with which those distinct operations are fulfilled.

Disturb not the order of battle. Forsake not the banner given to you by God. Wheresoever you may be, in the centre of whatsoever people circumstances may have placed you, be ever ready to combat for the liberty of that people, should it be necessary, but combat in such wise that the blood you shed may reflect glory, not on yourself alone, but on your country. Say not I, but We. Let each man among you strive to incarnate his country in himself. Let each man among you regard himself as a guarantor, responsible for his fellow-countrymen, and learn so to govern his actions as to cause his country to be loved and respected through him.

Your country is the sign of the Mission God has given you to fulfill towards Humanity. The faculties and forces of all her sons should be associated in the accomplishment of that mission. The true country is a community of free men and equals, bound together in fraternal concord to labour towards a common aim. You are bound to make it and to maintain it such. The country is not an aggregation, but an association. There is, therefore, no true country without a uniform right. There is no true country where the uniformity of that right is violated by the existence of caste privilege and inequality.

Where the activity of a portion of the powers and faculties of the individual is either cancelled or dormant; where there is not a common Principle, recognized, accepted, and developed by all, there is no true Nation, no People; but only a multitude, a fortuitous agglomeration of men whom circumstances have called together and whom circumstances may again divide. In the name of the love you bear your country, you must peacefully but untiringly combat the existence of privilege and inequality in the land that gave you life.

There is but one sole legitimate privilege, the privilege of Genius when it reveals itself united with virtue. But this is a privilege given by God, and when you acknowledge it, and follow its inspiration, you do so freely, exercising your own reason and your own choice. Every privilege which demands submission from you in virtue of power, inheritance, or any other right than the Right common to all, is a usurpation and a tyranny which you are bound to resist and destroy.

Be your country your Temple: God at the summit; a people of equals at the base.

Accept no other formula, no other moral law, if you would not dishonour alike your country and yourselves. Let all secondary laws be but the gradual regulation of your existence by the progressive application of this Supreme law. And in order that they may be such, it is necessary that all of you should aid in framing them. Laws framed only by a single fraction of the citizens, can never, in the very nature of things, be other than the mere expression of the thoughts, aspirations, and desires of that fraction; the representation, not of the country, but of a third or fourth part, of a class or zone of the country.

The laws should be the expression of the universal aspiration, and promote the universal good. They should be a pulsation of the heart of the nation. The entire nation should, either directly or indirectly, legislate.

By yielding up this mission into the hands of a few, you substitute the selfishness of one class for the Country, which is the union of all classes.

Source: Guiseppe Mazzini.

Country is not only a mere zone of territory. The true Country is the Idea to which it gives birth; it is the Thought of love, the sense of communion which unites in one all the sons of that territory.

So long as a single one amongst your brothers has no vote to represent him in the development of the national life, so long as there is one left to vegetate in ignorance where others are educated, so long as a single man, able and willing to work, languishes in poverty through want of work to do, you have no country in the sense in which Country ought to exist—the country of all and for all.

Education, labour, and the franchise, are the three main pillars of the Nation; rest not until you have built them thoroughly up with your own labour and exertions.

Be it yours to evolve the life of your country in loveliness and strength; free from all servile fears or sceptical doubts; maintaining as its basis the People; as its guide the principles of its Religious Faith, logically and energetically applied; its strength, the united strength of all; its aim, the fulfillment of the mission given to it by God.

And so long as you are ready to die for Humanity, the life of your country will be immortal.

Emma Goldman, "Patriotism: A Menace to Liberty"[67]

Emma Goldman (1869–1940) was an anarchist and a communist who strongly criticized government. Born in Lithuania, she moved to the United States and was later deported to Russia.

What is patriotism? Is it love of one's birthplace, the place of childhood's recollections and hopes, dreams and aspirations? Is it the place where, in childlike naivety, we would watch the fleeting clouds, and wonder why we, too, could not run so swiftly? The place where we would count the milliard glittering stars, terror-stricken lest each one "an eye should be," piercing the very depths of our little souls? Is it the place where we would listen to the music of the birds, and long to have wings to fly, even as they, to distant lands? Or the place where we would sit at mother's knee, enraptured by wonderful tales of great deeds and conquests? In short, is it love for the spot, every inch representing dear and precious recollections of a happy, joyous, and playful childhood?

If that were patriotism, few American men of today could be called upon to be patriotic, since the place of play has been turned into factory, mill, and mine, while deafening sounds of machinery have replaced the music of the birds. Nor can we longer hear the tales of great deeds, for the stories our mothers tell today are but those of sorrow, tears, and grief.

What, then, is patriotism? "Patriotism, sir, is the last resort of scoundrels," said Dr.[Samuel] Johnson [great English literary figure from the 1700's]. [Russian author] Leo Tolstoy, the greatest anti-patriot of our times, defines patriotism as the principle that will justify the training of wholesale murderers; a trade that requires better equipment for the exercise of man-killing than the making of such necessities of life as shoes, clothing, and houses; a trade that guarantees better returns and greater glory than that of the average workingman.

Gustave Herve, another great anti-patriot, justly calls patriotism a superstition—one far more injurious, brutal, and inhumane than religion. The superstition of religion originated in man's inability to explain natural phenomena. That is, when primitive man heard thunder or saw the lightning, he could not account for either, and therefore concluded that back of them must be a force greater than himself. Similarly he saw a supernatural force in the rain, and in the various other changes in nature. Patriotism, on the other hand, is a superstition artificially created and maintained through a network of lies and falsehoods; a superstition that robs man of his self-respect and dignity, and increases his arrogance and conceit.

Indeed, conceit, arrogance, and egotism are the essentials of patriotism. Let me illustrate. Patriotism assumes that our globe is divided into little spots, each one surrounded by an iron gate. Those who have had the fortune of being born on some particular spot, consider themselves better, nobler, grander, more intelligent than the living beings inhabiting any other spot. It is, therefore, the duty of everyone living on that chosen spot to fight, kill, and die in the attempt to impose his superiority upon all the others.

The inhabitants of the other spots reason in like manner, of course, with the result that, from early infancy, the mind of the child is poisoned with blood-curdling stories about the Germans, the French, the Italians, Russians, etc. When the child has reached manhood, he is thoroughly saturated with the belief that he is chosen by the Lord himself to defend HIS country against the attack or invasion of any foreigner. It is for that purpose that we are clamoring for a greater army and navy, more battleships and ammunition. It is for that purpose that America has within a short time spent four hundred million dollars. Just think of it—four hundred million dollars taken from the produce of the PEOPLE. For surely it is not the rich who contribute to patriotism. They are cosmopolitans, perfectly at home in every land. We in America know well the truth of this. Are not our rich Americans Frenchmen in France, Germans in Germany, or Englishmen in England? And do they not squander with cosmopolitan grace fortunes coined by American factory children and cotton slaves? Yes, theirs is the patriotism that will make it possible to send messages of condolence to a despot like the Russian Tsar [Russia's leader], when any mishap befalls him, as President Roosevelt did in the name of HIS people, when Sergius was punished by the Russian revolutionists.

It is a patriotism that will assist the arch-murderer, [Porfirio] Diaz [president of Mexico, 1876–1911], in destroying thousands of lives in Mexico, or that will even aid in arresting Mexican revolutionists on American soil and keep them incarcerated in American prisons, without the slightest cause or reason.

But, then, patriotism is not for those who represent wealth and power. It is good enough for the people. It reminds one of the historic wisdom of Frederic the Great, the bosom friend of Voltaire, who said: "Religion is a fraud, but it must be maintained for the masses."

That patriotism is rather a costly institution, no one will doubt after considering the following statistics. The progressive increase of the expenditures for the leading armies and navies of the world during the last quarter of a century is a fact of such gravity as to startle every thoughtful student of economic problems. It may be briefly indicated by dividing the time from 1881 to 1905 into five-year periods, and noting the disbursements of several great nations for army and navy purposes during the first and last of those periods. From the first to the last of the periods noted the expenditures of Great Britain increased from $2,101,848,936 to $4,143,226,885, those of France from $3,324,500,000 to $3,455,109,900, those of Germany from $725,000,200 to $2,700,375,600, those of the United States from $1,275,500,750 to $2,650,900,450, those of Russia from $1,900,975,500 to $5,250,445,100, those of Italy from $1,600,975,750 to $1,755,500,100, and those of Japan from $182,900,500 to $700,925,475.

The military expenditures of each of the nations mentioned increased in each of the five-year periods under review. During the entire interval from 1881 to 1905 Great Britain's outlay for her army increased fourfold, that of the United States was tripled, Russia's was doubled, that of Germany increased 35 per cent., that of France about 15 per cent., and that of Japan nearly 500 per cent. If we compare the expenditures of these nations upon their armies with their total expenditures for all the twenty-five years ending with 1905, the proportion rose as follows:

In Great Britain from 20 per cent. to 37; in the United States from 15 to 23; in France from 16 to 18; in Italy from 12 to 15; in Japan from 12 to 14. On the other hand, it is interesting to note that the proportion in Germany decreased from about 58 per cent. to 25, the decrease being due to the enormous increase in the imperial expenditures for other purposes, the fact being that the army expenditures for the period of 1901–5 were higher than for any five-year period preceding. Statistics show that the countries in which army expenditures are greatest, in proportion to the total national revenues, are Great Britain, the United States, Japan France, and Italy, in the order named.

The showing as to the cost of great navies is equally impressive. During the twenty-five years ending with 1905 naval expenditures increased approximately as follows: Great Britain, 300 per cent.; France 60 per cent.; Germany 600 per cent.; the United States 525 per cent.; Russia 300 per cent.; Italy 250 per cent.; and Japan, 700 per cent. With the exception of Great Britain, the United States spends more for naval purposes than any other nation, and this expenditure bears also a larger proportion to the entire national disbursements than that of any other power. In the period 1881–5, the expenditure for the United States navy was $6.20 out of each $100 appropriated for all national purposes; the amount rose to $6.60 for the next five-year period, to $8.10 for the next, to $11.70 for the next, and to $16.40 for 1901–5. It is morally certain that the outlay for the current period of five years will show a still further increase.

The rising cost of militarism may be still further illustrated by computing it as a per capita tax on population. From the first to the last of the five-year periods taken as the basis for the comparisons here given, it has risen as follows: In Great Britain, from $18.47 to $52.50; in France, from $19.66 to $23.62; in Germany, from $10.17 to $15.51; in the United States, from $5.62 to $13.64; in Russia, from $6.14 to $8.37; in Italy, from $9.59 to $11.24, and in Japan from 86 cents to $3.11.

It is in connection with this rough estimate of cost per capita that the economic burden of militarism is most appreciable. The irresistible conclusion from available data is that the increase of expenditure for army and navy purposes is rapidly surpassing the growth of population in each of the countries considered in the present calculation. In other words, a continuation of the increased demands of militarism threatens each of those nations with a progressive exhaustion both of men and resources.

The awful waste that patriotism necessitates ought to be sufficient to cure the man of even average intelligence from this disease. Yet patriotism demands still more. The people are urged to be patriotic and for that luxury they pay, not only by supporting their "defenders," but even by sacrificing their own children. Patriotism requires allegiance to the flag, which means obedience and readiness to kill father, mother, brother, sister.

The usual contention is that we need a standing army to protect the country from foreign invasion. Every intelligent man and woman knows, however, that this is a myth maintained to frighten and coerce the foolish. The governments of the world, knowing each other's interests, do not invade each other. They have learned that they can gain much more by international arbitration of disputes than by war and conquest. Indeed, as [historian and philosopher Thomas] Carlyle said, "War is a quarrel between two thieves too cowardly to fight their own battle; therefore they take boys from one village and another village; stick them into uniforms, equip them with guns, and let them loose like wild beasts against each other."

It does not require much wisdom to trace every war back to a similar cause. Let us take our own Spanish-American war, supposedly a great and patriotic event in the history of the United States. How our hearts burned with indignation against the atrocious Spaniards! True, our indignation did not flare up spontaneously. It was nurtured by months of newspaper agitation, and long after Butcher Weyler had killed off many noble Cubans and outraged many Cuban women [General Valeriano Weyler crushed a rebellion in Cuba, which at the time was a Spanish possession. He imprisoned hundreds of thousands of Cubans in concentration camps. His abuse galvanized the United States effort to free Cuba from Spanish rule]. Still, in justice to the American Nation be it said, it did grow indignant and was willing to fight, and that it fought bravely. But when the smoke was over, the dead buried, and the cost of the war came back to the people in an increase in the price of commodities and rent— that is, when we sobered up from our patriotic spree—it suddenly dawned on us that the cause of the Spanish-American war was the consideration of the price of sugar; or, to be more explicit, that the lives, blood, and money of the American people were used to protect the interests of American capitalists, which were threatened by the Spanish government [Goldman is referring to the Spanish-American War (1898)]. That this is not an exaggeration, but is based on absolute facts and figures, is best proven by the attitude of the American government to Cuban labor. When Cuba was firmly in the clutches of the United States, the very soldiers sent to liberate Cuba were ordered to shoot Cuban workingmen during the great cigarmakers' strike, which took place shortly after the war.

Nor do we stand alone in waging war for such causes. The curtain is beginning to be lifted on the motives of the terrible Russo-Japanese war, which cost so much blood and tears. And we see again that back of the fierce Moloch of war stands the still fiercer god of Commercialism. Kuropatkin, the Russian Minister of War during the Russo-Japanese struggle, has revealed the true secret behind the latter. The Tsar and his Grand Dukes, having invested money in Corean [Korean] concessions, the war was forced for the sole purpose of speedily accumulating large fortunes.

The contention that a standing army and navy is the best security of peace is about as logical as the claim that the most peaceful citizen is he who goes about heavily armed. The experience of every-day life fully proves that the armed individual is invariably anxious to try his strength. The same is historically true of governments. Really peaceful countries do not waste life and energy in war preparations, with the result that peace is maintained.

However, the clamor for an increased army and navy is not due to any foreign danger. It is owing to the dread of the growing discontent of the masses and of the international spirit among the workers. It is to meet the internal enemy that the Powers of various countries are preparing themselves; an enemy, who, once awakened to consciousness, will prove more dangerous than any foreign invader.

The powers that have for centuries been engaged in enslaving the masses have made a thorough study of their psychology. They know that the people at large are like children whose despair, sorrow, and tears can be turned into joy with a little toy. And the more gorgeously the toy is dressed, the louder the colors, the more it will appeal to the million-headed child . . .

We Americans claim to be a peace-loving people. We hate bloodshed; we are opposed to violence. Yet we go into spasms of joy over the possibility of projecting dynamite bombs from flying machines upon helpless citizens. We are ready to hang, electrocute, or lynch anyone, who, from economic necessity, will risk his own life in the attempt upon that of some industrial magnate. Yet our hearts swell with pride at the thought that America is becoming the most powerful nation on earth, and that it will eventually plant her iron foot on the necks of all other nations.

Such is the logic of patriotism.

Considering the evil results that patriotism is fraught with for the average man, it is as nothing compared with the insult and injury that patriotism heaps upon the soldier himself,—that poor, deluded victim of superstition and ignorance. He, the savior of his country, the protector of his nation,—what has patriotism in store for him? A life of slavish submission, vice, and perversion, during peace; a life of danger, exposure, and death, during war . . .

Questions for Contemplation and Discussion

1. What is Mazzini's main point, or thesis?

2. Do you agree with Mazzini's contention that "education, labor, and the franchise" are three main pillars of the nation.

3. In Goldman's view, in what ways can patriotism be dangerous?

4. Goldman cites statistics to support her opinion? What exactly does she cite? Does her use of statistics strengthen your argument (in other words, are you more impressed with her reasoning because she referred to statistics)?

5. Is it possible for a person to be too patriotic? Is it ever right for citizens to criticize and even condemn their own political leaders?

WHAT IS COMMUNISM?

Karl Marx and Friedrich Engels, The Communist Manifesto[68]

Karl Marx (1818–1883) and Frederick Engels (1820–1895) were the leading theoreticians of modern Communism. Their ideas were instrumental in the establishment of Communism in Russia, China, and elsewhere.

The history of all hitherto existing society is the history of class struggles. In the earlier epochs we find almost everywhere a complicated organization of society into various orders. In ancient Rome we have patricians, knights, plebeians, slaves; in the Middle Ages, feudal lords, vassals, guild masters, journeymen, apprentices, serfs.

The modern bourgeois [that class of individuals that are not born into wealth but have become wealthy through investment] society, which has sprung from the ruins of feudal society, has not done away with class antagonisms. It has only established new classes, new conditions of oppression, new forms of struggle in place of the old ones. Our epoch, the epoch of the bourgeois, possesses, however, this distinctive feature: it has simplified the class antagonisms. Society as a whole is more and more splitting up into two great hostile camps, into two great classes directly facing each other,—Bourgeoisie and Proletariat.

The discovery of America, the rounding of the Cape [the southern tip of South Africa, which was rounded by explorer Vasco de Gama on his way to India], opened up fresh fields for the rising bourgeoisie. The East Indian and Chinese markets, the colonization of America, gave to commerce, navigation, and industry an impulse never before known. The feudal system of industry, under which industrial production was monopolized by close guilds, now no longer sufficed for the growing demands of the new markets. The manufacturing system (on a small scale) took its place. The guild masters were pushed to one side by the manufacturing middle class; division of labor between the different corporate guilds vanished in the face of the division of labor in each single workshop.

Meantime the markets kept ever growing, the demand ever increasing. Production by hand no longer sufficed. Thereupon steam and machinery revolutionized industrial production. The place of handwork was taken by that giant, Modern Industry; the place of the industrial middle class, by industrial millionaires, the leaders of whole industrial armies,—the modern bourgeoisie. We see, therefore, how the modern bourgeoisie is itself the product of a long course of development, of a series of revolutions in the modes of production and of exchange.

The bourgeoisie, wherever it has got the upper hand, has put an end to all feudal; patriarchal, idyllic relations. It has pitilessly torn asunder the motley feudal ties that bound man to his "natural superiors," and has left no other tie between man and man than naked self-interest, callous "cash payment." It has drowned the heavenly ecstasies of religion, of chivalrous enthusiasm, of philistine sentimentalism, in the icy water of selfish business calculation. The bourgeoisie has stripped of its halo every occupation hitherto honored and looked up to with reverent awe. It has converted the physician, the lawyer, the priest, the poet, the man of science, into its paid wage laborers.

Constant revolutionizing of production, uninterrupted disturbance of all social conditions, everlasting uncertainty and agitation, distinguish the bourgeois epoch from all earlier periods. All fixed relations, with their ancient and venerable prejudices and opinions, are swept away; all new-formed ones become antiquated before they can solidify. All that is holy is profaned, and man is at last compelled to face with clear vision and without illusion his real conditions of life and his relations with his fellow-men.

The bourgeoisie, by the rapid spread of all instruments of production, by the immensely facilitated means of communication, draws even the most barbarous peoples into civilization. The low prices of its commodities are the heavy artillery with which it batters down all Chinese walls, with which it softens the barbarians' intensely obstinate hatred of foreigners. It compels all nations, on pain of extinction, to adopt the bourgeois mode of production; it forces them to introduce what it calls "civilization" into their midst, i.e. to become bourgeois themselves. In one word, it creates a world after its own image.

The bourgeoisie has subjected the country to the rule of the towns. It has created enormous cities, has greatly increased the urban population as compared with the rural, and has thus rescued a considerable part of the population from the stupidity of rural life. Just as it has made the country dependent on the towns, so it has made barbarian and semibarbarian countries dependent on the civilized ones, nations of peasants on nations of bourgeoisie, the East on the West.

The bourgeoisie, during its rule of scarce one hundred years, has created more colossal productive forces than have all preceding generations together. Subjection of Nature's forces to man, machinery, the application of chemistry to industry and agriculture, steam navigation, railways, electric telegraphs, clearing of whole continents for cultivation,—what earlier century had even a presentiment that such productive forces slumbered in the lap of social labor?

Source: Karl Marx & Friedrich Engels.

The arms with which the bourgeoisie felled feudalism to the ground are now turned against the bourgeoisie itself. It has not only forged the weapons for self-destruction; it has also called into existence the men who are to wield those weapons,—the modern working class,—the proletarians. In proportion as the bourgeoisie, i.e. capital, is developed, in the same proportion is the proletariat, i.e. the modern working class, developed, —a class of laborers, who live only so long as they find work, and who find work only so long as their labor increases capital. These laborers, who must sell themselves, are a commodity, like every other article of commerce, and are consequently exposed to all the vicissitudes of competition, to all the fluctuations of the market.

Owing to the extensive use of machinery and to division of labor, the work of the proletarians [working class people] has lost all individual character, and, consequently, all charm for the workman. He becomes an appendage of the machine, and it is only the most simple, most monotonous, and most easily acquired knack that is required of him.

Modern industry has converted the little workshop of the patriarchal master into the great factory of the industrial capitalist. Masses of laborers, crowded into the factory, are organized like soldiers. Not only are they slaves of the bourgeois class, and of the bourgeois State; they are daily and hourly enslaved by the machine, by the overseer, and, above all, by the individual bourgeois manufacturer himself. The less skill and exertion of strength is implied in manual labor, in other words, the more modern industry becomes developed, the more is the labor of men superseded by that of women.

But with the development of industry the proletariat not only increases in number; it becomes concentrated in greater masses, its strength grows, and it feels that strength more. The unceasing improvement of machinery, ever more rapidly developing, makes their livelihood more and more precarious; the collisions between individual workmen and individual bourgeois take more and more the character of collisions between two classes. Thereupon the workers begin to form combinations (trades unions) against the bourgeoisie; they club together in order to keep up the rate of wages. Here and there the contest breaks out into riots.

Just as, in an earlier period, a section of the nobility went over to the bourgeoisie, so now a portion of the bourgeoisie goes over to the proletariat, and, in particular, that portion of the bourgeois idealists who have raised themselves to the point of comprehending theoretically the historical movement as a whole.

All previous historical movements were movements of minorities, or in the interest of minorities. The proletarian movement is the self-conscious, independent movement of the immense majority. The proletariat, the lowest stratum of our present society, cannot stir, cannot raise itself without the whole superincumbent strata of official society being blown into the air.

It has become evident that the bourgeoisie is unfit any longer to be the ruling class in society and to impose its conditions of existence upon it. It is unfit to rule because it is incompetent to assure an existence to its slave in his slavery, because it cannot prevent his sinking into such a state that it has to feed him instead of being fed by him. Society can no longer live under this bourgeoisie; in other words, its existence is no longer compatible with society.

The essential condition for the existence and sway of the bourgeois class is the creation and increase of capital; the condition for capital is wage labor. Wage labor rests exclusively on competition between the laborers. The advance of industry, whose involuntary promoter is the bourgeoisie, replaces the isolation of the laborers, due to competition, by their revolutionary combination, due to association. The development of modern industry, therefore, cuts from under its feet the very foundation of capitalist production and distribution of wealth. What the bourgeoisie therefore produces, above all, are its own gravediggers. Its fall and the victory of the proletariat are inevitable.

Vladmir Ilyich Ulyanov, or Lenin, What is to be Done?[69]

Vladmir Lenin (1870–1924) was the leader of the Bolshevik Party, which seized control of Russia in 1917 and established the Soviet Union in 1922.

. . . The organisation of the revolutionaries must consist first and foremost of people who make revolutionary activity their profession (for which reason I speak of the organisation of *revolutionaries*, meaning revolutionary Social-Democrats). In view of this common characteristic of the members of such an organisation, *all distinctions as between workers and intellectuals,* not to speak of distinctions of trade and profession, in both categories, *must be effaced.*

. . . Our very first and most pressing duty is to help to train working-class revolutionaries who will be on the same level *in regard to Party activity* as the revolutionaries from amongst the intellectuals (we emphasise the words "in regard to Party activity", for, although necessary, it is neither so easy nor so pressingly necessary to bring the workers up to the level of intellectuals in other respects). Attention, therefore, must be devoted *principally* to *raising* the workers to the level of revolutionaries . . .

Source: From *On The Intelligentsia* by V. I. Lenin (Moscow: Progress Publishers; 1983).

. . . As the spontaneous rise of their movement becomes broader and deeper, the working-class masses promote from their ranks not only an increasing number of talented agitators, but also talented organisers, propagandists, and "practical workers" in the best sense of the term (of whom there are so few among our intellectuals who, for the most part, in the Russian manner, are somewhat careless and sluggish in their habits). When we have forces of specially trained worker-revolutionaries who have gone through extensive preparation (and, of course, revolutionaries "of all arms of the service"), no political police in the world will then be able to contend with them, for these forces, boundlessly devoted to the revolution, will enjoy the boundless confidence of the widest masses of the workers. We are directly *to blame* for doing too little to "stimulate" the workers to take this path, common to them and to the "intellectuals", of professional revolutionary training, and for all too often dragging them back by our silly speeches about what is "accessible" to the masses of the workers, to the "average workers", etc.

Mao Zedong, Speech, June 30, 1949[70]

Mao Zedong (1893–1976), sometimes spelled Tse-Tung, was the leader of the Chinese Communist Party from 1935 to his death. He spearheaded the revolution that established the People's Republic of China in 1949.

The Chinese people will win final victory in the great War of Liberation. Even our enemy no longer doubts the outcome. . .

In the long period of more than twenty years from the counter-revolutionary coup d'état of April 12, 1927 down to the present day, have not the Chinese reactionaries headed by Chiang Kai-shek [1887–1975, anti-communist leader of the Republic of China. Ruled from Taiwan, since the communists had taken over China itself] and his ilk given proof enough that they are a gang of blood-stained executioners who slaughter people without blinking? Have they not given proof enough that they are a band of professional traitors and the running dogs of imperialism? Think it over, everybody! . . .

We hold that the Chinese people's revolutionary camp must expanded and must embrace all who are willing to join the revolutionary cause at the present stage. The Chinese people's revolution needs a main force and also needs allies, for an army without allies cannot defeat the enemy. The Chinese people, now at the high tide of revolution, need friends and they should remember their friends and not forget them. In China there are undoubtedly many friends faithful to the people's revolutionary cause, who try to protect the people's interests and are opposed to protecting the enemy's interests, and undoubtedly none of these friends should be forgotten or cold-shouldered. Also, we hold that we must consolidate the Chinese people's revolutionary camp and not allow bad elements to sneak in or wrong views to prevail. Besides keeping their friends in mind, the Chinese people, now at the high tide of revolution, should also keep their enemies and the friends of their enemies firmly in mind. As we said above, since the enemy is cunningly using the method of "peace" and the method of sneaking into the revolutionary camp to preserve and strengthen his position, whereas the fundamental interests of the people demand that all reactionary forces be destroyed thoroughly and that the aggressive forces of U.S. imperialism be driven out of China, those who advise the people to take pity on the enemy and preserve the forces of reaction are not friends of the people, but friends of the enemy.

Theodore White, Fire in the Ashes[71]

Theodore White (1915–1986) was a journalist who covered politics. He was the author of a series of books entitled *The Making of the President*. He won a Pulitzer prize in 1962.

Communism—The Challenge

Americans are so frightened by the evil in communism that they fail to see that the greatest danger is not the evil but the attraction in it. Only Americans live in a society in which communism can seduce no healthy mind. Most of our senior Allies and the myriadman countries who live outside our Alliance are made of people who stand transfixed by fear of communism and its sinister charm at the same time.

The magic appeal in the Communist faith is simple. It is the belief that pure logic applied to human affairs is enough to change the world and cure it of all its human miseries. It is buttressed by the belief that the processes of history are governed by certain "scientific" laws, which automatically guarantee the triumph of communism when the situation is ripe, if only its protestants have the courage to strike and act.

This simple credo carries an almost irresistible attraction to two kinds of people everywhere in the world: first, to small coteries of able and ambitious young men hungry for the ecstasy of leadership, and, secondly, to larger masses of miserable ignorant people who have just begun to hope.

Source: From *Selected Military Writings of Mao Tse-Tung* (Peking: Foreign Languages Press; 1967).
Source: From *Fire in the Ashes* by Theodore H. White. Copyright © 1953 by Theodore H. White. Reprinted by permission.

To both these schools of converts, the fatal flaw in the Communist faith is neither apparent nor important. This fatal flaw is embedded in the nature of human beings whenever they gather politically. Human beings tend to be illogical. The logic of which communism boasts is never certain, therefore, of success in any political operation unless simultaneously it imposes so rigid a discipline as to make ordinary people mere bodies in the sequence of their masters' planning. Logic cannot succeed if its premises are to be shaken over and over again by vagrant human emotions allowed freely to express themselves in all their passion and frailty. Any political organization which sets out to be totally logical thus calls for total discipline; total discipline inevitably requires police, and police bring terror.

But the weakness of communism lies less in the calculated immorality of terror than in the inevitable internal appetite of the discipline. The discipline feeds on itself; it shrinks the area of discussion and decision into ever narrower, ever tighter, ever more cramped circles. Fewer and fewer men have less and less access to the raw facts which are necessary for wise judgment. The discipline they control and impose inevitably sneaks back to weaken them, to blind or deafen them into stupidity and error.

To those who come to communism out of ambition or out of misguided intelligence, this flaw is not immediately apparent. Each of this type of convert cherishes the illusion until too late that the ever-shrinking circle of discipline will leave him safe at its center of creative leadership, rather than crushed and tortured as discipline contracts about his own soft human body. To the second category of converts, those who come to it out of hunger and ignorance, this flaw in communism (even if it could be explained to them) seems unimportant. They have always been excluded from decision and control over their own lives. Communism promises them simply "more"; they are ready to believe. The hungrier and more ignorant they are, the more difficult it is to explain to them that their own hopes and welfare are directly dependent on the freedom of creative minds, with which they are unfamiliar, to think independently of all discipline.

To the Western world, so challenged by communism, this flaw in the adversary presents a grotesque problem. Communism's prison-logical system of human organization grows in strength decade by decade even as its leadership becomes less and less capable of wise and sensible decision. For all its dynamism and strength, the Communist world falls into blunders with increasing frequency, blunders which are only rectified by great wrenchings of policy that shake the world with disaster. To deal with communism, one must recognize both its strength and its blunders clearly.

Communist strength today is radiant with power at two levels. It possesses, in Russia, a base of physical force adorned with every instrument of compulsion and combat, still in flood tide of expansion, carried on by the momentum of those warped geniuses who made the Russian revolution. It also possesses, still, the fire and power of a missionary faith, seducing men's minds everywhere with the simplicity of its logic. Its achievements and physical strength within its Russian base marry with its evangelical kinetic outside Russia to give it the sweep and appearance of an irresistible tide. Yet, by its own internal laws, as its area of control and success spreads, its discipline must become ever tighter and ever more constricting. And this process, extending and deepening, not only on the periphery of satellite and associate states, but ever more ruthlessly at the center in Moscow, has already begun to addle the thinking, fuddle the judgment, provoke the unrest, and produce those inevitable blunders which give the Western world its opportunities.

Questions for Contemplation and Discussion

1. Marx writes that there are two great classes in society: bourgeoisie and proletariat. Is this possibly an example of an either/or fallacy? What questions should be asked in order to question Marx's assumption? Explain.

2. In Marx's view, what were some problems with the economy and society of his day? Do his criticisms, in your opinion, have relevance today? Explain.

3. What was Lenin's vision for the party? Do you think all workers would have agreed with his philosophy? Explain.

4. What is Mao's main message to the Chinese people? How does he try to persuade his readers? Explain.

5. In White's view what is the "fatal flaw" of Communism? Does the fact that White was not a communist influence your opinion of White's analysis? Would his argument have been more persuasive if White had been writing as a former communist? Explain.

WHAT DOES IT MEAN TO LIVE UNDER A TOTALITARIAN REGIME?

The Mind of a Nazi: Adolf Eichmann[72]

Adolf Eichmann (1906–1962) was a leading Nazi who helped plan out the Holocaust. Sometimes he has been referred to as the Third Reich's "Chief Executioner." After years on the run, he was captured, placed on trial, convicted, and executed by hanging. To this day he is the only person ever executed in the modern country of Israel. Hannah Arendt (1906–1975) was a historian/philosopher who wrote many books, including *On Totalitarianism*.

In Jerusalem, confronted with documentary proof of his extraordinary loyalty to Hitler and the Führer's order, Eichmann tried a number of times to explain that during the Third Reich "the Führer's words had the force of law" (*Führerworte haben Gesetzeskraft*), which meant, among other things, that if the order came directly from Hitler it did not have to be in writing. He tried to explain that this was why he had never asked for a written order from Hitler (no such document relating to the Final Solution has ever been found; probably it never existed), but had demanded to see a written order from Himmler. To be sure, this was a fantastic state of affairs, and whole libraries of very "learned" juridical comment have been written, all demonstrating that the Führer's *words,* his oral pronouncements, were the basic law of the land. Within this "legal" framework, every order contrary in letter or spirit to a word spoken by Hitler was, by definition, unlawful. Eichmann's position, therefore, showed a most unpleasant resemblance to that of the often-cited soldier who, acting in a normal legal framework, refuses to carry out orders that run counter to his ordinary experience of lawfulness and hence can be recognized by him as criminal. The extensive literature on the subject usually supports its case with the common equivocal meaning of the word "law," which in this context means sometimes the law of the land—that is, posited, positive law—and sometimes the law that supposedly speaks in all men's hearts with an identical voice. Practically speaking, however, orders to be disobeyed must be "manifestly unlawful" and unlawfulness must "fly like a black flag above [them] as a warning reading: 'Prohibited!' "—as the judgment pointed out. And in a criminal regime this "black flag" with its "warning sign" flies as "manifestly" above what normally is a lawful order—for instance, not to kill innocent people just because they happen to be Jews—as it flies above a criminal order under normal circumstances. To fall back on an unequivocal voice of conscience—or, in the even vaguer language of the jurists, on a "general sentiment of humanity" (Oppenheim-Lauterpacht in *International Law,* 1952)—not only begs the question, it signifies a deliberate refusal to take notice of the central moral, legal, and political phenomena of our century.

To be sure, it was not merely Eichmann's conviction that Himmler was now giving "criminal" orders that determined his actions. But the personal element undoubtedly involved was not fanaticism, it was his genuine, "boundless and immoderate admiration for Hitler" (as one of the defense witnesses called it)—for the man who had made it "from lance corporal to Chancellor of the Reich." It would be idle to try to figure out which was stronger in him, his admiration for Hitler or his determination to remain a law-abiding citizen of the Third Reich when Germany was already in ruins. Both motives came into play once more during the last days of the war, when he was in Berlin and saw with violent indignation how everybody around him was sensibly enough getting himself fixed up with forged papers before the arrival of the Russians or the Americans. A few weeks later, Eichmann, too, began to travel under an assumed name, but by then Hitler was dead, and the "law of the land" was no longer in existence, and he, as he pointed out, was no longer bound by his oath. For the oath taken by the members of the S.S. differed from the military oath sworn by the soldiers in that it bound them only to Hitler, not to Germany.

The case of the conscience of Adolf Eichmann, which is admittedly complicated but is by no means unique, is scarcely comparable to the case of the German generals, one of whom, when asked at Nuremberg [site of trials of many leading Nazis in 1946], "How was it possible that all you honorable generals could continue to serve a murderer with such unquestioning loyalty?," replied that it was "not the task of a soldier to act as judge over his supreme commander. Let history do that or God in heaven." (Thus General Alfred Jodl, hanged at Nuremberg.) Eichmann, much less intelligent and without any education to speak of, at least dimly realized that it was not an order but a law which had turned them all into criminals. The distinction between an order and the Führer's word was that the latter's validity was not limited in time and space, which is the outstanding characteristic of the former. This is also the true reason why the Führer's order for the Final Solution was followed by a huge shower of regulations and directives, all drafted by expert lawyers and legal advisers, not by mere administrators; this order, in contrast to ordinary orders, was treated as a law. Needless to add, the resulting legal paraphernalia, far from being a mere symptom of German pedantry or thoroughness, served most effectively to give the whole business its outward appearance of legality.

Source: From *Eichmann in Jersusalem* by Hannah Arendt, copyright © 1963, 1964 by Hannah Arendt, copyright renewed © 1991, 1992 by Lotte Kohler. Used by permission of Viking Penguin, a division of Penguin Group (USA), Inc.

And just as the law in civilized countries assumes that the voice of conscience tells everybody "Thou shalt not kill," even though man's natural desires and inclinations may at times be murderous, so the law of Hitler's land demanded that the voice of conscience tell everybody: "Thou shalt kill," although the organizers of the massacres knew full well that murder is against the normal desires and inclinations of most people. Evil in the Third Reich had lost the quality by which most people recognize it—the quality of temptation. Many Germans and many Nazis, probably an overwhelming majority of them, must have been tempted *not* to murder, *not* to rob, *not* to let their neighbors go off to their doom (for that the Jews were transported to their doom they knew, of course, even though many of them may not have known the gruesome details), and not to become accomplices in all these crimes by benefiting from them. But, God knows, they had learned how to resist temptation. . .

The trouble with Eichmann was precisely that so many were like him, and that the many were neither perverted nor sadistic, that they were, and still are, terribly and terrifyingly normal. From the viewpoint of our legal institutions and of our moral standards of judgment, this normality was much more terrifying than all the atrocities put together, for it implied—as had been said at Nuremberg over and over again by the defendants and their counsels—that this new type of criminal, who is in actual fact *hostis generis humani*, commits his crimes under circumstances that make it well-nigh impossible for him to know or to feel that he is doing wrong.

Cult of Personality. "A Hymn to Stalin"[73]

Joseph Stalin (1879–1953), the subject of this poem, was one of the leaders of the Bolshevik Party, general secretary of the Soviet Union and the most powerful person in the country for the last twenty-five years of his life. He was responsible for the deaths of tens of millions of Soviet citizens. To this day he is regarded as one of the most ruthless leaders in history.

Thank you, Stalin. Thank you because I am joyful. Thank you because I am well. Centuries will pass, and the generations still to come will regard us as the happiest of mortals, as the most fortunate of men, because we lived in the century of centuries, because we were privileged to see Stalin, our inspired leader.

The men of all ages will call on thy name, which is strong, beautiful, wise and marvellous. Thy name is engraven on every factory, every machine, every place on the earth, and in the hearts of all men.

> O great Stalin, O leader of the peoples,
> Thou who broughtest man to birth.
> Thou who fructifiest the earth,
> Thou who restorest to centuries,
> Thou who makest bloom the spring,
> Thou who makest vibrate the musical chords . . .
> Thou, splendour of my spring, O Thou,
> Sun reflected by millions of hearts . . .

Source: A. O. Avdienko.

Questions for Contemplation and Discussion

1. What is Arendt's main conclusion about Eichmann? How is her conclusion applicable today?

2. Although Eichmann said that he was following the orders of his Nazi superiors, he was executed. Do you agree with the verdict? Are soldiers always obligated to obey their superiors, even if the soldiers believe they are being asked to break moral laws?

3. Sometimes the phrase "cult of personality" is used to describe the praise of a leader which has become too intense. At the same time, it is expected that leaders should be admired and supported. Would you agree that the author of the "Hymn to Stalin" has crossed the line into cult of personality? Explain by making reference to words and phrases in the hymn.

WAS IT RIGHT FOR THE UNITED STATES TO DROP THE ATOMIC BOMB ON JAPAN DURING WORLD WAR II?

Gar Alperovitz, The Decision to Use the Atomic Bomb and the Architecture of an American Myth[74]

Professor Gar Alperovitz is Lionel R. Bauman Professor of Political Economy at the University of Maryland, College Park, and President of the National Center for Economic and Security Alternatives.

Repeated polls over the years have shown that the vast majority of Americans have raised very few questions about the bombing of Hiroshima and Nagasaki. The conventional wisdom that the atomic bomb saved hundreds of thousands—perhaps a million—lives persists. . .

Quite simply, it is not true that the atomic bomb was used because it was the only way to save the "hundreds of thousands" or "millions" of lives as was subsequently claimed. The readily available options were to modify the surrender terms and/or await the shock of the Russian attack. Three months remained before a November Kyushu landing could take place even in theory; there were six or seven months before the spring invasion of Honshu could begin under the existing planning assumptions . . .

However, the evidence—especially from the MAGIC intercepts, the records of the Joint Chiefs of Staff, the 1945 intelligence studies, numerous statements by military leaders close to the decision process, and the Leahy, Stimson, Forrestal, McCloy, and Brown diaries—allows us to go beyond this. It is impossible to peer into the hearts and minds of men fifty years after the fact. Nevertheless, although matters of nuance and degree can be endlessly debated, it is quite clear that alternatives to using the bomb existed—and that the president and his advisers were aware of them. . .

Modern evidence—reinforced, again, by the information which has been discovered in the course of research for this book—suggests not only that the president and Byrnes knew Japan was on the verge of surrender, but that once the new weapon had been successfully tested, rushing to end the war before an expected mid-August Red Army attack was indisputably a major concern. . .

It is sometimes held that no real "decision" to use the atomic bomb ever took place, that the "momentum" of the war (or of bureaucracy, etc.) produced the bombings—and that, besides, there is no surviving contemporaneous evidence that anyone directly challenged the decision.

As a historian who once subscribed to—indeed, helped launch—one version of the "no-decision," momentum theory, I know the temptation this view offers: Among other things, if there was no human decision, no burden of judgment must be borne—and no human responsibility is to be assigned. . .

The truth is that at least three very clear and explicit decisions (and probably more) were made which set the terms of reference for the bomb's subsequent seemingly "inevitable" use. Indeed, once they were made, they so tightly framed the remaining issues as to make it all but impossible thereafter to oppose the bombings.

The first decision involved rejection of the recommendation that to offer any meaningful possibility of surrender a statement to Japan would have to allow enough time for the development of a serious response. . .

The second and more fundamental choice was the decision not to offer Japan assurances for the Emperor. Once this decision had been made—and the Japanese were allowed to believe the Emperor might be removed and possibly hanged as a war criminal—it was obvious to all concerned that the fighting would continue. . .

The third fundamental choice has now also been fully documented. It was the decision not to test the impact of the Russian declaration of war—indeed, to weaken the military challenge posed to Japan by attempting to put off an event which all understood would have extraordinary impact. This decision, too, was made at the political level. . .

In the decades since World War II, writers who have defended the bombings have repeatedly pointed to the hard-line Japanese army faction which was opposed to surrender and which was clearly preparing to defend against a possible invasion. Some have even offered dramatic, detailed descriptions of battles which in theory might possibly have been fought. . .

In the first place it is an obvious non sequitur to argue from the fact that preparations were going forward that what was "planned" was also what, in fact, was likely to happen. The U.S. military, after all, was also engaged in preparations and plans for an invasion. It is quite clear that the Japanese both wished to be prepared for an invasion and wanted to make sure U.S. officials believed they would fight to the death if invaded.

Much more important, no knowledgeable historian would dispute the idea that so long as the Emperor's position was in doubt—as it was throughout the entire period—the Japanese would likely have resisted to the end. The army faction held all

---

Source: From *The Decision to Use The Atomic Bomb* by Gar Alperovitz, copyright © 1995 by Gar Alperovitz. Used by permission of Alfred A. Knopf, a division of Random House, Inc.

the cards so long as the Emperor was threatened. And so long as the Russians were neutral they could also argue it was not totally insane to continue the war.

Nor is it surprising that after the war some Japanese leaders honestly recalled that they had planned to fight on. That is, in fact, what they had expected to do, given that U.S. policy continued to threaten the Emperor. This was what the fundamental debate was all about inside the U.S. government—and precisely why American military leaders urged the president to offer Japan assurances for the Emperor. . .

We are not the only people who have struggled with questions of this nature about the past. None have found them easy. We recognize quite easily, however, that it is important for modern Germans, Japanese, Russians, and others—people who themselves also had little to do with decisions made by earlier leaders—to acknowledge their past, to learn from it, even to make reparation. Some Germans today have come to admit the (far greater) evils of their past. The Japanese have a long way to go but many also have begun to realize some of the all too many outrages committed during World War II. Russians—recently even in the case of the Katyn massacres [1940 massacre of Polish officers by the Soviet Union]—have sometimes acknowledged crimes from the past committed by another generation. Perhaps one day we Americans will come to terms with Hiroshima.

President Harry S. Truman[75]

Harry S. Truman (1884–1972) was the thirty-third president of the United States. He became president after President Franklin Delano Roosevelt died in office in 1945. Truman made the critical decision to drop the atomic bomb in Japan.

December 12, 1946

My Dear Mr. Bohnen:

I appreciated very much your letter of December second and thank you for suggesting to Mr. Mayer of M.G.M. that I become a movie star. In the first place I haven't the talent to be a movie star and, in the second place, I am sure you will do the part creditably.

The only objection to the film, as it was, was that it appeared to have been a snap judgment program. It was anything but that—the use of the atomic bomb was deliberated for long hours and many days and weeks, and it was discussed with the Secretary of State, the Secretary of War, the Secretary of the Navy and the General Staff of the Allied Armies, as well as with Mr. Churchill and Mr. Attlee.

When it was finally demonstrated in New Mexico that the operation of the bomb was a successful one, it was decided to give the Japanese ample warning before the bomb was dropped. I have no qualms about it whatever for the simple reason that it was believed the dropping of not more than two of these bombs would bring the war to a close. The Japanese in their conduct of the war had been vicious and cruel savages and I came to the conclusion that if two hundred and fifty thousand young Americans could be saved from slaughter the bomb should be dropped, and it was.

A survey was made and the cities on which the bombs were dropped were those which were devoted almost exclusively to the manufacture of ammunition and weapons of destruction.

As I said before, the only objection to the film was that I was made to appear as if no consideration had been given to the effects or the result of dropping the bomb—that is an absolutely wrong impression.

Sincerely yours,

HARRY S. TRUMAN

Mr. Boman Bohnen
10537 Valley Spring Lane
North Hollywood, California

Source: Letter to Mr. Bohnen.

Questions for Contemplation and Discussion

1. What is Alperovitz's thesis, or main point?

2. What kinds of evidence does Alperovitz cite to support his argument?

3. Alperovitz's thesis is controversial, to be sure. If a history professor born after World War Two agreed with his thesis, and a World War Two veteran without any formal history training disagreed with it, who do you think would be more credible? What would each have to do to persuade you that their view of the Alperovitz thesis was correct?

4. Does President Truman's letter contain information that effectively refutes Alperovitz? Would Truman have agreed at all with Alperovitz? Explain.

5. How valuable is Truman's letter as historical evidence? What kind of attitude should historians bring when relying on letters and other such documents?

6. Some would say that a former president's memoirs, when they are being considered for their value as historical evidence, should be approached skeptically. Do you agree?

7. Is it appropriate for anyone, even a historian, to criticize a decision made in the heat of the moment, such as during a war? Explain.

SHOULD THE UNITED STATES HELP END COMMUNISM IN VIETNAM?[76]

The Cold War between the United States and the Soviet Union lasted from the end of World War II in 1945 to the fall of the Soviet Union in 1991. As an international conflict the Cold War developed over a period of time. Relations between the United States and the Soviet Union had been on friendly terms at various times during the history of the two nations. But, in the early 1950s the U. S. became concerned with Soviet expansionism in Eastern Europe and, that this expansionism would come to challenge U. S. world dominance. Both countries had expansionist backgrounds. The Soviet Union had expanded over land and U. S. expansion included westward expansion on the North American continent and world wide expansion.

U. S. strategy to contain the Soviet Union ultimately led to U.S. rearmament and military conflict between the two countries in various parts of the world. One area of conflict was in Vietnam. Vietnam, located in Southeast Asia was a country of small farmers. The country had resisted foreign invades for centuries prior to the Cold War; most recently the Chinese, French, and Japanese. The Vietnamese struggle was for independence, to live life according to their religious and political beliefs. During French colonial rule that began in 1867, a political party developed as the opposition to French exploitation. Gradually the Communist party grew as the legitimate opposition to the French. It soon attracted intellectuals, college students and nationalists. One of those was Ho Chi Minh. It is this Communist party that will lead to Vietnam being drawn into the conflict between the Soviet Union and the United States. The Communist party in Vietnam was a nationalist party not connected to the expansionism of the Soviet Union.

During the Cold War when "spheres of influence" became a major part of the conflict between the U. S. and the Soviet Union every piece of territory in the world and its ideological affiliation became important. So when the Vietnamese began fighting the French for independence this conflict was viewed within the contest of the Cold War. When the French pulled out of Vietnam in 1954 the U. S. expanded its involvement to include sending in ground forces in 1964. American involvement lasted until the fall of South Vietnam in 1975.

The documents below are examples of this Cold War conflict. Direct interaction is between the United States and Vietnam and not the United States and the Soviet Union. That is the way in which this conflict was waged. The United States and the Soviet Union did not enter into military conflict directly but through surrogate nations. Webster defines the Cold War as "an extended period of conflict between nations that does not include direct warfare.

The Vietnamese Declaration of Independence

Although the French did not leave Vietnam until years later, independence was declared in 1945.

The Vietnamese Declaration of Independence, 1945

All men are created equal; they are endowed by their Creator with certain unalienable Rights; among these are Life, Liberty, and the pursuit of Happiness.

This immortal statement was made in the Declaration of Independence of the United States of America in 1776. In a broader sense, this means: All the peoples on the earth are equal from birth, all the peoples have a right to live, to be happy and free.

The Declaration of the French Revolution made in 1791 on the Rights of Man and the Citizen also states: "All men are born free and with equal rights, and must always remain free and have equal rights."

Those are undeniable truths.

Nevertheless, for more than eighty years, the French imperialists, abusing the standard of Liberty, Equality, and Fraternity, have violated our Fatherland and oppressed our fellow citizens. They have acted contrary to the ideals of humanity and justice.

In the field of politics, they have deprived our people of every democratic liberty.

They have enforced inhuman laws; they have set up three distinct political regimes in the North, the Center, and the South of Viet-Nam in order to wreck our national unity and prevent our people from being united.

They have built more prisons than schools. They have mercilessly slain our patriots; they have drowned our uprisings in rivers of blood.

They have fettered public opinion; they have practiced obscurantism against our people.

To weaken our race they have forced us to use opium and alcohol.

In the field of economics, they have fleeced us to the backbone, impoverished our people and devastated our land.

They have robbed us of our rice fields, our mines, our forests, and our raw materials. They have monopolized the issuing of bank notes and the export trade.

They have invented numerous unjustifiable taxes and reduced our people, especially our peasantry, to a state of extreme poverty.

They have hampered the prospering of our national bourgeoisie; they have mercilessly exploited our workers.

In the autumn of 1940, when the Japanese fascists violated Indochina's territory to establish new bases in their fight against the Allies, the French imperialists went down on their bended knees and handed over our country to them.

Thus, from that date, our people were subjected to the double yoke of the French and the Japanese. Their sufferings and miseries increased. The result was that, from the end of last year to the beginning of this year, from Quang Tri Province to the North of Viet-Nam, more than two million of our fellow citizens died from starvation. On March 9 [1945], the French troops were disarmed by the Japanese. The French colonialists either fled or surrendered, showing that not only were they incapable of "protecting" us, but that, in the span of five years, they had twice sold our country to the Japanese.

On several occasions before March 9, the Viet Minh League urged the French to ally themselves with it against the Japanese. Instead of agreeing to this proposal, the French colonialists so intensified their terrorist activities against the Viet Minh members that before fleeing they massacred a great number of our political prisoners detained at Yen Bay and Cao Bang.

Notwithstanding all this, our fellow citizens have always manifested toward the French a tolerant and humane attitude. Even after the Japanese *Putsch* of March, 1945, the Viet Minh League helped many Frenchmen to cross the frontier, rescued some of them from Japanese jails, and protected French lives and property.

From the autumn of 1940, our country had in fact ceased to be a French colony and had become a Japanese possession.

After the Japanese had surrendered to the Allies, our whole people rose to regain our national sovereignty and to found the Democratic Republic of Viet-Nam.

The truth is that we have wrested our independence from the Japanese and not from the French.

The French have fled, the Japanese have capitulated, Emperor Bao Dai has abdicated. Our people have broken the chains which for nearly a century have fettered them and have won independence for the Fatherland. Our people at the same time have overthrown the monarchic regime that has reigned supreme for dozens of centuries. In its place has been established the present Democratic Republic.

For these reasons, we, members of the Provisional Government, representing the whole Vietnamese people, declare that from now on we break off all relations of a colonial character with France; we repeal all the international obligation that France has so far subscribed to on behalf of Viet-Nam, and we abolish all the special rights the French have unlawfully acquired in our Fatherland.

The whole Vietnamese people, animated by a common purpose, are determined to fight to the bitter end against any attempt by the French colonialists to reconquer their country.

We are convinced that the Allied nations, which at Teheran and San Francisco have acknowledged the principles of self-determination and equality of nations, will not refuse to acknowledge the independence of Viet-Nam.

A people who have courageously opposed French domination for more than eighty years, a people who have fought side by side with the Allies against the fascists during these last years, such a people must be free and independent.

For these reasons, we, members of the Provisional Government of the Democratic Republic of Viet-Nam, solemnly declare to the world that Viet-Nam has the right to be a free and independent country—and in fact it is so already. The entire Vietnamese people are determined to mobilize all their physical and mental strength, to sacrifice their lives and property in order to safeguard their independence and liberty.

Eisenhower's Explanation of the Domino Theory

Dwight David Eisenhower (1890–1969) was President of the United States from 1953 to 1961. This document is from 1954.

Eisenhower Explains the Domino Theory, 1954

Q, ROBERT RICHARDS, COPLEY PRESS: Mr. President, would you mind commenting on the strategic importance of Indochina to the free world? I think there has been, across the country, some lack of understanding on just what it means to us.

THE PRESIDENT: You have, of course, both the specific and the general when you talk about such things.

First of all, you have the specific value of a locality in its production of materials that the world needs.

Then you have the possibility that many human beings pass under a dictatorship that is inimical to the free world.

Finally, you have broader considerations that might follow what you would call the "falling domino" principle. You have a row of dominoes set up, you knock over the first one, and what will happen to the last one is the certainty that it will go over very quickly. So you could have a beginning of a disintegration that would have the most profound influences.

Now, with respect to the first one, two of the items from this particular area that the world uses are tin and tungsten. They are very important. There are others, of course, the rubber plantations and so on.

Then with respect to more people passing under this domination, Asia, after all, has already lost some 450 million of its peoples to the Communist dictatorship, and we simply can't afford greater losses.

But when we come to the possible sequence of events, the loss of Indochina, of Burma, of Thailand, of the Peninsula, and Indonesia following, now you begin to talk about areas that not only multiply the disadvantages that you would suffer through loss of materials, sources of materials, but now you are talking about millions and millions and millions of people.

Finally, the geographical position achieved thereby does many things. It turns the so-called island defensive chain of Japan, Formosa, of the Philippines and to the southward; it moves in to threaten Australia and New Zealand.

It takes away, in its economic aspects, that region that Japan must have as a trading area or Japan, in turn, will have only one place in the world to go—that is, toward the Communist areas in order to live.

So, the possible consequences of the loss are just incalculable to the free world.

Lyndon B. Johnson's Explanation of why Americans Fight in Vietnam.

Lyndon Baines Johnson (1908–1973) served as Vice President under President John F. Kennedy. After Kennedy's assassination, he became president, serving until January 1969. This explanation of the Vietnam War is from 1965.

Lyndon B. Johnson Explains Why Americans Fight in Vietnam, 1965

Why must this nation hazard its ease, its interest, and its power for the sake of a people so far away?

We fight because we must fight if we are to live in a world where every country can shape its own destiny, and only in such a world will our own freedom be finally secure.

This kind of world will never be built by bombs or bullets. Yet the infirmities of man are such that force must often precede reason and the waste of war, the works of peace.

We wish that this were not so. But we must deal with the world as it is, if it is ever to be as we wish.

The world as it is in Asia is not a serene or peaceful place.

The first reality is that North Viet-Nam has attacked the independent nation of South Viet-Nam. Its object is total conquest.

Of course, some of the people of South Viet-Nam are participating in attack on their own government. But trained men and supplies, orders and arms, flow in a constant stream from North to South.

This support is the heartbeat of the war.

And it is a war of unparalleled brutality. Simple farmers are the targets of assassination and kidnapping. Women and children are strangled in the night because their men are loyal to their government. And helpless villages are ravaged by sneak attacks. Large-scale raids are conducted on towns, and terror strikes in the heart of cities.

The confused nature of this conflict cannot mask the fact that it is the new face of an old enemy.

Over this war—and all Asia—is another reality: the deepening shadow of Communist China. The rulers in Hanoi are urged on by Peking. This is a regime which has destroyed freedom in Tibet, which has attacked India and has been condemned by the United Nations for aggression in Korea. It is a nation which is helping the forces of violence in almost every continent. The contest in Viet-Nam is part of a wider pattern of aggressive purposes.

Why are these realities our concern? Why are we in South Viet-Nam?

We are there because we have a promise to keep. Since 1954 every American President has offered support to the people of South Viet-Nam. We have helped to build, and we have helped to defend. Thus, over many years, we have made a national pledge to help South Viet-Nam defend its independence.

And I intend to keep that promise.

To dishonor that pledge, to abandon this small and brave nation to its enemies, and to the terror that must follow, would be an unforgivable wrong.

We are also there to strengthen world order. Around the globe from Berlin to Thailand are people whose well being rests in part on the belief that they can count on us if they are attacked. To leave Viet-Nam to its fate would shake the confidence of all these people in the value of an American commitment and in the value of America's word. The result would be increased unrest and instability, and even wider war.

We are also there because there are great stakes in the balance. Let no one think for a moment that retreat from Viet-Nam would bring an end to conflict. The battle would be renewed in one country and then another. The central lesson of our time is that the appetite of aggression is never satisfied. To withdraw from one battlefield means only to prepare for the next. We must say in Southeast Asia—as we did in Europe—in the words of the Bible: "Hitherto shalt thou come, but no further."

There are those who say that all our effort there will be futile—that China's power is such that it is bound to dominate all Southeast Asia. But there is no end to that argument until all of the nations of Asia are swallowed up.

There are those who wonder why we have a responsibility there. Well, we have it there for the same reason that we have a responsibility for the defense of Europe. World War II was fought in both Europe and Asia and when it ended we found ourselves with continued responsibility for the defense of freedom.

Our objective is the independence of South Viet-Nam and its freedom from attack. We want nothing for ourselves—only that the people of South Viet-Nam be allowed to guide their own country in their own way.

We will do everything necessary to reach that objective and we will do only what is absolutely necessary.

In recent months attacks on South Viet-Nam were stepped up. Thus, it became necessary for us to increase our response and to make attacks by air. This is not a change of purpose. It is a change in what we believe that purpose requires.

We do this in order to slow down aggression.

We do this to increase the confidence of the brave people of South Viet-Nam who have bravely borne this brutal battle for so many years with so many casualties.

And we do this to convince the leaders of North Viet-Nam—and all who seek to share their conquest—of a simple fact:

We will not be defeated.

We will not grow tired.

We will not withdraw, either openly or under the cloak of a meaningless agreement.

We know that air attacks alone will not accomplish all of these purposes. But it is our best and prayerful judgment that they are a necessary part of the surest road to peace.

We hope that peace will come swiftly. But that is in the hands of others besides ourselves. And we must be prepared for a long continued conflict. It will require patience as well as bravery—the will to endure as well as the will to resist.

I wish it were possible to convince others with words of what we now find it necessary to say with guns and planes: armed hostility is futile—our resources are equal to any challenge—because we fight for values and we fight for principle, rather than territory or colonies, our patience and our determination are unending.

Once this is clear, then it should also be clear that the only path for reasonable men is the path of peaceful settlement. . . .

These countries of Southeast Asia are homes for millions of impoverished people. Each day these people rise at dawn and struggle through until the night to wrestle existence from the soil. They are often wracked by diseases, plagued by hunger, and death comes at the early age of forty.

Stability and peace do not come easily in such a land. Neither independence nor human dignity will ever be won though by arms alone. It also requires the works of peace. The American people have helped generously in times past in these works, and now there must be a much more massive effort to improve the life of man in that conflict-torn corner of our world.

The first step is for the countries of Southeast Asia to associate themselves in a greatly expanded co-operative effort for development. We would hope that North Viet-Nam would take its place in the common effort just as soon as peaceful co-operation is possible.

The United Nations is already actively engaged in development in this area, and as far back as 1961 I conferred with our authorities in Viet-Nam in connection with their work there. And I would hope tonight that the Secretary General of the United Nations could use the prestige of his great office and his deep knowledge of Asia to initiate, as soon as possible, with the countries of that area, a plan for co-operation in increased development.

For our part I will ask the Congress to join in a billion dollar American investment in this effort as soon as it is underway.

And I would hope that all other industrialized countries, including the Soviet Union, will join in this effort to replace despair with hope and terror with progress.

The task is nothing less than to enrich the hopes and existence of more than a hundred million people. And there is much to be done.

The vast Mekong River can provide food and water and power on a scale to dwarf even our own T.V.A.

The wonders of modern medicine can be spread through villages where thousands die every year from lack of care.

Schools can be established to train people in the skills needed to manage the process of development.

And these objectives, and more, are within the reach of a cooperative and determined effort.

I also intend to expand and speed up a program to make available our farm surpluses to assist in feeding and clothing the needy in Asia. We should not allow people to go hungry and wear rags while our own warehouses overflow with an abundance of wheat and corn and rice arid cotton.

So 1 will very shortly name a special team of outstanding, patriotic, and distinguished Americans to inaugurate our participation in these programs. This team will be headed by Mr. Eugene Black, the very able former president of the World Bank.

This will be a disorderly planet for a long time. In Asia, and elsewhere, the forces of the modern world are shaking old ways and uprooting ancient civilizations. There will be turbulence and struggle and even violence. Great social change—as we see in our own country—does not always come without conflict.

We must also expect that nations will on occasion be in dispute with us. It may be because we are rich, or powerful, or because we have made some mistakes, or because they honestly fear our intentions. However, no nation need ever fear that we desire their land, or to impose our will, or to dictate their institutions.

But we will always oppose the effort of one nation to conquer another nation.

We will do this because our own security is at stake.

But there is more to it than that. For our generation has a dream. It is a very old dream. But we have the power, and now we have the opportunity to make that dream come true.

For centuries nations have struggled among each other. But we dream of a world where disputes are settled by law and reason. And we will try to make it so.

For most of history men have hated and killed one another in battle. But we dream of an end to war. And we will try to make it so.

For all existence most men have lived in poverty, threatened by hunger. But we dream of a world where all are fed and charged with hope. And we will help to make it so.

A Vietnamese Recruit Explains why He Joined the Revolution.

This document dates from 1961.

A Vietcong Recruit Explains Why He Joined the Revolution

I joined the VC [Vietcong] when I was thirty-five years old. I was married and had four children. I was leasing farmland—one hectare [about 2.5 acres]—that was very poor in quality, almost sterile. That was why the owner rented it out to us. Despite working hard all year round, we got only about 100 *gia* of rice out of it. Of this amount, 40 *gia* went to the landlord. We borrowed money to buy ducks and geese. We lived a very hard life, But I cultivated the land carefully, and in time it became fertile. When it did, the owner took it back; my livelihood was gone. I had to go back to my parents, to raise ducks for my father.

I was poor. I had lost my land and I didn't have enough money to take care of my children. In 1961 propaganda cadres of the Front [National Liberation Front] contacted me. These guys had joined the resistance against the French, and after Geneva they had stayed underground in the South. They came to all the poor farmers and made an analysis of the poor and rich classes. They said that the rich people had always served the French and had used the authority of the French to oppress the poor. The majority of the people were poor, not because they wasted their money but because they had been exploited by the landlords who had worked with the French. In the past, the ancestors of the poor had broken ground for tillage. Then powerful people had seized their land. Without any other means to live, the poor had become slaves of the landlords. The cadres told us that if the poor people don't stand up the rich people, we would be dominated by them forever. The only way to ensure freedom and a sufficient life was to overthrow them.

When I heard the cadres, I thought that what they said was correct. In my village there were about forty-three hundred people. Of these, maybe ten were landlords. The richest owned five hundred hectares [1,236 acres], and the others had at least twenty hectares [49 acres] apiece. The rest of the people were tenants or honest poor farmers. I knew that the rich oppressed the poor. The poor had nothing to eat, and they also had no freedom. We had to get rid of the regime that allowed a few people to use their money and authority to oppress the others.

So I joined the Liberation Front. I followed the VC to fight for freedom and prosperity for the country. I felt that this was right.

Source: From *Portrait of the Enemy* by David Chanoff and Doan Van Toai, Copyright © 1986 by David Chanoff and Doan Van Toai. Used by permission of Random House, Inc.

Questions for Contemplation and Discussion

1. What reasons did the Vietnamese give for their fight for independence?

2. How does Eisenhower explain the Domino Theory?

3. How does Lyndon Johnson connect the war for independence in Vietnam to the spread of communism?

4. How did the personal goals of the Vietcong recruit in Document 4 connect to the goals of the war for independence in Vietnam?

5. From the four documents provided in this section you can see that the Vietnamese and the U. S. viewed the Vietnam War differently. What would you suggest to both sides as a way of addressing these differences?

WHAT WAS APARTHEID IN SOUTH AFRICA?

A. L. Geyer[77]

The following material comes from a speech given before the Rotary Club of London on August 19, 1953.

This brings me to the question of the future. To me there seems to be two possible lines of development: Apartheid or Partnership. Partnership means Cooperation of the individual citizens within a single community, irrespective of race . . . . (It) demands that there shall be no discrimination whatsoever in trade and industry, in the professions and the Public Service. Therefore, whether a man is black or a white African, must according to this policy be as irrelevant as whether in London a man is a Scotsman or an Englishman. I take it: that Partnership must also aim at the eventual disappearance of all social segregation based on race. This policy of Partnership admittedly does not envisage immediate adult suffrage. Obviously, however, the loading of the franchise in order to exclude the great majority of the Bantu could be no worse than a temporary expedient . . . . (In effect) "there must one day be black domination, in the sense that power must pass to the immense African majority. Need I say more to show that this policy of Partnership could, in South Africa, only mean the eventual disappearance of the white South African nation? And will you be greatly surprised if I tell you that this white nation is not prepared to commit national suicide, not even by slow poisoning?

The only alternative is a policy of apartheid, the policy of separate development. The germ of this policy is inherent in almost all of our history, implanted there by the force of circumstances . . . . Apartheid is a policy of self preservation. We make no apology for possessing that very natural urge. But it is more than that. It is an attempt at self-preservation in a manner that will enable the Bantu [dominant language family in sub-Saharan Africa] to develop fully as a separate people.

We believe that, for a long time to come, political power will have to remain with the whites, also in the interest of our still very immature Bantu. But we believe also, in the words of a statement by the Dutch Reformed Church in 1950, a Church that favours *apartheid*, that "no people in the world worth their salt, would be content indefinitely with no say or only indirect say in the affairs of the State or in the country's socio-economic organisation in which decisions are taken about their interests and their future."

The immediate aim is, therefore, to keep the races outside the Bantu areas apart as far as possible, to continue the process of improving the conditions and standards of living of the Bantu, and to give them greater responsibility for their own local affairs. At the same time the long-range aim is to develop the Bantu areas both agriculturally and industrially, with the object of making these areas in every sense the national home of the Bantu-areas in which their interests are paramount, in which to an ever greater degree all professional and other positions are to be occupied by them, and in which they are to receive progressively more and more autonomy.

Archbishop Desmond Tutu[78]

Archbishop Tutu (1931–) was the first person of color appointed archbishop in the Anglican Church in South Africa. His vocal opposition to apartheid won him the 1984 Nobel Peace Prize.

I speak out of a full heart, for I am about to speak about a land that I love deeply and passionately; a beautiful land of rolling hills and gurgling streams, of clear starlit skies, of singing birds, and gamboling lambs; a land God has richly endowed with the good things of the earth, a land rich in mineral deposits of nearly every kind; a land of vast open spaces, enough to accommodate all its inhabitants comfortably; a land capable of feeding itself and other lands on the beleaguered continent of Africa, a veritable breadbasket; a land that could contribute wonderfully to the material and spiritual development and prosperity of all Africa and indeed of the whole world. It is endowed with enough to satisfy the material and spiritual needs of all its peoples.

And so we would expect that such a land, veritably flowing with milk and honey, should be a land where peace and harmony and contentment reigned supreme. Alas, the opposite is the case. For my beloved country is wracked by division, by alienation, by animosity, by separation, by injustice, by avoidable pain and suffering. It is a deeply fragmented society, ridden by fear and anxiety, covered by a pall of despondency and a sense of desperation, split up into hostile, warring factions.

It is a highly volatile land, and its inhabitants sit on a powder-keg with a very short fuse indeed, ready to blow us all up into kingdom come. There is endemic unrest, like a festering sore that will not heal until not just the symptoms are treated but the root causes are removed.

Source: From *Union of South Africa Government: Information Pamphlet*, 1953 (New York).
Source: © 1984 by United Nations. Reprinted by permission.

South African society is deeply polarized. Nothing illustrates this more sharply than the events of the past week. While the black community was in the seventh heaven of delight because of the decision of that committee in Oslo, and while the world was congratulating the recipient of the Nobel Peace prize, the white government and most white South Africans, very sadly, were seeking to devalue that prize. An event that should have been the occasion of uninhibited joy and thanksgiving revealed a sadly divided society . . .

Over 100,000 black students are out of school, boycotting—as they did in 1976—what they and the black community perceive as an inferior education designed deliberately for inferiority. An already highly volatile situation has been ignited several times and, as a result, over 80 persons have died. There has been industrial unrest, with the first official strike by black miners taking place, not without its toll of fatalities among the blacks . . .

But there is little freedom in this land of plenty. There is little freedom to disagree with the determinations of the authorities. There is large-scale unemployment because of the drought and the recession that has hit most of the world's economy. And it is at such a time that the authorities have increased the prices of various foodstuffs and also of rents in black townships—measures designed to hit hardest those least able to afford the additional costs. It is not surprising that all this has exacerbated an already tense and volatile situation.

So the unrest is continuing, in a kind of war of attrition, with the casualties not being large enough at any one time to shock the world sufficiently for it to want to take action against the system that is the root cause of all this agony. We have warned consistently that unrest will be endemic in South Africa until its root cause is removed. And the root cause is apartheid—a vicious, immoral and totally evil, and unchristian system . . .

White South Africans are not demons; they are ordinary human beings, scared human beings, many of them; who would not be, if they were outnumbered five to one? Through this lofty body I wish to appeal to my white fellow South Africans to share in building a new society, for blacks are not intent on driving whites into the sea but on claiming only their rightful place in the sun in the land of their birth.

We deplore all forms of violence, the violence of an oppressive and unjust society and the violence of those seeking to overthrow that society, for we believe that violence is not the answer to the crisis of our land.

We dream of a new society that will be truly non-racial, truly democratic, in which people count because they are created in the image of God.

We are committed to work for justice, for peace, and for reconciliation. We ask you, please help us; urge the South African authorities to go to the conference table with the authentic representatives of all sections of our community . . .

I say we will be free, and we ask you: Help us, that this freedom comes for all of us in South Africa, black and white, but that it comes with the least possible violence, that it comes peacefully, that it comes soon.

Questions for Contemplation and Discussion

1. What is the main point or thesis of Geyer?

2. Is Geyer's statement that "the only alternative is a policy of apartheid" at all logically problematic? Explain

3. What is the main point or thesis of Archbishop Tutu?

4. In what ways are Tutu's values different from Geyer? Explain

5. In the 1980's, when apartheid was still policy in South Africa, many people protested the policy by boycotting any product coming from South Africa. What are some strengths and weaknesses of such a boycott?

6. Would you spend money in a country that denied citizens their civil rights? Why? Why not?

WHAT ARE THE CAUSES OF AFRICA'S PROBLEMS?

Kevin Shillington[79]

Kevin Shillington earned a Ph.D. in African History from the University of London. Formerly a professor at the University of Botswana, he now is a freelance journalist who has written several books on Africa's past.

The problems which Africans and their governments have had to face since independence have, very largely, been the product of their history. This is not to suggest that the misdirection, corruption or incompetence of some African leaders or even ecological factors have not been partly to blame for Africa's continuing underdevelopment. But the roots of many of Africa's recurrent problems in the final decades of the twentieth century are to be found in the period of colonial rule of the previous eighty years or more.

The Political Legacy of Colonial Rule

It was only on the eve of independence that Europeans had imposed upon Africa their own systems of parliamentary democracy with all its inappropriate European ceremony and formality. By then Europeans preferred to overlook the point that colonial rule had been largely established and sustained in Africa by brutal military conquest. The real political legacy of colonial government in Africa was that of an alien dictatorship, benevolent at times, but always prepared to crush outspoken opposition. Many of Africa's independence leaders had suffered periods of detention without trial for daring to speak out against the unjust and arbitrary nature of colonial authority.

The boundaries of the countries themselves were mostly totally artificial. They had been created at the whim of European politicians with little or no regard for Africa's multitude of pre-colonial nation states and 'stateless' village communities. Peoples of widely differing languages and political and cultural traditions had been cobbled together for European convenience. The widespread colonial use of 'indirect rule' (see pp. 355-8) further served to emphasise the differences. These people were now suddenly expected to feel at ease with systems of multi-party parliamentary democracy that had only evolved in the nation-states of Europe after centuries of conflict.

The artificiality of Africa's national boundaries caused serious problems of 'national' unity after independence. African politicians may have been united in their anti-colonial sentiments, but they were yet to think of themselves as part of a single nation.

One-Party States Most of Africa's ruling politicians quickly rejected the multi-party parliamentary system as unworkable. They pleaded the particular circumstances of their country's crying need for national unity in order to achieve rapid social and economic development. Within a few years of independence most African governments had established some form of 'one-party state'. By the late 1980s only Botswana, with its low population of one million people, had maintained an unbroken record of multi-party parliamentary democracy since independence. The argument in favour of a one-party system was that parliamentary opposition based upon regional ethnic interests was destructive rather than constructive opposition. Democratic choice, it was argued, could just as easily be exercised within a single party system.

The Economic Legacy of Underdevelopment and Dependency

European colonial governments left Africa with a mounting economic crisis that had been the end-product of eighty years of colonial misrule. The African economies, such as they were, had been directed towards exporting cheap agricultural raw materials and unprocessed minerals to Europe and in return importing relatively expensive manufactured goods. There had been little or no attempt to develop African economic self-sufficiency, for that would have defeated the purpose of Europe's possessing colonies. Not only the nature of the products, but also the 'terms of trade' were determined by Europe at the expense of African interests. Prices for Africa's export commodities were controlled in the so-called 'developed economies' of Europe and north America. Thus in times of European depression Africa was paid less for her exports, and in times of European inflation Africans had to pay more for their imports. Each year more and more African effort had to be turned to producing cash crops for the European market in order to import the same amount of manufactured goods. As a result of these 'adverse terms of trade,' Africa was a net exporter of wealth to Europe and north America.

At the same time, as more effort was put into cash-crop production and labouring in the mines, subsistence cultivation for Africa's basic food was neglected. By the 1950s Africa had become a net importer of food. In other words Africans on average were growing less than half of their own food needs. The crisis was heightened by the growing level of urban unemployment.

Source: Extracts from *History of Africa* by Kevin Shillington © Kevin Shillington first published by Macmillan Education 1989 & 1995 reprinted by permission of the publisher.

From the late 1940s and early 1950s more and more people migrated to the towns in a desperate attempt to escape increasing rural poverty or forced cropping and forced labour schemes.

Another poor legacy from the colonial period was Africa's transport systems which were totally inadequate for the continent's internal development. Most of the railways had been built around the turn of the century to ease the export of the continent's wealth to Europe. By independence they were badly in need of repair and simply linked a country's mines or main source of cash crops to the sea. Roads were poorly developed and most of Africa's road and rail networks showed no concern for the country's internal development. Furthermore, there were virtually no regional road or rail links to help promote trade between one African country and another, unless as a route from a land-locked country to the sea. Telecommunications were the same. Internal rural networks were almost non-existent, and it was easier to telephone from Africa to Europe than it was to telephone from one African capital to another.

African governments inherited two particularly repressive economic policies from their colonial predecessors: poll tax and agricultural marketing boards. The former was charged on all adult males regardless of income. The latter paid fixed low prices to farmers, while selling their produce for higher prices abroad and keeping the difference as government revenue. Both repressive policies provided such important sources of government income that they were initially retained in many countries after independence.

The lack of education was a further debilitating legacy of the colonial period. Across most of tropical Africa barely ten per cent of the population was literate at independence.

Thomas Sowell[80]

Thomas Sowell (1930–) is a holder of the Rose and Milton Friedman fellowship at the Hoover Institution, which is on the campus of Stanford University, Stanford, California. He holds the Ph.D. in Economics from the University of Chicago and has written widely on economics, race, politics, and child psychology.

Although Africans have had patterns common to other conquered peoples, they have also been distinctive in some ways. Unlike either the American colonies or Britain under the Roman empire, African countries were in most cases neither replicas of the imperial society nor truly integrated into its legal system or social traditions. Though many newly independent African nations imitated the outward forms of Western democratic societies, the relatively brief period of Western rule could hardly have replicated the centuries of tradition which made democratic institutions viable in Europe and in European offshoot societies overseas. Few of these democratic institutions survived for long after independence in Africa.

The economic achievements of Europe were likewise not readily transferable to Africa, partly because of the severe geographical and climatic handicaps which long retarded economic, cultural, and political development in many parts of the continent. Moreover, the relatively brief history of Africa's exposure to European culture made widespread economic replication of European economic progress no more likely than replication of European democracy. Nevertheless, to some extent European culture did have an effect on Africans. This limited transfer of culture took place in many ways, ranging from unconscious influence to formal study. However, despite an obvious desire in many newly independent African nations to imitate the West, by building industrial manufacturing plants, for example, little of the science, technology, or organizational management skills of the Western world were transferred to Africans.

Although many Africans destined to become leaders of their countries spent years, and in some cases decades, living and studying in Europe or the United States, what they brought back from the West were not the practical or scientific knowledge and skills behind the wealth and power of the West, but rather the social theories and moral speculations of European and American intellectuals. Much of the painful history of the first quarter of a century of African independence was a history of African leaders, without the practical knowledge or experience of either Africa or the West, attempting sweeping social experiments on their own people, based on the untested theories of Western intellectuals.

Source: From *Conquests and Cultures: An International History* by Thomas Sowell (New York; Basic Books: 1998).

Questions for Contemplation and Discussion

1. In Shillington's view, has Africa's colonial legacy helped or hurt Africa? Explain

2. Shillington briefly mentions that a lack of education has hurt Africa. Why do you think literacy is so important for a country or a continent? How would a well-educated nation, such as the United States, be different if only 10% of the population could read? Explain.

3. What does Sowell say about the causes of Africa's problems? Explain.

4. Do Shillington and Sowell give adequate attention to the role of the spread of AIDS? Is this a weakness in their arguments? Explain.

5. Some would say that Africa's problems should be solved by Africans only, that Western nations should stay out. Which values are at play in that kind of argument? Do you agree with this argument? Explain.

WHY DID THE SOVIET UNION COLLAPSE?

Edwin Meese III[81]

Edwin Meese (1931–) served as attorney general of the United States during the second term of President Reagan. Meese earlier worked with the President when he was Governor of California.

From Reagan's many statements on this topic, and from the various 'policies initiated on his watch, a clear, coherent, and comprehensive Cold War strategy emerged. Though there were occasional setbacks along the way, the main elements of this strategy never altered:

1. In the Cold War confrontation between East and West, there was no "moral equivalence." At the level of ultimate values, we were right, and they were wrong. Freedom was in every way superior to tyranny. This did not mean that we were perfect, that we wanted war, or that we wouldn't negotiate. But it did mean that we should never blur the key distinctions between a free society and the regimented system of our adversaries.

2. Given the totalitarian and expansionist ambitions of the Soviets, converging in their huge military establishment and worldwide program of subversion, it was essential that we vigorously defend ourselves. Wishful-thinking strategies—seeking peace through weakness and accommodation—only encouraged the expansionism of the communists. America, and the West in general, needed a policy of peace through strength.

3. Despite its armed might (and in part because of it), the Soviet system was inherently weak—it could not command the allegiance of its captive peoples, and its economic system could not produce the goods required to shelter, feed, and clothe them. A free society was superior to communism on both these counts.

4. Communism was accordingly torn by fatal contradictions—its global and military ambitions on the one hand, its internal economic and political problems on the other. In any full-scale competition with the United States and other Western powers, therefore, communism would be forced to choose between maintaining its global empire and solving its domestic problems.

5. It followed that the United States and the Western world in general should stop retreating before the communist challenge, stop imposing artificial limitations on themselves, and begin competing in earnest against the Soviets; this meant refurbishing our defenses, assisting anticommunist resistance forces around the world, and giving greater emphasis to the scientific/technological strength afforded by the free society.

6. It further followed, finally, that the West should stop bailing the communists out of their technical and economic difficulties. This implied an end to one-sided arms agreements that tilted the strategic balance toward the Kremlin; it meant no longer giving the Soviets and their proxies a free hand in subverting Third World countries; and it meant cutting back on technology transfer from East to West, on strategic trade that helped to build the Soviet war machine, and on economic credits that eased the problems of the communist system.

On this basis, the President believed, the Soviets would have to come to terms on authentically peaceable agreements, not because they were trustworthy (although he eventually came to have a relatively high regard for Soviet President Gorbachev), but because they had no other choice. The "objective factors," to use a communist phrase, would lead inexorably to a stand-down from the Cold War. . .

From a post-Cold War perspective, the main principles of the Reagan program may seem self-evident. Given accurate data about the communist system, indeed, they are the very essence of common sense. Viewing the rubble of the Berlin Wall, the upheavals that have transformed Eastern Europe, and the internal collapse of the Soviet regime, hardly anyone can doubt that communism was indeed an "evil empire" and a failed economic system. Such points have been affirmed by the former leaders of the communist world itself.

Yet at the time Reagan was making these statements and pursuing these policies, there was nothing self-evident about it. On the contrary, he was roundly attacked both for his general analysis of the situation, and for nearly all the specific steps he took in carrying out his policy—the defense buildup, INF deployments, aid to anticommunist resistance forces, curtailment of technology transfer, SDI [Strategic Defense Initiative or "Star Wars": President Reagan's idea of using missles to prevent a nuclear attack], and so on.

In fact, even in the aftermath of the communist collapse Reagan critics were reluctant to credit the President with the accuracy of his vision or the correctness of his policy. Many discussions of the communist debacle completely ignore the impact

Source: From the book *With Reagan: The Inside Story* by Edwin Meese III. Copyright © 1992. Published by Regnery Publishing, Inc. All rights reserved. Reprinted by special permission of Regnery Publishing, Inc., Washington, D.C.

of the Reagan strategy, attributing the demise of the evil empire to a change of heart on the part of the communists, or to unnamed forces that somehow brought about the toppling of the system.

Perhaps the most famous example of this tendency was the issue of *Time* magazine celebrating the virtual end of communism and proclaiming Mikhail Gorbachev [final leader of the Soviet Union, 1985–1991] "Man of the Decade." The role of Ronald Reagan in all of this was scarcely mentioned, nor was much notice given to the fact that the establishment view had been mistaken at every step along the way. Instead, *Time* concluded that the collapse of communism proved the "doves" had been right all along! Margaret Thatcher provided a more accurate view at a 1991 Heritage Foundation dinner in Washington, when she summed up the President's accomplishments abroad: "He won the Cold War without firing a shot."

Glen Bowman[82]

Glen Bowman (1968–) holds a Ph.D. in History from the University of Minnesota and is Associate Professor of History at Elizabeth City State University. He is also the author of *The Razor's Edge*.

Problems started to develop in 1989. Economic growth slipped to 1.5%, and many consumer goods were in short supply. By the end of 1989, shortages were common: out of a list of 1200 goods, all but fifty of them were in short supply. Another previously hidden problem came to the surface—the deficit. Between 1985 and 1988, it was at 131 billion rubles; this total took into account the costs of pulling out of Afghanistan and of bailing out unprofitable enterprises. The deficit in 1989 was an astounding 720 billion rubles. Inflation rose to double digits in 1989 as the government continued pumping the economy full of rubles . . .

In 1991, the economy collapsed: total output, for example, dropped by 17%, the most since the dark years of the Nazi invasions during World War II. The deficit, which was only 2.4% of GNP in 1985, had mushroomed to 17%. Total trade plunged 38%. Inflation, about zero in 1985, had gone into triple digits. The State Committee for Statistics of the former Soviet Union estimated that in 1991, GDP dropped 17%, industrial output, 8%, and agricultural output, 7%.

Perhaps the most noticeable effects of these deep economic woes were the mercurial rise in prices and food shortages . . . Soviet citizens certainly noticed that the economy had gone sour. The dominant sentiments were not hope, but rather anger, despair, and cynicism. Such desperation bred paranoia: food shortages were blamed on "the mafia" (apparently an invisible scapegoat) and foreign workers, especially Vietnamese ones. Millions of Soviet citizens were plunged into poverty, and some into homelessness . . . The last year of the Soviet Union indeed was, at least in economics, a disaster.

Now that the Soviet Union is gone, it is certain that many will look to Gorbachev's tenure and insist that his policies were the principal cause for the Soviet Union's economic ruin. There is some truth to this appraisal: Gorbachev was definitely more than a passive observer of the economic disintegration of his country, though it may be an exaggeration to agree with Lewin that Gorbachev inherited an economic crisis which had been brewing since the 1930's. He enacted some bold policies, and in hindsight . . . it would appear that most of them failed . . . Still, it is also true that the Soviet Union had been in a twenty-year economic slump back in 1978, when Brezhnev hired him to restore agricultural strength. It is simply not fair to blame him for most of his country's economic woes, though it is also only fair to point out that his ambitious reforms perhaps hastened an inevitable slide into ruin, If Gorbachev were on a ship, he would be the person hired on the spot to patch the gaping holes made by others. Those who bored the holes would probably already be on a lifeboat, watching him try in vain to patch the boat as water pours in all around him.

There were numerous "holes" in the Soviet economy, most of which got only larger as Gorbachev tried to repair them. First, it is apparent that the U.S.S.R. mishandled their natural resources: on one hand, it left vast resources untapped . . . On the other hand, the Soviet Union polluted its environment and thus abused other natural resources. In 1988, industry in just the Ukraine emitted 22 billion pounds of toxic chemicals (for the entire U.S., it was 2.7 billion). In the city of Magnitogorsk, the air contained nine times the maximum-safe level of benzene and four times the level of sulfur compounds. The Aral Sea has gradually become dangerously salty: salinity increased from 10% in 1960 to 23% in the late 1980's, probably because water was taken to irrigate the cotton fields of Central Asia. There are other forms of water pollution. In 1988, 17 billion gallons of toxic petrochemical waste was dumped in the Caspian Sea, killing the beloved sturgeon and poisoning the water supply so much that boiling it would not make it potable. According to another report, industrial and agricultural enterprises in the 1980's dumped 10 million gallons of contaminated water in the Dnesti River. These practices have lowered life expectancies: the average Muscovite lives ten years less than did his or her parents. There have been epidemics of other diseases, which may or may not be related to environmental problems—plague, diphtheria, polio, dysentery, whooping-cough, and botulism, among others.

The damage to the environment becomes even grimmer when one includes the steep environmental costs caused by the careless use of nuclear technology. One scientist from the Kazakh region said that the total release of radioactive substances in the U.S.S.R. reached, in the late 1980's, 3 trillion curies, which is about half of the entire world's output. Numbers of this magnitude, however, do not reveal the problems of radioactivity as clearly as do relative comparisons. The estimated total radioactive waste from the 1979 accident at Three Mile Island near Limerick, Pennsylvania, was 15 curies of radionucleides; at Chernobyl, the site of a 1986 accident, the total release was around 50 **million** curies. The population there, to put it mildly, has suffered: nearly every native resident suffers from tuberculosis, and their bones, on average, contain 10–20 times the safe level of lead—210 and 100 times the safe level of cesium—1.37. Chernobyl, though, is not the site of the worst nuclear pollution. At the Chelyabinsk area, a site of tests on surface and air nuclear missiles, the level of curies is an astounding 1.2 billion curies, over twenty times more than that at Chernobyl. Even more surprising, there are parts around the Barents, White, and Kara Seas which have curie-levels between 1-3.5 billion . . .

Another problem was . . . with the transportation and distribution of crops. Even though average annual output for both grain and meat was 20% higher between 1986 and 1990 than it was between 1981 and 1985, around 30% of grain and 50% of potatoes and vegetables were lost in the decade's final five years due to poor transportation, storage, and processing . . . Industry had perhaps even greater problems. Quantity, not quality, was usually the primary goal; this policy encouraged slipshod work. For example, the Samarkand Refrigerator Factory had won many awards for going well beyond its goals for production. The factory's refrigerators, however, were constructed and inspected so poorly that they had to be sent back to the plant. This potentially embarrassing incident did not hurt the company that much: the government continued to subsidize the factory. There have been other problems with shoddy work. Heat pipelines routinely burst in cold weather; new roads collapsed soon after construction; and televisions caught on fire.

This emphasis on output was also wasteful: there was little incentive to conserve materials. There were reports of wood piles being left to rot outside of railway stations and of batteries left to age in factories. Expensive trucks rusted away in Siberia; if new trucks were needed to construct a road, the state would provide them. There are other examples of peculiar approaches to road construction: scarce, expensive materials were used when cheaper ones just as effective existed . . . Employees with creative ideas were discouraged from offering their suggestions, perhaps because managers feared that implementing new ideas would slow production . . . Another problem was employee theft: workers would steal items and either sell or barter them on the black market, or give them to public officials. Of course, such problems are a part of the workplace in even Western, free-market societies; it would seem, though, that these dilemmas were even worse in the Soviet Union.

The U.S.S.R. also failed to keep up with technology. For instance, in 1955, a new method for bleaching wood pulp in the making of paper (this approach used oxygen) was discovered. Although this discovery was known to Soviet managers it had not yet been implemented thirty years later. According to another estimate, industrial equipment is replaced less frequently than in the United States: whereas American companies bring in new machines, on average, every ten to twelve years, the wait in the U.S.S.R. is almost twice as long . . .

A tragedy of the abysmal condition of the Soviet economy in its final years is that problems did not end when the Soviet Union ceased to exist. Nuclear contamination from Chernobyl will not go away for thousands of years. Recent reports have noted that Russia's life expectancy is still in decline due to diseases such as diphtheria . . .

In the 1950's, many Soviet leaders saw it as inevitable that their empire would surpass the economic power of the West. To many of them, capitalism had been discredited by the depression of the 1930's; moreover, the postwar economic rise of the Soviet Union was to them proof that central planning was the route to optimum economic growth. By the 1970's, most Soviet officials, it would appear, had lost much of this optimism. The goal now was to keep pace with the West; surpassing it was apparently viewed as unlikely. By the 1990's, the primary goal was mere survival in face of food shortages, triple-digit inflation, environmental pollution, and widespread disease.

By this point, it was clear that increased defense spending in the mid to late-1980's had done more harm than good to the economy, but it may be an exaggeration to conclude that a bloated military budget was the Soviet Union's "Achilles heel". The U.S.S.R., had it invested adequately in research and development, may have been able to continue its rivalry with the United States. At one point, the U.S.S.R. and the U.S. were equally-matched in technology; perhaps in the late 1950's, when it launched *Sputnik,* the Soviet Union might have been the most technologically advanced nation on earth. After this peak in the late-1950's, Soviet technology, as well as its economy, started to decline. By the mid-1960's, the U.S.S.R. was lagging behind the U.S. in the number of prototypes of machines, equipment, instruments, and computers. Not surprisingly, the economy was also by this time starting to weaken; it continued to do so until the mid-1980's, when Gorbachev sought to reform not only the economy, but also the defense, both of which—almost together—had been sinking deeper into decline for decades.

A balanced conclusion might be that on one hand, his increases in defense spending almost definitely hurt the economy by increasing the national debt. On the other hand, the defense perhaps would not have been in such shambles had it been financed by a vibrant economy. In some ways, then, the arms race helped bankrupt the economy of the U.S.S.R., but it was arguably going toward insolvency anyway. Increased defense spending probably accelerated, but not necessarily caused, economic collapse.

Questions for Contemplation and Discussion

1. What is the main argument, or thesis, of the excerpt from Edwin Meese's book?

2. Meese was the U.S. Attorney General under President Reagan. Do you think it was therefore impossible for Meese to be completely objective? Explain.

3. What kinds of evidence does Bowman cite to support his own thesis? What are some possible questions one should ask about the evidence before accepting it? Explain.

4. Bowman blames the collapse of the Soviet Union largely on the economy. What other possible causes should one consider, not just about the reasons behind the Soviet Union's collapse, but about the decline of ANY country, past or present? Explain.

WHO SHOULD CONTROL PALESTINE?

Theodore Herzl[83]

Theodore Herzl (1860–1904) was an Austrian Jew who founded the Zionist movement.

No one can deny the gravity of the situation of the Jews. Wherever they live in perceptible numbers, they are more or less persecuted. Their equality before the law, granted by statute, has become practically a dead letter. They are debarred from filling even moderately high positions, either in the army, or in any public or private capacity. And attempts are made to thrust them out of business also: "Don't buy from Jews!"

We are one people—our enemies have made us one without our consent, as repeatedly happens in history. Distress binds us together, and, thus united, we suddenly discover our strength. Yes, we are strong enough to form a State, and, indeed, a model State. We possess all human and material resources necessary for the purpose.

This is therefore the appropriate place to give an account of what has been somewhat roughly termed our "human material." But it would not be appreciated till the broad lines of the plan, on which everything depends, has first been marked out.

The Plan

The whole plan is in its essence perfectly simple, as it must necessarily be if it is to come within the comprehension of all.

Let the sovereignty be granted us over a portion of the globe large enough to satisfy the rightful requirements of a nation; the rest we shall manage for ourselves.

The creation of a new State is neither ridiculous nor impossible. We have in our day witnessed the process in connection with nations which were not largely members of the middle class, but poorer, less educated, and consequently weaker than ourselves. The Governments of all countries scourged by Anti-Semitism will be keenly interested in assisting us to obtain the sovereignty we want.

Palestine is our ever-memorable historic home. The very name of Palestine would attract our people with a force of marvellous potency. If His Majesty the Sultan [term meaning "political leader" in many Muslim countries] were to give us Palestine, we could in return undertake to regulate the whole finances of Turkey. We should there form a portion of a rampart of Europe against Asia, an outpost of civilization as opposed to barbarism. We should as a neutral State remain in contact with all Europe, which would have to guarantee our existence. The sanctuaries of Christendom would be safeguarded by assigning to them an extra-territorial status such as is well-known to the law of nations. We should form a guard of honor about these sanctuaries, answering for the fulfilment of this duty with our existence. This guard of honor would be the great symbol of the solution of the Jewish Question after eighteen centuries of Jewish suffering.

The Palestinian National Charter: Resolutions of the Palestine National Council, July 1–17, 1968[84]

This is the written constitution of the Palestinian Liberation Organization, which was created in the 1960s to set up an independent Palestine.

Article 1: Palestine is the homeland of the Arab Palestinian people; it is an indivisible part of the Arab homeland, and the Palestinian people are an integral part of the Arab nation.

Article 2: Palestine, with the boundaries it had during the British Mandate, is an indivisible territorial unit.

Article 3: The Palestinian Arab people possess the legal right to their homeland and have the right to determine their destiny after achieving the liberation of their country in accordance with their wishes and entirely of their own accord and will.

Article 4: The Palestinian identity is a genuine, essential, and inherent characteristic; it is transmitted from parents to children. The Zionist occupation and the dispersal of the Palestinian Arab people, through the disasters which befell them, do not make them lose their Palestinian identity and their membership in the Palestinian community, nor do they negate them.

Source: From *The Jewish State: An Attempt at a Modern Solution of the Jewish Question* by Theodor Herzl. Copyright © 1946 by American Zionist Emergency Council. Reprinted by permission of the American Zionist Movement.
Source: Palestine National Charter.

Article 5: The Palestinians are those Arab nationals who, until 1947, normally resided in Palestine regardless of whether they were evicted from it or have stayed there. Anyone born, after that date, of a Palestinian father—whether inside Palestine or outside it—is also a Palestinian.

Article 6: The Jews who had normally resided in Palestine until the beginning of the Zionist invasion will be considered Palestinians.

Article 7: That there is a Palestinian community and that it has material, spiritual, and historical connection with Palestine are indisputable facts. It is a national duty to bring up individual Palestinians in an Arab revolutionary manner. All means of information and education must be adopted in order to acquaint the Palestinian with his country in the most profound manner, both spiritual and material, that is possible. He must be prepared for the armed struggle and ready to sacrifice his wealth and his life in order to win back his homeland and bring about its liberation . . .

Article 9: Armed struggle is the only way to liberate Palestine. This it is the overall strategy, not merely a tactical phase. The Palestinian Arab people assert their absolute determination and firm resolution to continue their armed struggle and to work for an armed popular revolution for the liberation of their country and their return to it. They also assert their right to normal life in Palestine and to exercise their right to self-determination and sovereignty over it . . .

Article 11: The Palestinians will have three mottoes: national (wataniyya) unity, national (qawmiyya) mobilization, and liberation.

Article 12: The Palestinian people believe in Arab unity. In order to contribute their share toward the attainment of that objective, however, they must, at the present stage of their struggle, safeguard their Palestinian identity and develop their consciousness of that identity, and oppose any plan that may dissolve or impair it.

Article 13: Arab unity and the liberation of Palestine are two complementary objectives, the attainment of either of which facilitates the attainment of the other. Thus, Arab unity leads to the liberation of Palestine, the liberation of Palestine leads to Arab unity; and work toward the realization of one objective proceeds side by side with work toward the realization of the other . . .

Article 15: The liberation of Palestine, from an Arab viewpoint, is a national (qawmi) duty and it attempts to repel the Zionist and imperialist aggression against the Arab homeland, and aims at the elimination of Zionism in Palestine. Absolute responsibility for this falls upon the Arab nation—peoples and governments—with the Arab people of Palestine in the vanguard . . .

Article 16: The liberation of Palestine, from a spiritual point of view, will provide the Holy Land with an atmosphere of safety and tranquility, which in turn will safeguard the country's religious sanctuaries and guarantee freedom of worship and of visit to all, without discrimination of race, color, language, or religion. Accordingly, the people of Palestine look to all spiritual forces in the world for support.

Article 17: The liberation of Palestine, from a human point of view, will restore to the Palestinian individual his dignity, pride, and freedom. Accordingly the Palestinian Arab people look forward to the support of all those who believe in the dignity of man and his freedom in the world.

Article 18: The liberation of Palestine, from an international point of view, is a defensive action necessitated by the demands of self-defense. Accordingly the Palestinian people, desirous as they are of the friendship of all people, look to freedom-loving, and peace-loving states for support in order to restore their legitimate rights in Palestine, to re-establish peace and security in the country, and to enable its people to exercise national sovereignty and freedom.

Article 19: The partition of Palestine in 1947 and the establishment of the state of Israel are entirely illegal, regardless of the passage of time, because they were contrary to the will of the Palestinian people and to their natural right in their homeland, and inconsistent with the principles embodied in the Charter of the United Nations; particularly the right to self-determination . . .

Article 22: Zionism is a political movement organically associated with international imperialism and antagonistic to all action for liberation and to progressive movements in the world. It is racist and fanatic in its nature, aggressive, expansionist, and colonial in its aims, and fascist in its methods . . .

Article 23: The demand of security and peace, as well as the demand of right and justice, require all states to consider Zionism an illegitimate movement, to outlaw its existence, and to ban its operations, in order that friendly relations among peoples may be preserved, and the loyalty of citizens to their respective homelands safeguarded.

Article 24: The Palestinian people believe in the principles of justice, freedom, sovereignty, self-determination, human dignity, and in the right of all peoples to exercise them.

Article 25: For the realization of the goals of this Charter and its principles, the Palestine Liberation Organization will perform its role in the liberation of Palestine in accordance with the Constitution of this Organization . . .

Article 29: The Palestinian people possess the fundamental and genuine legal right to liberate and retrieve their homeland. The Palestinian people determine their attitude toward all states and forces on the basis of the stands they adopt vis-a-vis to the Palestinian revolution to fulfill the aims of the Palestinian people.

Questions for Contemplation and Discussion

1. Columnist Cal Thomas interprets Article 15 of the charter to mean "In the view of the Palestinians, no co-existence with Jews, much less an Israeli state, is possible."[73] Is a careful reading of the charter consistent with Thomas's interpretation?

2. Are there any articles in the charter that contradict each other? If so, identify them and explain how they are, or could appear to be, inconsistent.

3. What is Theodor Herzl's main point?

4. Some would say that an international body such as the United Nations should determine the answer to the question, "Who should control Palestine?" Would you agree? If so, why? If not, why not?

WHAT IS FUNDAMENTALISM?

The Fundamentals[85]

The Fundamentals: A Testimony to the Truth was published in the early 1900's by the Bible Institute of Los Angeles (California) as a series of pamphlets in defense of the inspiration of the Bible, the virgin birth, miracles, and other supernatural teachings, as well as the literal six-day creation. This book represents Protestant fundamentalism.

PROOF OF THE BIBLE'S INSPIRATION

How does the Bible prove itself to be a divinely inspired, heaven-given book, a communication from a Father to His children, and thus a revelation?

First, by the fact that, as does no other sacred book in the world, it condemns man and all his works. It does not praise either his wisdom, his reason, his art, or any progress that he has made; but it represents him as being in the sight of God, a miserable sinner, incapable of doing anything good, and deserving only death and endless perdition. Truly, a book which is able thus to speak, and in consequence causes millions of men, troubled in conscience, to prostrate themselves in the dust, crying, "God be merciful to me a sinner," must contain more than mere ordinary truth.

Secondly, the Bible exalts itself far above all merely human books by its announcement of the great incomprehensible mystery that, "God so loved the world that He gave His only begotten Son; that whosoever believeth in Him should not perish, but have everlasting life" (John 3:16). Where is there a god among all the heathen nations, be he Osiris, Brahma, Baal, Jupiter or Odin, that would have promised those people that, by taking upon himself the sin of the world and suffering its punishment, he would thus become a savior and redeemer to them?

Thirdly, the Bible sets the seal of its divine origin upon itself by means of the prophecies. Very appropriately does God inquire, through the prophet Isaiah, "Who, as I, shall call, and shall declare it, and set it in order for Me since I established the ancient people? and the things that are coming and shall come to pass, let them declare" (Isa Ch. 44:7). Or says again, "I am God, declaring the end from the beginning, and from ancient times, things not yet done, saying, My counsel shall stand, and I will do all My pleasure; calling a ravenous bird from the east, and the man of My counsel from afar country. Yea, I have spoken, I will also bring it to pass; I have purposed, I will also do it" (Isa Ch. 46 :10, 11). Or, addressing Pharaoh, "Where are thy wise men, and let them tell thee, and let them know what the Lord of Hosts hath purposed upon Egypt" (Isa Ch. 19:12).

Again we say, where is there a god, or gods, a founder of religion, such as Confucius, Buddha, or Mohammed, who could, with such certainty, have predicted the future of even his own people? Or where is there a statesman who in these times can foretell what will be the condition of things in Europe one hundred or even ten years from now? Nevertheless the prophecies of Moses and his threatened judgments upon the Israelites have been literally fulfilled. Literally also have been fulfilled, (although who at the time would have believed it?) the prophecies respecting the destruction of those great ancient cities, Babylon, Nineveh and Memphis [Egypt, not Tennessee]. Who in these times would believe a like prophecy respecting London, Paris, or New York?

Moreover, in a literal way has been fulfilled what the prophets David and Isaiah foresaw concerning the last sufferings of Christ—His death on the cross, His drinking of vinegar, and the casting of lots for His garments. And there are other prophecies which will still be most literally fulfilled, such as the promises made to Israel, the final judgment, and the end of the world. "For," as Habakkuk says, "the vision is yet for an appointed time, and will not lie. Though it tarry, wait for it; it will surely come" (Isa Ch. 2:3).

Furthermore, the Bible has demonstrated its peculiar power by its influence with the martyrs. Think of the hundreds of thousands who, at different times and among different peoples, have sacrificed their all, their wives, their children, all their possessions, and finally life itself, on account of this book. Think of how they have, on the rack and at the stake, confessed the truth of the Bible, and borne testimony to its power. However, O ye critics and despisers of God's Word, if you will only write such a book and then die for it, we will believe you.

Lastly, the Bible shows itself every day to be a divinely given book by its beneficent influence among all kinds of people. It converts to a better life the ignorant and the learned, the beggar on the street and the king upon his throne, yonder poor woman dwelling in an attic, the greatest poet and the profoundest thinker, civilized Europeans and uncultured savages. Despite all the scoffing and derision of its enemies, it has been translated into hundreds of languages, and has been preached by thousands of missionaries to millions of people. It makes the proud humble and the dissolute virtuous; it consoles the unfortunate, and teaches man how to live patiently and die triumphantly. No other book or collection of books accomplishes for man the exceeding great benefits accomplished by this book of truth.

MODERN CRITICISM AND ITS RATIONALISTIC METHOD

In these times there has appeared a criticism which, constantly growing bolder in its attacks upon this sacred book, now decrees, with all self-assurance and confidence, that it is simply a human production. Besides other faults found with it, it is declared to be full of errors, many of its books to be spurious, written by unknown men at later dates than those assigned, etc., etc. But we ask, upon what fundamental principle, what axiom, is this verdict of the critics based? It is upon the idea that, as [French philosopher Ernest] Renan expressed it, reason is capable of judging all things, but is itself judged by nothing. That is surely a proud dictum, but an empty one if its character is really noticed. To be sure, God has given reason to man, so that, in his customary way of planting and building, buying and selling, he may make a practical use of created nature by which he is surrounded. But is reason, even as respects matters of this life, in accord with itself? By no means. For, if that were so, whence comes all the strife and contention of men at home and abroad, in their places of business and their public assemblies, in art and science, in legislation, religion and philosophy? Does it not all proceed from the conflicts of reason? The entire history of our race is the history of millions of men gifted with reason who have been in perpetual conflict one with another. Is it with such reason, then, that sentence is to be pronounced upon a divinely given book? A purely rational revelation would certainly be a contradiction of terms; besides, it would be wholly superfluous. But when reason undertakes to speak of things entirely supernatural, invisible and eternal, it talks as a blind man does about colors, discoursing of matters concerning which it neither knows nor can know anything; and thus it makes itself ridiculous. It has not ascended up to heaven, neither has it descended into the deep; and therefore a purely rational religion is no religion at all.

INCOMPETENCY OF REASON FOR SPIRITUAL TRUTH

Reason alone has never inspired men with great sublime conceptions of spiritual truth, whether in the way of discovery or invention; but usually it has at first rejected and ridiculed such matters. And just so it is with these rationalistic critics, they have no appreciation or understanding of the high and sublime in God's Word. They understand neither the majesty of Isaiah, the pathos of David's repentance, the audacity of Moses' prayers, the philosophic depth of Ecclesiastes, nor the wisdom of Solomon which "uttereth her voice in the streets." According to them ambitious priests, at a later date than is commonly assigned, compiled all those books to which we have alluded; also they wrote the Sinaitic law, and invented the whole story of Moses' life. ("A magnificent fiction"—so one of the critics calls that story.) But if all this is so, then we must believe that cunning falsifiers, who were, however, so the critics say, devout men, genuine products of their day (although it calls for notice that the age in which those devout men lived, should, as was done to Christ, have persecuted and killed them, when usually an age loves its own children); that is to say, we must believe not only that shallow-minded men have uncovered for us eternal truths and the most distant future, but also that vulgar, interested liars, have declared to us the inexorable righteousness of a holy God! Of course, all that is nonsense; no one can believe it.

But if these critics discourse, as sometimes they do, with great self-assurance upon topics such as the history of Israel, the peculiar work of the prophets, revelation, inspiration, the essence of Christianity, the difference between the teachings of Christ and those of Paul, anyone who intelligently reads what they say is impressed with the idea that, although they display much ingenuity in their efforts, after all they do not really understand the matters concerning which they speak. In like manner they talk with much ingenuity and show of learning about men with whom they have only a far-off acquaintance; and they discuss events in the realm of the Spirit where they have had no personal experience. Thus they both illustrate and prove the truth of the Scripture teaching that "the natural man receiveth not the things of the Spirit of God." These critics say that God, not being a man, cannot speak; consequently there is no word of God!

Also, God cannot manifest Himself in visible form; therefore all the accounts of such epiphanies are mythical tales! Inspiration, they tell us, is unthinkable; hence all representations of such acts are diseased imagination! Of prophecy there is none; what purports to be such was written after the events! Miracles are impossible; therefore all the reports of them, as given in the Bible, are mere fictions! Men always seek, thus it is explained, their own advantage and personal glory, and just so it was with those "prophets of Israel." Such is what they call "impartial science," "unprejudiced research," "objective demonstration."

Ayatollah Imam Sayyid Ruhollah al-Musavi al-Khomeini[86]

Khomeini (1900–1989) became the Supreme Leader of Iran after Muslim fundamentalists led a revolution to overthrown the Shah, who had the support of many Western powers.

Imam Sayyid Ruholtah al-Musavi al-Khomeini

Islamic Government
Hukournat-i Islami

Islam is the religion of militant individuals who are committed to truth and justice. It is the religion of those who desire freedom and independence. It is the school of those who struggle against imperialism. But the servants of imperialism have presented Islam in a totally different light. They have created in men's minds a false notion of Islam. The defective version of Islam, which they have presented in the religious teaching institution, is intended to deprive Islam of its vital, revolutionary aspect and to prevent Muslims from arousing themselves in order to gain their freedom, fulfill the ordinances of Islam, and create a government that will assure their happiness and allow them to live lives worthy of human beings.

For example, the servants of imperialism declared that Islam is not a comprehensive religion providing for every aspect of human life and has no laws or ordinances pertaining to society. It has no particular form of government. Islam concerns itself only with rules of ritual purity after menstruation and parturition. It may have a few ethical principles, but it certainly has nothing to say about human life in general and the ordering of society.

This kind of evil propaganda has unfortunately had an effect.

Quite apart from the masses, the educated class—university students and also many students at the religious teaching institutions—have failed to understand Islam correctly and have erroneous notions. Just as people may, in general, be unacquainted with a stranger, so too they are unacquainted with Islam; Islam lives among the people of this world as if it were a stranger. If somebody were to present Islam as it truly is, he would find it difficult to make people believe him. In fact, the agents of imperialism in the religious teaching institutions would raise a hue and cry against him.

In order to demonstrate to some degree how great the difference is between Islam and what is presented as Islam, I would like to draw your attention to the difference between the Qur'an and the books of hadith, on the one hand, and the practical treatises of jurisprudence, on the other. The Qur'an and the books of hadith, which represent the sources for the commands arid ordinances of Islam, are completely different from the treatises written by the mujtahids of the present age both in breadth of scope and in the effect they are capable of exerting on time life of society.

The ratio of Qur'anic verses concerned with the affairs of society to those concerned with ritual worship is greater than a hundred to one. Of the approximately fifty sections of the corpus of hadith containing all the ordinances of Islam, not more than three or four sections relate to matters of ritual worship and the duties of man toward his Creator and Sustainer. A few more are concerned with questions of ethics, and all the rest are concerned with social, economic, legal, and political questions—in short, the gestation of society.

You who represent the younger generation and who, God willing, will be of service to Islam in the future must strive diligently all your lives to pursue the aims I will now set forth and to impart the laws and ordinances of Islam. In whatever way you deem most beneficial, in writing or in speech, instruct the people about the problems Islam has had to contend with since its inception and about the enemies and afflictions that now threaten it.

Do not allow the true nature of Islam to remain hidden, or people will imagine that Islam is like Christianity (nominal, not true Christianity), a collection of injunctions pertaining to man's relation to God, and the mosque will be equated with the church.

At a time when the West was a realm of darkness and obscurity—with its inhabitants living in a state of barbarism and America still peopled by half-savage redskins and the two vast empires of Iran and Byzantium were under the rule of tyranny, class privilege, and discrimination, and the powerful dominated all without any trace of law oraopular government, God, Exalted and Almighty, by means of the Most Noble Messenger (peace and blessings be upon him), sent laws that astound us with their magnitude. He instituted laws and practices for all human affairs and laid down injunctions for man extending from even before the embryo is formed until after he is placed in the tomb. In just the same way that there are laws setting forth the duties of worship for man, so too there are laws, practices, and norms for the affairs of society and government. Islamic law is a progressive, evolving, and comprehensive system of law. All the voluminous books that have been compiled from the earliest

---

Source: Excerpts from *Islamic Government: Governance of the Jurist* by Imam Sayyid Ruhollah Al-Musavi Al-Khomeini, translated and annotated by Dr. Hamid Algar. Copyright © by Islamic Publications International. Reprinted by permission.

dines on different areas of law, such as judicial procedure, social transactions, penal law, retribution, international relations, regulations pertaining to peace and war, private and public law—taken together, these contain a mere sample of the laws and injunctions of Islam. There is not a single topic in human life for which Islam has not provided instruction and established a norm. . . .

This is all the result of the wave of propaganda that has now reached the religious teaching institution and imposed on us the duty of proving that Islam also possesses rules of government. That is our situation then—created for us by the foreigners through their propaganda and their agents. They have removed from operation all the judicial processes and political laws of Islam and replaced them with European importations, thus diminishing the scope of Islam and ousting it from Islamic society. For the sake of exploitation they have installed their agents in power.

So far, we have sketched the subversive and corrupting plan of imperialism. We must now take into consideration as well certain internal factors, notably the dazzling effect that the material progress of the imperialist countries has had on some members of our society. As the imperialist countries attained a high degree of wealth and affluence—the result both of scientific and technical progress and of their plunder of the nations of Asia and Africa—these individuals lost all self-confidence and imagined that the only way to achieve technical progress was to abandon their own laws and beliefs. When the moon landings took place, for instance, they concluded that Muslims should jettison their laws! But what is the connection between going to the moon and the laws of Islam? Do they not see that countries having opposing laws and social systems compete with each other in technical and scientific progress and the conquest of space! Let them go all the way to Mars or beyond the Milky Way; they will still be deprived of true happiness, moral virtue, and spiritual advancement and be unable to solve their own social problems. For the solution of social problems and the relief of human misery require foundations in faith and morals; merely acquiring material power and wealth conquering nature and space, have no effect in this regard. They must be supplemented by, and balanced with, the faith, the conviction, and the morality of Islam in order truly to serve humanity instead of endangering it. This conviction, this morality, these laws that are needed, we already possess. So as soon as someone goes somewhere or invents something, we should not hurry to abandon our religion and its laws, which regulate the life of man and provide for his well-being in this world and the hereafter.

The same applies to the propaganda of the imperialists. Unfortunately, some members of our society have been influenced by their hostile propaganda, although they should not have been.

The imperialists have propagated among us the view that Islam does not have a specific form of government or governmental institutions. They say further that even if Islam does have certain laws, it has no method for enforcing them, so that its function is purely legislative. This kind of propaganda forms part of the overall plan of the imperialists to prevent the Muslims from becoming involved in political activity and establishing an Islamic government. It is in total contradiction with our fundamental beliefs.

We believe in government and believe that the Prophet (upon whom be peace) was bound to appoint a successor, as he indeed did.

Was a successor designated purely for the sake of expounding law! The expounding of law did not require a successor to the Prophet.

He himself, after all, had expounded the laws; it would have been enough for the laws to be written down in a book and put into the people's hands to guide them in their actions. It was logically necessary for a successor to be appointed for the sake of exercising government. Law requires a person to execute it. The same holds true in all countries of the world, for the establishment of a law is of little benefit in itself and cannot secure the happiness of man. After a law is established, it is necessary also to create an executive power. If a system of law or government lacks all executive power, it is clearly deficient. Thus Islam, just as it established laws, also brought into being an executive power.

There was still a further question: who was to hold the executive power! If the Prophet (upon whom be peace and blessings) had not appointed a successor to assume the executive power, he would have failed to complete his mission, as the Qur'an testifies. The necessity for the implementation of divine law, the need for an executive power, and the importance of that power in fulfilling the goals of the prophetic mission and establishing a just order that would result in the happiness of mankind—all of this made the appointment of a successor synonymous with the completion of the prophetic mission. In the time of the Prophet, laws were not merely expounded and promulgated; they were also implemented. The Messenger of God was an executor of the law.

For example, he implemented the penal provisions of Islam: he cut off the hand of the thief and administered lashings and stonings. The successor to the Prophet must do the same; his task is not legislation, but the implementation of the divine laws that the Prophet has promulgated. It is for this reason that the formation of a government and the establishment of executive organs are necessary. Belief in the necessity for these is part of the general belief in the Imamate, as are, too, exertion and struggle for the sake of establishing them.

Questions for Contemplation and Discussion

1. Would you agree with the fundamentalist position that life would be better if every person obeyed every teaching in the Bible? Why? Why not?

2. Is it impossible for reason to comprehend matters of faith?

3. What is Khomeini's main point?

4. What is Khomeini's interpretation of Islam? What kind of religion is it?

5. What does Khomeini say about the "West"? Is he right? Explain your answer with evidence and reasoning.

6. Fundamentalists often believe that women should be treated as less than men. Other than leaving, what can and should women do in countries, such as Iran, that are led by fundamentalists?

BIBLIOGRAPHY

Africapacific.com. Accessed December 21, 2006.

Alperovitz, Gar. *The Decision to Use the Atomic Bomb and the Architecture of an American Myth.* New York: Alfred Knopf, 1995.

Althouse.blogspot.com. Accessed December 21, 2006.

Arendt, Hannah. *Eichmann in Jerusalem: A Report on the Banality of Evil.* New York: The Viking Press, 1963.

Aristotle, *The Nicomachean Ethics of Aristotle.* Translated by F.H. Peters. London: Kegan Paul, 1893.

Aston, W.G. trans. *Nihongi: Chronicles of Japan from the Earliest Times to A.D. 607, Transactions and Proceedings of The Japan Society, Supplement 1* (London: Kegan, Paul, 1896.

de Azurara, Gomes Eannes. *The Chronicle of the Discovery and Conquest of Guinea.* Translated by C.R. Beazley and Edgar Prestage. London: Hakluyt Society, 1896.

Bettex, F. "The Bible and Modern Criticism," *The Fundamentals: A Testimony to the Faith.*, ed. R. A. Torrey. Chicago: Testimony, 1910.

Blake, William. *Songs of Innocence and Songs of Experience.* London: R.B. Johnson, 1901.

Boccaccio. *The Decameron*, translated by M. Rigg. London: David Campbell, 1921.

Bourne, Edward G., ed. *Journal of the First Voyage of Columbus.* New York: Scribner and Sons, 1906.

Bowman, Glen. "The Decline and Fall of the Soviet Union." Unpublished paper.

The Breviary of Eberhard of Bamberg ed. Zeumer in MG.LL. Sec V, Formulae, p. 650. translated in University of Pennsylvania Translations and Reprints. Philadelphia: University of Pennsylvania Press, 1898.

Brown, Flora B., ed. Elizabeth City State University

Christian Classic Ethereal Library. Accessed on February 11, 2005 at www.ccel.org

Chang, Iris. *The Rape of Nanking: The Forgotten Holocaust of World War II.* New York: Basic Books, 1997.

Clarkson, Thomas. *The History of the Rise, Progress and Accomplishment of the Abolition of the African Slave-Trade, by the British Parliament.* London: J. W. Parker, 1839.

Davis, William Stearns, ed. *Readings in Ancient History: Illustrative Extracts from the Sources.* 2 Vols. Boston: Allyn and Bacon, 1913.

Deathpenaltyinfo.org. Accessed December 21, 2006.

Defoe. *History of the Plague in London.* New York: American Book Company, 1894.

Dewey. *Democracy and Education: An Introduction to the Philosophy of Education.* New York: MacMillan, 1916.

Dickens, Charles. *American Notes, Reprinted Pieces: The Works of Charles Dickens.* NY: Peter Fenelon Collier, 1900.

Equiano, Olaudah. *The Life of Olaudah Equiano, or Gustavus Vassa, the African.* Boston: Knapp, 1837.

Francke, Kuno, ed. *The German Classics of The Nineteenth and Twentieth Centuries, Vol. X: Prince Otto Von Bismarck, Count Helmuth Von Moltke, Ferdinand Lassalle.* 1914.

Gibbon, Edward. *The Decline and Fall of the Roman Empire.* 6 volumes. Edited by Oliphant Smeaton. New York: Dutton, 1910.

Giles, Lionel, ed. *Sun Tzu on the Art of War.* London, 1910.

Goldman, Emma. "Patriotism: A Menace to Liberty", in *Anarchism & Other Essays.* New York: Mother Earth Publishing, 1911.

Gordon, Ruth E., and Clive J. Talbot, eds. *From Dias to Vorster: Source material on South African history 1488–1975.* Cape Town: Nasou, 1977.

Harper, Robert Francis, ed. *The Code of Hammurabi, King of Babylon.* Chicago: University of Chicago Press, 1904.

Herzl, Theodor. *The Jewish State: An Attempt at a Modern Solution of the Jewish Question.* New York: American Zionist Emergency Council, 1946.

Hobbes. *Leviathan.* London: Andrew Crooke, 1651.

Hume, David. *An Enquiry Concerning Human Understanding.* Edited by L.A. Selby-Bigge. Oxford: Oxford University Press, 1902.

Islam-pedia.com. Accessed December 21, 2006.

Jack, Homer, ed. *The Gandhi Reader: A Source Book of His Life and Writings.* New York: AMS Press, 1956.

Kaegl, Walter Emil, Jr., and Peter White, eds. *Readings in Western Civilization.* Chicago: University of Chicago Press, 1986.

Kramer, Heinrich, and James Sprenger. *Malleus Maleficarum.* Translated by Montague Summers. New York: Benjamin Blum, 1920, 1970.

Laqueur, Walter, and Barry Rubin, eds. *The Human Rights Reader.* New York: Penguin Books, 1990.

Lenin, V.I. *On the Intelligentsia.* Edited by S.A. Fedyukin and I.K. Eldarova. Moscow: Progress Publishers, 1983.

Li, Dun J. ed. *The Civilization of China.* New York: Charles Scribner's Sons, 1975.

Lim, Richard, and David Kammerling Smith, eds. *The West in the Wider World: Sources and Perspectives, Volume 1.* Boston and New York: Bedford/St. Martin's, 2003.

Locke. *Two Treatises of Government.* London, 1688.

Locke, John. *Two Treatises on Civil Government.* Edited by Henry Morley. London: Routledge, 1884.

Lugard, F.D. *The Rise of Our East African Empire.* London: William Blackwood and Sons, 1893.

Luther. *The Smalcald Articles.* translated by F. Bente and W. H. T. Dau. St. Louis: Concordia Publishing House, 1921.

Mazzini, Guiseppe. *An Essay On the Duties of Man Addressed to Workingmen.* New York: Funk & Wagnalls, 1898.

Meese, Edwin, III, *With Reagan: The Inside Story.* Washington, D.C.: Regnery Gateway, 1992.

Mideastweb.org. Accessed December 17, 2004.

Newadvent.org. Accessed January 18, 2005.

Norton, Arthur O., *Readings in the History of Education: Mediaeval Universities.* Cambridge, MA: Harvard University Press, 1909.

Nyconsulate.prchina.org. Accessed January 4, 2005.

Olson, Julius E., ed. *The Voyages of the Northmen.* New York: Scribner and Sons, 1906.

Ponet, John. *Short Treatise of Politic Power.* London, 1556.

Procopius. *The History of the Wars, Volumes I and II.* translated by H.B. Dewing. London: Heinemann, 1914.

Prothero, G.W., ed. *Select Statutes and Other Constitutional Documents Illustrative of the Reigns of Elizabeth and James I.* Oxford: Clarendon Press, 1913.

Rigby, T.H., ed. *Stalin.* Englewood Cliffs, NJ: Prentice Hall, 1966.

Riley, Philip F., et al (four additional editors), ed. *The Global Experience: Readings in World History to 1500.* Englewood Cliffs, NJ: Prentice Hall, 1992.

Robinson, James Harvey, ed. *Readings in European History.* 2 volumes. Boston: Ginn and Company, 1904 and 1906.

Robinson, James Harvey, and Charles A. Beard, eds. *Readings in Modern European History.* 2 volumes. Boston: Ginn and Company, 1908 and 1909.

Rodwell, J. M., trans. *The Koran.* London and New York: J.M. Dent and E.P. Dutton, 1909.

Rogers, Perry, ed. *Aspects of Western Civilization: Problems and Sources in History.* 2 volumes. Englewood Cliffs, NJ: Prentice-Hall, 1988.

Rottenberg, Annette T. *Elements of Argument: A Text and Reader.* Boston: Bedford Books of St. Martin's Press, 1991.

Shillington, Kevin. *History of Africa.* Oxford: Oxford University Press, 1995.

Smith, Adam. *An Inquiry into the Nature and Causes of the Wealth of Nations.* London: Dent, 1904.

Snyder, Louis L., ed. *Documents of German History.* Westport, CT: Greenwood Press, 1958.

Sowell, Thomas. *Conquest and Cultures: An International History.* New York: Basic Books, 1998.

Stanton, Elizabeth Cady, S.B. Anthony and M.J. Gage, eds. *A History of Women's Suffrage.* 2 volumes. Rochester, N.Y.: Fowler and Wells, 1889.

Thatcher, Oliver J., ed. *The Library of Original Sources.* 7 volumes. New York: University Research Extension, 1907.

Thatcher, Oliver J., and Edgar Holmes McNeal, eds. *A Source Book for Medieval History.* New York: Scribners, 1905.

Trumanlibrary.org. Accessed January 19, 2005.

Tse-Tung, Mao. *Selected Military Writings of Mao Tse-Tung.* Peking: Foreign Languages Press, 1967.

Tutu, Desmond. "The Question of South Africa," *Africa Report* 30 (January_February 1985): 50–52

Urbancure.org. Accessed December 21, 2006.

Vetter, Herbert F., ed. *Speak Out Against the New Right.* Boston: Beacon Press, 1982.

Waterworth, J., ed. and translator. *The Council of Trent, The Twenty-Fifth Session. The canons and decrees of the sacred and ecumenical Council of Trent.* London: Dolman, 1848.

Weber, Eugen, ed. *The Western Tradition, Volume 1.* Lexington, MA: D.C. Heath and Company, 1990.

White, Theodore. *Fire in the Ashes.* New York: William Sloane Associates Publishers, 1953.

Wikipedia.org. Accessed December 21, 2006.

Williams, Eric. *Capitalism and Slavery.* Chapel Hill: University of North Carolina Press, 1940; reprinted, New York: G. P. Putnam's Sons, 1966.

Wilson, Epiphanius, ed. *Chinese Literature Comprising the Analects of Confucius, the Sayings of Mencius, the Shi-King, the Travels of Fâ-Hien, and the Sorrows of Han.* New York: The Colonial Press, 1900.

Winsor, Justin. *Christopher Columbus and How He Received and Impaired the Spirit of Discovery.* Boston: Houghton Mifflin, 1892.

Wollstonecraft, Mary. *A Vindication of the Rights of Woman.* London: Walter Scott, 1891.

Wu-chi, Liu, ed. *An Introduction of Chinese Literature.* Bloomington, IN: Indiana University Press, 1966.

www.wandea.org.pl. Accessed December 20, 2006. Khomeini. *Islamic Government.* Translated by Hamid Alger. 1970.

ENDNOTES

[1] From the King James Version

[2] From W.G. Aston, trans. *Nihongi: Chronicles of Japan from the Earliest Times to A.D. 607, Transactions and Proceedings of The Japan Society, Supplement 1* (London: Kegan, Paul, 1896), 1–45.

[3] Robert Francis Harper, ed. *The Code of Hammurabi, King of Babylon* (Chicago: University of Chicago Press, 1904), 11–81.

[4] Dun J. Li, ed. *The Civilization of China* (New York: Charles Scribner's Sons, 1975), 259–269.

[5] Oliver J. Thatcher, ed. *The Library of Original Sources* (New York: University Research Extension, 1907), 1:385, 388, 389, 392, 399, 401, 402, 403, 405, 407.

[6] Aristotle, *The Nicomachean Ethics of Aristotle*, trans. F.H. Peters (London: Kegan Paul, 1893).

[7] From the King James Version

[8] Heinrich Kramer and James Sprenger, *Malleus Maleficarum*, trans. Montague Summers (New York: Benjamin Blum, 1928, 1970), 43–45.

[9] Mary Wollstonecraft, *A Vindication of the Rights of Woman* (London: Walter Scott, 1891).

[10] James Harvey Robinson, ed. *Readings in European History* (Boston: Ginn and Company, 1906), 2:219–221.

[11] Locke, *Two Treatises on Civil Government*, ed. Henry Morley (London: Routledge, 1884).

[12] Oliver J. Thatcher, ed. *The Library of Original Sources*, 4:361–363.

[13] David Hume, *An Enquiry Concerning Human Understanding*, ed. L.A. Selby-Bigge (Oxford, 1902)

[14] James Harvey Robinson and Charles A. Beard, eds. *Readings in Modern European History* (Boston: Ginn and Company, 1909), 2: 251–253.

[15] Elizabeth Cady Stanton, S.B. Anthony and M.J. Gage, eds. *A History of Women's Suffrage*, vol. 1 (Rochester, N.Y.: Fowler and Wells, 1889), 70–71.

[16] Liu Wu-chi, ed. *An Introduction of Chinese Literature* (Bloomington, IN: Indiana University Press, 1966), 82–83.

[17] Kuno Francke, ed. *The German Classics of The Nineteenth and Twentieth Centuries, Vol. X: Prince Otto Von Bismarck, Count Helmuth Von Moltke, Ferdinand Lassalle* (1914).

[18] Epiphanius Wilson, ed. *Chinese Literature Comprising the Analects of Confucius, the Sayings of Mencius, the Shi-King, the Travels of Fâ-Hien, and the Sorrows of Han* (New York: The Colonial Press, 1900).

[19] Arthur O. Norton, *Readings in the History of Education: Mediaeval Universities* (Cambridge, MA: Harvard University Press, 1909).

[20] Dewey, *Democracy and Education: An Introduction to the Philosophy of Education* (New York: MacMillan, 1916).

[21] Iris Chang, *The Rape of Nanking: The Forgotten Holocaust of World War II* (New York: Basic Books, 1997), 92–93.

[22] "Execution of the Jews at Dubno, October 5, 1942," in Louis L. Snyder, ed. *Documents of German History* (Westport, CT: Greenwood Press, 1958), 462–464.

[23] James Harvey Robinson, ed. *Readings in European History*, 1:313.

[24] Ibid., 2:130–131.

[25] Ibid., 2:380–381.

[26] Lionel Giles, ed. *Sun Tzu on the Art of War* (London, 1910).

[27] Oliver J. Thatcher, and Edgar Holmes McNeal, eds., *A Source Book for Medieval History* (New York: Scribners, 1905), 417–418.

[28] *The Koran*, trans. J.M. Rodwell (London and New York: J.M. Dent ; E.P. Dutton, 1909).

[29] Adopted at the Third Session of the Fifth National People's Congress on September 10,1980,and amended in accordance with "Decision Regarding the Amendment (of Marriage Law of the People's Republic of China)" passed at 21st. Session of the Standing Committee of the Ninth National People's Congress on April 28, 2001. Accessed on January 4, 2005 at www.nyconsulate.prchina.org/eng/lsqz/laws/t42222.htm

[30] Boccaccio, *The Decameron*, trans. M. Rigg, (London: David Campbell, 1921), 1:5–11.

[31] Defoe, *History of the Plague in London* (New York: American Book Company, 1894).

[32] John Ponet, *Short Treatise of Politic Power* (London, 1556).

[33] Gandhi, "On Home Rule," in Homer Jack, ed. *The Gandhi Reader: A Source Book of His Life and Writings* (New York: AMS Press, 1956), 112–113.

[34] Walter Emil Kaegl, Jr. and Peter White, eds. *Readings in Western Civilization* (Chicago: University of Chicago Press, 1986), 2:284–289.

[35] Adam Smith, *An Inquiry into the Nature and Causes of the Wealth of Nations* (London: Dent, 1904).

[36] William Stearns Davis, ed., *Readings in Ancient History: Illustrative Extracts from the Sources*, 2 Vols. (Boston: Allyn and Bacon, 1913), 2:166–172.

[37] Oliver J. Thatcher, ed. *The Library of Original Sources*, 5: 71–75.

[38] Hobbes, *Leviathan* (London: Andrew Crooke, 1651).

[39] Locke, *Two Treatises of Government* (London, 1688).

[40] James Harvey Robinson and Charles A. Beard, eds. *Readings in Modern European History*, 2: 431–433.

[41] "An Act for the Relief of the Poor," Elizabeth I, 1563, in G.W. Prothero, *Select Statutes and Other Constitutional Documents Illustrative of the Reigns of Elizabeth and James I* (Oxford: Clarendon Press, 1913), 41–43.

[42] Charles Dickens, *American Notes, Reprinted Pieces: The Works of Charles Dickens* (NY: Peter Fenelon Collier, 1900).

[43] *The Breviary of Eberhard of Bamberg* ed. Zeumer in *MG.LL. Sec V, Formulae*, p. 650. translated in University of Pennsylvania Translations and Reprints (Philadelphia: University of Pennsylvania Press, 1898), 4:4:7–9.
[44] From the King James Version.
[45] Victor F. Weisskopf, "On Avoiding Nuclear Holocaust," in Herbert F. Vetter, ed. *Speak Out Against the New Right* (Boston: Beacon Press, 1982), 183–184.
[46] Oliver J. Thatcher, ed. *The Library of Original Sources*, 1:72–73.
[47] *The Koran*, trans. J.M. Rodwell, J. M.
[48] Oliver J. Thatcher, ed. *The Library of Original Sources*, 1: 211–213.
[49] Edward Gibbon, *The Decline and Fall of the Roman Empire*, ed. Oliphant Smeaton (New York: Dutton, 1910), 4:175–176.
[50] Augustine, *St. Augustine's City of God and Christian Doctrine*, ed. Philip Schaff (New York: The Christian Literature Publishing Co., 1890). Accessed on February 11, 2005 at http://www.ccel.org/ccel/schaff/npnf102.html
[51] Procopius, *The History of the Wars, Volumes I and II*, trans. H.B. Dewing (London: Heinemann, 1914).
[52] *The Voyages of the Northmen*, ed. Julius E. Olson (New York: Scribner and Sons, 1906).
[53] *Journal of the First Voyage of Columbus* Ed. by Edward G. Bourne (New York: Scribner and Sons, 1906).
[54] Pope Leo XIII, "Quarto Abeunte Saeculo, Encyclical promulgated on July 16, 1892." Accessed on January 18, 2005 at http://www.newadvent.org/library/docs_le13qs.htm. Accessed January 18
[55] Justin Winsor, *Christopher Columbus and How He Received and Impaired the Spirit of Discovery* (Boston: Houghton Mifflin, 1892).
[56] Gomes Eannes de Azurara, *The Chronicle of the Discovery and Conquest of Guinea*, trans. C.R. Beazley and Edgar Prestage (London: Hakluyt Society, 1896), 1:81–83.
[57] Olaudah Equiano, *The Life of Olaudah Equiano, or Gustavus Vassa, the African* (Boston: Knapp, 1837).
[58] Luther, *The Smalcald Articles*, trans. F. Bente and W. H. T. Dau (St. Louis: Concordia Publishing House, 1921), 453–529.
[59] *The Council of Trent, The Twenty-Fifth Session. The canons and decrees of the sacred and ecumenical Council of Trent*, ed. and trans. J. Waterworth (London: Dolman, 1848), 232–236.
[60] Thomas Clarkson, *The History of the Rise, Progress and Accomplishment of the Abolition of the African Slave-Trade, by the British Parliament* (London: J.W. Parker, 1839).
[61] Eric Williams, *Capitalism and Slavery* (Chapel Hill: University of North Carolina Press, 1940; reprinted, New York: G.P. Putnam's Sons, 1966).
[62] F.D. Lugard, *The Rise of Our East African Empire* (London: William Blackwood and Sons, 1893), 1:380–82.
[63] James Harvey Robinson and Charles A. Beard, eds. *Readings in Modern European History*, 2: 452–453.
[64] William Blake, *Songs of Innocence and Songs of Experience* (London: R.B. Johnson, 1901).
[65] James Harvey Robinson and Charles A. Beard, eds. *Readings in Modern European History*, 2: 485–487.
[66] Guiseppe Mazzini, *An Essay On the Duties of Man Addressed to Workingmen* (New York: Funk & Wagnalls, 1898), 59–63.
[67] Emma Goldman, "Patriotism: A Menace to Liberty", in *Anarchism & Other Essays* (New York: Mother Earth Publishing, 1911).
[68] James Harvey Robinson and Charles A. Beard, eds. *Readings in Modern European History*, 2: 489–493.
[69] V.I. Lenin, *What is To be Done*, in *On the Intelligentsia*, S.A. Fedyukin and I.K. Eldarova, eds.(Moscow: Progress Publishers, 1983), 36–37.
[70] Mao Tse-Tung, *Selected Military Writings of Mao Tse-Tung* (Peking: Foreign Languages Press, 1967), 383, 386, 388, 389.
[71] Theodore White, *Fire in the Ashes* (New York: William Sloane Associates Publishers, 1953), 318–320.
[72] Hannah Arendt, *Eichmann in Jerusalem: A Report on the Banality of Evil* (New York: The Viking Press, 1963), 148–50, 276.
[73] T.H. Rigby, ed. *Stalin* (Englewood Cliffs, NJ: Prentice Hall (division of Simon and Schuster), 1966), 111–112.
[74] Gar Alperovitz, *The Decision to Use the Atomic Bomb and the Architecture of an American Myth* (New York: Alfred Knopf, 1995), 627–639.
[75] Harry S. Truman, "Letter from Harry S. Truman to Roman Bohnen, December 12, 1946," from Truman Presidential Museum and Library. Accessed on January 19, 2005 at www.trumanlibrary.org..
[76] Edited by Flora B. Brown, Professor of History, Elizabeth City State University
[77] Ruth E. Gordon and Clive J. Talbot, eds. *From Dias to Vorster : source material on South African history 1488–1975* (Cape Town: Nasou, 1977), 410.
[78] Desmond Tutu, "The Question of South Africa," *Africa Report* 30 (January-February 1985): 50–52.
[79] Kevin Shillington, *History of Africa* (Oxford: Oxford University Press, 1995), 190–191.
[80] Thomas Sowell, *Conquest and Cultures: An International History* (New York: Basic Books, 1998), 172–173.
[81] Edwin Meese III, *With Reagan: The Inside Story* (Washington, D.C.: Regnery Gateway, 1992), 168–173.
[82] Glen Bowman, "The Decline and Fall of the Soviet Union." Unpublished paper.
[83] Theodor Herzl, *The Jewish State: An Attempt at a Modern Solution of the Jewish Question* (New York: American Zionist Emergency Council, 1946), 85, 92, 96.
[84] "THE PALESTINIAN NATIONAL CHARTER: Resolutions of the Palestine National Council, July 1–17, 1968," Accessed on December 17, 2004 at http://www.mideastweb.org/plocha.htm.
[85] F. Bettex, "The Bible and Modern Criticism," *The Fundamentals: A Testimony to the Faith*, ed. R.A. Torrey (Chicago: Testimony, 1910–1915).
[86] Khomeini, *Islamic Government* (1970), trans. Hamid Alger. Accessed December 20, 2006 at www.wandea.org.pl